The Sacred
Mirror

OMEGA BOOKS

The OMEGA BOOKS series from Paragon House is dedicated to classic and contemporary works about human development and the nature of ultimate reality, encompassing the fields of mysticism and spirituality, psychic research and paranormal phenomena, the evolution of consciousness, and the human potential for self-directed growth in body, mind, and spirit.

John White, M.A.T., Series Editor of OMEGA BOOKS, is an internationally known author and educator in the fields of consciousness research and higher human development.

MORE TITLES IN OMEGA BOOKS

The Sacred Mirror

Nondual Wisdom & Psychotherapy

Edited by

John J. Prendergast
Peter Fenner
Sheila Krystal

Published in the United States by

Paragon House
3600 Labore Road
St. Paul, Minnesota 55110

The Omega Books series from Paragon House is dedicated to classic and contemporary works about human development and the nature of ultimate reality.

Library of Congress Cataloging-in-Publication Data

The sacred mirror : nondual wisdom & psychotherapy / edited by John J. Prendergast, Peter Fenner, Sheila Krystal.-- 1st ed.
    p. cm. -- (Omega books)
Includes bibliographical references and index.
    ISBN 1-55778-824-3 (pbk. : alk. paper)
1. Psychotherapy--Philosophy. 2. Psychotherapy--Religious aspects. 3. Advaita. I. Prendergast, John J., 1950- II. Fenner, Peter. III. Krystal, Sheila, 1945- IV. Title. V. Series: Omega books (St. Paul, MN.)
RC437.5.S237 2003
616.89'14'01--dc21

                                                              2003011009

10 9 8 7 6 5 4
For current information about all releases from Paragon House,
visit the web site at www.paragonhouse.com

for

The one inner sage
and
its many outer forms

Contents

Acknowledgments

Chapter 2, "Nonduality and Therapy: Awakening the Unconditioned Mind" by Peter Fenner. The T. S. Eliot poem is printed with permission from Faber and Faber, and Harcourt Brace.

Chapter 7, "Being Intimate with What Is: Healing the Pain of Separation" by Dorothy Hunt. The Rumi poem is printed with permission from Coleman Barks.

1

Introduction

John J. Prendergast

Overview

At the beginning of the twenty-first century we are witnessing an increasingly intimate conversation between Western psychotherapists and teachers from the Eastern wisdom traditions.[1] This conversation has been happening simultaneously on a number of different levels. The most obvious and outward level is intellectual, evidenced by the growing stream of books and journal articles (mostly Buddhist), as well as by conferences and academic classes that include a Transpersonal or Integral orientation. However, a less obvious but more important part of this conversation is happening experientially and intuitively as psychotherapists sit silently in meditation and dialogue with Indian and Southeast Asian sages, Japanese and Korean Zen masters, Middle Eastern Sufis, Taoist masters, Tibetan lamas and *rinpoches*, and more recently with some of their long-term Western students who have become teachers in their own right. In fact, this conversation between Eastern-oriented dharma teachers and Western psychotherapists is a smaller part of a much larger dialogue that includes millions of nonpsychotherapists as well as teachers in the Christian, Jewish, and native mystical traditions. In addition, increasing numbers of individuals in the West are reporting spontaneous and profound, life transforming awakenings without prior exposure to any spiritual teachers, teachings, or practices.[2] Surveying these developments, we see the emergence of an essential dialogue, stripped of its cultural forms and roles, between the conditioned mind and that awareness which is unconditioned, open, and unknown. Reality seems to be enjoying this conversation with itself, since it is happening with increasing frequency and depth.

The fruit of this dialogue has been an accelerated awakening of nondual wisdom. Nonduality is a rather curious and uncommon word that so far has been used by a relatively small number of scholars and teachers.[3] It derives from the Sanskrit word *advaita* which means "not-two." Nondual wisdom refers to the understanding and direct experience of a fundamental consciousness that underlies the apparent distinction between perceiver and perceived. From the nondual perspective, the split between self and other is a purely mental construct. This understanding, rooted in the direct experience of countless sages through millennia, is at the heart of Hindu Vedanta, most schools of Buddhism, and Taoism, and mystical Christianity, Judaism, and Islam. Nonduality is a particularly elegant and clear formulation, since it describes reality in terms of what it is not (unsplit, undivided) rather than what it is. It has the added advantage of being nonsectarian, unhinged to any particular religious or psychospiritual tradition, yet adaptable to many. It is a word that points to that which is before and beyond the projections of a separative, self-reflexive mind. What is pointed to can never be adequately conceptualized. It can only be lived in the timeless now.

Nondual wisdom expresses itself as and through a radiant heart (love) and illumined mind (wisdom). While essentially without qualities, it is commonly experienced as being vast, free, spacious, heartfelt, and present-centered. Many people report feeling a subtle joy, love, compassion, peace, gratitude, and sense of connectedness with all of life when they directly attune with it. There are many signs that this awareness is emerging in the West. Why now? Perhaps it is as the historian Charles Beard (Rogers, 1980; see bibliography) observed, "When the skies grow dark, the stars begin to shine."

This flowering of nondual wisdom is presenting new challenges and opportunities for the field of psychotherapy. While Wilber (2000, 1996) and other Integral/Transpersonal philosophers and psychologists have mapped out nondual awareness as the pinnacle of self-realization, it has been presented as a rarefied condition. Surprisingly, this no longer appears to be as true. As a result, a new generation of clinicians and teachers has begun to explore how this awareness directly impacts the way psychotherapists work.

The title of this book, *The Sacred Mirror,* refers to the capacity of the therapist to reflect back the essential nature of the client—that awareness that is prior to and inclusive of all thoughts, feelings, and sensations. Sacred mirroring is multidimensional, reflecting both personal and impersonal dimensions of being. This capacity implies a high degree of maturity by therapists who are awakening to the realization that they are not only who they have taken themselves to be. They realize, at least to some degree, that they are not limited to being a "therapist" (although they may function in that role), or even a "person." Their locus of identity is either resting in or moving toward unconditioned awareness, or Presence. The result is the emergence of a natural simplicity, transparency, clarity, and warm acceptance of whatever arises within themselves and their clients. Since they increasingly do not take themselves as some "thing," they also do not take their clients as objects separate from themselves. They understand that there is no separate mirror and someone mirrored; there is only mirroring. As Rumi (1995) said, "We are the mirror, as well as the face in it."

Through their Presence and skillful therapeutic means, awakening psychotherapists may spontaneously assist some of their clients to see through their various limited identities and gradually rest in an unknown openness, even as they fully honor, accept, and explore whatever mental, emotional, and somatic contractions arise. This expansive role complements and increasingly overlaps with the traditional role of the spiritual teacher or director, and raises a number of interesting questions.

First, we may ask whether we are witnessing the emergence of a new school of psychotherapy—one that is "nondual." Certainly one could reasonably propose this. Perhaps a modern set of principles and practices that enhance awakening and transformation could be articulated and taught. Maybe, as one of the editors (Peter Fenner) suggests, nondual therapy is what the sages, Buddha included, have been doing all along and we are simply encountering an old wine—Buddhadharma—in a new wineskin. On the other hand, there are good reasons to be cautious about trying to codify or reify nondual awareness into yet another framework that will eventually be added to the compost pile along with all of the psychological models that preceded it. By its nature, that which is nondual is undivided and nonconceptual. The conceptual mind can never nail it down. It is not limited by a set of principles since it is the source of all principles. Nor can it be confined to any particular set of practices, since reality uses all tools at its disposal at any given moment, including death, disease, pain, shock, and suffering, to point us to our true nature. Nonduality can never be confined by any philosophy or psychospiritual practice, although such practices may play a vital role in preparing the ground for awakening or facilitating a glimpse of our true nature. It is not limited to any object or subtle state of consciousness, even as it includes these. It is both no-thing and everything, empty yet full of pure potentiality. It is immanent and transcendent, formed and formless. And it is none of this. It is *what is* and *what we are* and little more of any meaning can be said about it. Mainly we can describe what it is not, and even that in time will be seen to be untrue.

Even though nondual awareness cannot be objectified,

awakening to it changes one's life profoundly. How may we assess its impact on the field of psychotherapy? It may be helpful to think of psychotherapy, and all of life for that matter, as having a horizontal and vertical dimension. The horizontal refers to the realm of form—the evolution of phenomenal life in time and space. The vertical refers to that which is formless and exists outside of time and space. Psychology, like all disciplines, evolves on the horizontal plane as new information about the development and functioning of the human body/mind is discovered and synthesized, leading to new schools of thought. While the *concept* of nondual awareness has already been incorporated horizontally into Transpersonal and Integral frameworks, its main effect occurs vertically as practitioners deepen in their intimacy with their true nature.

Awakening nondual awareness adds a depth dimension to any of the existing schools of psychology, regardless of their orientation, through the psychotherapist's deepening awareness. Whether their model is neoanalytic (object relations, self psychology, intersubjectivity), Jungian, cognitive/behavioral, humanistic/existential, or Integral/Transpersonal, awakening psychotherapists bring a quality of awareness that transforms their work. It is not so much that therapists integrate Being, as they are absorbed by it. As they more deeply attune with and embody the ground of Being, Presence is enhanced. Their thoughts, feelings, and actions tend to spontaneously radiate out from this open awareness. Authentic transformation arises from the therapist and client's coexploration of *what is.*

Presence can be described as Being aware of Itself. Its effects are contagious. When we are in the Presence of an individual who has awakened from the dream of "me," we can sense an unpretentiousness, lucidity, transparency, joy, and ease of being. Those same qualities are elicited within ourselves. What is normally background may temporarily be called into the foreground of attention. When Presence is particularly strong and we are particularly open, it may feel as if a fire has been ignited. The German-Canadian sage Eckhart Tolle (1999) has commented on this:

When a log that has only just started to burn is placed next to one that is burning fiercely, and after a while they are separated again, the first log will be burning with much greater intensity. After all, it is the same fire. To be such a fire is one of the functions of a spiritual teacher. Some therapists may also be able to fulfill that function, provided they have gone beyond the level of mind and can create and sustain a state of intense conscious presence while they are working with you.

Tolle's proviso that therapists must transcend the mind is critically important.

Does this mean that psychotherapy is evolving into a Western vehicle for the transmission of the flame of dharma, or truth? Are awakening psychotherapists in the same lineage as the Buddha or India's other illustrious sages? It seems obvious that any awakening or awakened beings will transmit their understanding according to their capacities and limitations in any moment. This holds true for psychotherapists and nonpsychotherapists alike. In some ways being a psychotherapist may make awakening more difficult, especially if there are strong attachments to theories about the mind. On the other hand, psychotherapists are in a unique position in modern society to offer a sanctuary for individuals to sort out their lives and more intimately explore their direct experience. Further, people may be more at ease working individually with a therapist who has a nondual orientation than with joining a spiritual organization or community that has its own specialized rules, roles, and rituals.

Having identified the flowering of Presence as the primary impact of awakening, we can also recognize a number of powerful secondary effects. One obvious area is in our self-identity as a "psychotherapist." When we awaken from the sense of personal identity, we also awaken from all of our role identities, even as these roles continue. We are like the actor who snaps out of his trance while onstage and suddenly realizes that he had lost himself in his role. Even though we continue our roles as Mr. or Ms. Jones, we do not forget that it is just a play. Therapy is what we do, it is not who we are. As a result, we take ourselves much more lightly. The role of psychotherapist has its legitimate and socially relevant function, yet we no longer allow it to become a screen or mask to hide behind. Freed of the role identity, we are more authentic, transparent, available, and creative in the moment. We are no longer problem solvers facing problem holders. Instead, we are Being meeting itself in one of its infinite and intriguing disguises.

If we no longer take ourselves as problem solvers, it is also true that we can no longer find any real problems. This radical understanding can be disorienting. Clearly, nearly all clients come in presenting problems that therapists are taught to carefully assess in their initial sessions. If there is no problem, what is there to do? We meet the client where they are. If they believe that they have a problem, and certainly there will be compelling evidence to support such an interpretation, we join them there and begin the process of intimately exploring what the actual experience of the "problem" is. As apparent problems are gradually unpacked and clients deepen in their self-intimacy, they will eventually encounter a profound sense of emptiness that has been fiercely defended against. They discover that their prior problems were all outcomes from and compensatory expressions of this defense against what at first appears to be annihilation and in time reveals itself as unconditional love. When we believe that we are not enough, we think, feel, and act in all kinds of ways that create suffering for ourselves and others. Yet even this avoidance of emptiness is not seen as a problem. It is simply a misunderstanding of our true nature that *is* fundamentally empty—of everything we have taken to be true about ourselves and the world. This misunderstanding is also part of the divine play. Facing emptiness either will or will not occur depending upon the motivation and readiness of the client. It is not up to the therapist, who is free of any agenda, to change things as they are.

Another impact of an awakening nondual awareness is an enhanced capacity to be with *what is*. All mainstream schools of psychotherapy understand the importance of acceptance, yet the dualistic mind can never be an agent of complete acceptance. The mind only accepts *what is* conditionally, hoping that if something is accepted, it will change. The living insight of nondual awareness is that everything already is accepted and embraced just as it is. As awakening deepens, the judging mind loses its grip and attention becomes increasingly innocent, intimate, and impersonally affectionate. Attention drops from the head to the heart. Without any conscious intention on the part of the therapist, an optimal field of loving acceptance arises that facilitates transformation. What has been unmet is waiting to be fully embraced before it can transform. Unconditional love is the greatest transformative power. A flower bud naturally unfolds to the caress of sunlight; it cannot be willed to open.

Awakening nondual awareness fully discloses the therapeutic encounter as a shared field and enhances the phenomenon of empathic resonance (Hart, 2000). When we are no longer protecting and projecting a personal identity, we are multidimensionally open and available to our clients. A remarkable intimacy may evolve, depending in part upon the availability of the client, where we are able to experience our client's world as if from the inside. Interpersonal boundaries become very fluid and permeable yet without the merging and confusion that is typical of unconscious relationships. The therapist intimately experiences without becoming identified with or caught in whatever is being experienced, a blending of love and wisdom. We can touch the core of a client's contraction even as we retain a sense of spacious detachment. Interestingly, clients consciously participate in these encounters, knowing when a therapist's heart and sensitivity have touched them where they have never been met before. This empathic resonance helps heal the pain of separation.

The awakening of nondual awareness also facilitates the depth and transformative power of inquiry. Discernment is significantly enhanced. As therapists learn to live in the unknown, increasingly free of conclusions, they are better able to assist their clients to do the same. They see thoughts for what they are—just thoughts, recognizing the different layers of their clients' stories and assisting in their gradual deconstruction when this is appropriate. They know the peace and freedom of living without attachment to any story of how things are or should be. This is especially the case with the story of being a separate self, which is unquestioned by all conventional psychotherapies. The unfolding of nondual awareness allows therapists to authentically pose or support the investigation of essential questions such as "Who am I?" "What do I really want?" and "Is it true?" and follow the process of undoing fundamental beliefs to their end beyond the conceptual mind. This is in marked contrast to the process of purely cognitive or intellectual inquiry that stays limited to the surface, rational mind. The illumined intellect (*buddhi* in Sanskrit) shines more freely as nondual awareness awakens to itself, allowing a natural resting in not-knowing.

We should also briefly address the issue of methods and skills. Since nondual awareness is all-inclusive, it will at times use skillful means to assist its own unfolding. Wisdom and love work through many "little methods." In psychotherapy this may look like silent listening, empathic reflections, inquiries, interpretations, educating through teaching stories and metaphors, invitations to be attentive to something, or to look, listen, or sense in a new way. Therapy can use nature, breath work, movement, bilateral stimulation, dream work, free association, toning, gazing, journaling, art, or a gentle touch of the hand. When effective, it almost always engages the body on some level. The critical question is whether the therapist's awareness is centered in the moment and creatively responsive to *what is*. Are we entering a session fixed to an agenda and protocol, or are we able to let everything go and be fresh and truly available? Can we let the session be naked and unfurnished at any moment? Are we able to rest in the Unknown?

The Sacred Mirror is primarily about how awakening impacts the psychotherapist and secondarily about how it affects psychotherapy. Yet awakening is not something that the conditioned mind can "do." It is out of the ego's control and happens of its own. We cannot pretend to be awake when we are not (this is still part of being in the dream of a separate self), nor can we completely deny or refuse our underlying nature as Awakeness. When awakening happens, it is an impersonal event and belongs to no one. It is *from*, not *for* the person. As the European sage Jean Klein (1988) observes, "Awakening happens when we are convinced that there is no one who awakens." It is enough to be where we are, as we are—lucidly allowing our experience in the moment, whether we are at war or peace with reality. The love of truth, manifesting as the surrender to Silence and an active investigation into all of our cherished beliefs, gradually leads us to greater authenticity. The rest takes care of itself. Living this way brings a sense of transparency to our lives and our work as psychotherapists. In time and without any conscious effort or intent we become like stained glass, more adequate forms for the transmission of light. Our individuality is liberated and enhanced as we knowingly share this common ground with all beings.

The Authors and Chapters

All of the chapters in *The Sacred Mirror* have been specifically written for this volume—a rarity for anthologies. Each of the authors has some degree of firsthand familiarity with nondual awareness, either through spontaneous openings or through a lengthy association with nondual teachers and teachings. The authors have publicly presented their work over a series of small conferences entitled Nondual Wisdom & Psychotherapy held annually in California since 1998. Their descriptions and innovations reflect the cutting edge of this confluence. Each of the authors is either a seasoned clinician (Dan Berkow, Stephan Bodian, Dorothy Hunt,

Sheila Krystal, Lynn Marie Lumiere, Richard Miller, John Prender-gast, John and Jennifer Welwood, and Bryan Wittine) or an experienced spiritual teacher (Adyashanti and Peter Fenner). Most of them know each other to some degree and some are good friends. These chapters, then, are a kind of conversation among friends, a small sampling of the much larger conversation that we spoke of earlier. The view, however, is not synoptic and this book is not gospel. After all, friends can differ. It is an exploration in progress.

The chapters are not ordered according to any sense of their relative importance, however, more theoretical essays are generally followed by ones that are more practical.

The volume begins with Peter Fenner's "Nonduality and Therapy: Awakening the Unconditioned Mind" in which he lays the foundations for a nondual therapy, which, paradoxically, cannot be defined:

> In the same way that we can talk about Buddhism, schools of Buddhism, Buddhist traditions, and the realization that Buddhism doesn't exist, similarly we can talk about a nondual therapy. And at the same time we know there is no such thing as nondual therapy. What makes nondual therapy unique is that it doesn't exist.

According to Fenner, a nondual approach to therapy focuses on "awakening an experience of the unconditioned mind for the therapist and client, and the ongoing cultivation of this experience." The chapter's first section surveys general characteristics of a therapy inspired by nonduality: the healing power of the unconditioned mind, the capacity to go beyond suffering, a homing instinct toward openness and acceptance, the reconditioning of thought patterns and emotions, living in the here and now, embodying transcendence, and the union of love and wisdom. The second section identifies obstacles to experiencing the unconditioned mind: attachment to suffering, the habitual need to do something, the need to know and to create meaning, and fearful projections about the unconditioned mind. The third section describes preparatory and supporting practices: observing fixations, discovering a desireless way of being, achieving completion in the moment, broadening "the river of life," developing serenity, and resting in healing bliss. In the final section, Fenner identifies some distinctive features of a nondual approach to therapy: pure listening and speaking, the practice of noninterference, deconstructing fixations, natural koans, checking the purity of the unconditioned experience, and dancing in the paradoxes of nondual logic.

In "Love Returning for Itself" two of the editors (Prendergast and Krystal) interview Adyashanti, a San Francisco Bay Area native who underwent a series of awakenings after years of traditional Zen Buddhist practice. In two wide-ranging and illuminating discussions Adyashanti explores a number of nuances at the interface of spiritual awakening and psychotherapy, including the nature of emptiness, the transformation of the ego upon awakening, what he calls "watching-experiencing," full embodiment, the power of core beliefs, and the overlapping roles of the spiritual teacher and psychotherapist. The interview's title refers to Adyashanti's description of his own experience of a spontaneous movement of awakeness to lovingly return and fully touch whatever is unawake and suffering in one's own or another's body-mind.

> There is a movement of inherent love for everything in the body-mind that had any amount of conflict, of suffering. This beingness or awakeness inherently had a tendency to move toward unawakeness or suffering—to welcome it back into its true nature.

When asked how therapists can facilitate awakening in their clients, his response is direct and uncompromising: "Be awakened yourself." He cautions therapists to know the territory firsthand if they are going to invite their clients to inquire into their essential nature. Further, some clients may not be ready for this invitation. He questions whether there can be a spiritual psychotherapy as such even as he acknowledges that spiritual psychotherapists are the most important element of therapy:

> There's a whole other facility which has to do with who and what [psychotherapists] are, which is as potent or powerful as anything they might be doing as a human being.

John Prendergast describes a way of *being together* with some of his clients that uses a relaxed, nonintentional mutual eye gazing which tends to invite Presence and a sense of shared spaciousness into the foreground of awareness in "The Sacred Mirror: Being Together." This may occur spontaneously or be informally initiated by the therapist. Sacred mirroring includes an essential, impersonal, and timeless dimension of being, distinctive from more conventional forms of mirroring that focus on the contents of a client's awareness or seek to validate the client's worth. This highly intimate and direct approach also tends to evoke reactions and defenses as well as their gradual resolution:

> In addition to inviting presence, this powerful contact inevitably brings up deeply entrenched defenses against intimacy and letting go that are usually directly related to the client's presenting problems. Compelling negative beliefs, powerful emotions and intense somatic constrictions are frequently uncovered and gradually worked through. This transformative process is particularly important since it is of limited value to evoke presence in order to temporarily bypass difficult personal material. Instead, approaching the knots and veils of personal difficulties from a much larger shared space allows them to open or dissolve more easily, even as they are accepted as they are.

Prendergast outlines his discovery of this form of mirroring, the qualities of awareness that support or obstruct it, the phenomenon of a consciously shared field of awareness, common client experiences, as well as cautions and contraindications. In a detailed case study, he describes three phases of exploration that unfolded with his client. He ends by suggesting that:

> "Being Together" offers a simple and elegant way for the self to meet itself in the apparent other. In so doing psychotherapy becomes a sacred mirror for both client and therapist.

Sheila Krystal, in "A Nondual Approach To EMDR: Psychotherapy as Satsang," briefly describes psychotherapy from a nondual perspective and suggests that it is comparable to satsang where people come together in conversation in the now as seekers of truth and the company of God. The concepts of entrainment or therapeutic resonance and no mind or empty mind are discussed in the context of satsang:

> As the therapist rests in nondual awareness with an empty mind, without attending to any inner commentary other than an intuitive impulse or direction, entrainment or therapeutic resonance can occur. The therapist's empty, peaceful and quiet mind is contagious and clients begin to experience their own peace and truth. Clients are naturally invited into a deeper level of reality beyond their belief systems, concepts, conditioning and tribal consciousness. Essence comes into the foreground from the background shadows, allowing healing and peaceful contentment to occur.

A case study demonstrates that long-lasting healthful results can occur when nondual wisdom joins EMDR (eye movement desensitization and reprocessing)—an integrative approach to psychotherapy. The coming together of therapist and client in satsang can be greatly assisted by skillful means such as EMDR. Krystal describes a special Transpersonal EMDR protocol that she has developed for processing mental, emotional, and bodily distractions from the experience of constant contentment and nondual realization that she blended with the traditional EMDR protocol in her case study

John Welwood addresses the need for a balanced view of nonduality, one that equally values transcendent and immanent dimensions of human existence, in "Double Vision: Duality and Nonduality in Human Experience." Between the prehuman dualistic ego-mind and the transhuman nondual ground of being lies the human realm: vulnerable, evolving, and, above all, relational. Welwood cautions against a one-sided transcendentalism that dehumanizes human experience by emphasizing its illusory nature. "What is needed," he argues, "is a liberation spirituality that helps people recognize nondual presence as a basis for fully inhabiting their humanity...." Welwood reviews Martin Buber's immanent perspective ("a higher octave of dualism") that values the sacred other, the importance of authentic dialogue, and the acceptance of each individual's unique particularity and process of individuation. Welwood notes, however, that Buber did not recognize the importance of transcendence. He introduces the reader to the nondual teachings of Swami Prajnanpad, an Indian Advaitan, as an example of a balanced nondual view that emphasizes the full embrace of human differences as a path to undermine self-centeredness. The heart of Welwood's approach accents unconditional presence—"learning to be present with your experience just as it is." He observes that historically transcendental nondual wisdom has not deeply impacted worldly life and sees our primary evolutionary challenge awaiting us in the field of human relationships:

> Developing more conscious relationships is an important next frontier in human evolution. And this will require a capacity to marry nondual realization—which dissolves

fixation on the separate self—with careful attention to personal relational patterns that block or distort the free flow of loving presence.

In "Being Intimate with What Is: Healing the Pain of Separation," Dorothy Hunt describes the healing that unfolds when *that which is awake* directly and intimately touches *what is*. This intimacy is not a product of the conceptual mind. Suffering ceases when we do not separate ourselves from our essential being or from the truth of the moment. Therapists will not be able to invite their clients to experience the truth of their being or the intimate touch of awakeness unless they have done so themselves. She points out that there are no "nondual" techniques for the mind to learn; our effectiveness as therapists requires an *unlearning* and a mind that rests in unknowing. Hunt identifies two main ways that healing manifests: by simply *being* together without any agenda to go anywhere or change anything and by continually inviting the direct experience of the moment as it is. She describes different levels of awakening that include the mind, the heart, and the body, and concludes by writing:

> When "bare *nothingness*" intimately touches itself as *something*: when what is radiantly clear meets its own confusion; when what is looking through our own eyes sees itself looking back—this awakeness we *are* is awake to itself. When what is unconditionally loving meets the places in itself that have felt unloved; when what is innocent embraces fully what was been shamed; when what is infinitely open meets its own finite contractions—we experience healing.

In "A Psychology of No-thingness: Seeing Through the Projected Self," Dan Berkow suggests that "the human being is that which is not-a-thing"—neither an independently existing subject nor object. Psychological problems arise as a result of mistaking a self-object construct for "an independent observer, doer and experiencer." According to Berkow the foundations of a psychology of no-thingness are: a) knowing that one is not-a-thing b) understanding and resolving anxieties arising from intrusions of groundlessness and related projections and defenses, and c) using therapy to question assumptions that divide experience. Berkow envisions therapy as:

> a relinquishment of attachment and illusion, not a promotion of positive mindsets and self-images. It is growth through letting go, rather than an accumulation of new ideas.

The therapist does not impose any view or expectation for the client to either change or stay the same. Instead, a spontaneous process of therapeutic inquiry rooted in present-centered openness to *what is* facilitates the seeing through of the projected self. Berkow presents several case examples where his clients gradually saw through aspects of the projected self, resulting in a common tone of inner quietness and outer receptivity. The resolution of projection is nonconceptual:

> The key insight into projection is not a conceptual analysis of how projection occurs or what it is; it is the simple openness in which projection is not the case.

Richard Miller explores the therapeutic applications of the ancient discipline of Yoga Nidra in his chapter "Welcoming All That Is: Nonduality, Yoga Nidra, and the Play of Opposites in Psychotherapy." After briefly surveying Yoga Nidra's traditional roots and describing his first profound encounter with it over thirty years ago, Miller outlines two distinctive phases of its use in his work with clients. In the first or constructive phase, clients are guided to develop a better integrated psychological identity by attending to naturally occurring opposites or polarities in their thoughts, feelings, and sensations. During a second, deconstructive phase, awareness itself is accented rather than the contents of awareness. Miller suggests that suffering is sustained by our inability to fully allow (and thus transcend) pairs of opposites such as grief *and* joy that are complementary polarities. Welcoming the splits within the ego or separative self that has been ruled by the "tyranny of shoulds" gradually allows for a deeper inquiry into the fundamental polarity of self and other. The fruition of this inquiry is the discovery of one's essential nondual nature that includes both transcendent and immanent dimensions. Miller notes,

> Yoga Nidra and psychotherapy entail the art of listening, which is an openness free of direction or preconception. It is this capacity of therapists and clients to be present and listen, without an agenda or judgment that enables them to explore and reveal hidden and disregarded aspects of self that otherwise sustain conflict, suffering, and the myth of separation. Hidden within every conflict is its solution.

In "Deconstructing the Self: The Uses of Inquiry in Psychotherapy and Spiritual Practice," Stephan Bodian briefly surveys the history of spiritual and psychological inquiry, touching upon Zen, Tibetan Dzogchen/Mahamudra and Advaita Vedanta as well as conventional psychoanalytic and existential-humanistic approaches. Bodian states that there is no attempt to change or get rid of anything with deconstructive inquiry in a nondual approach to psychotherapy:

> The only purpose is to shine the light of inquiry onto the contents of experience in order to discriminate between the true and the false, the real and the unreal, in Advaita terms. Instead of seeking answers or solutions, which are understood to be merely additional conceptual overlays, the inquiry is focused on revealing the concepts, stories,

and beliefs that cause suffering, knowing that once they're recognized for what they are, rather than taken to be true, suffering and conflict will spontaneously disperse.

Bodian acknowledges that clients will often resist inquiry into their "self and world construct" system, preferring a familiar if painful point of view to the apparent groundlessness of the unknown. Once directly encountered, however, emptiness reveals itself as wholeness or completeness, accompanied by profound peace and unexpected joy. Bodian also describes "The Work" of Byron Katie—a particularly potent form of deconstructive inquiry that helps clients undo their core beliefs. He writes:

> By encouraging direct experience of feelings and sensations unmitigated by the mind while inquiring into the beliefs and stories that cause suffering, a nondual approach to therapy invites clients to deconstruct the "self and world construct system" entirely.

Lynn Marie Lumiere explores the healing power of now in conjunction with the use of Somatic Experiencing (SE) in "Healing Trauma in the Eternal Now." While maintaining that "Our past traumas can be resolved only in the here and now," Lumiere acknowledges that skillful means are usually necessary to "facilitate being present with the nervous system's experience of trauma in the body." She outlines the basic structure of SE developed by its founder Peter Levine, focusing on three key concepts: pendulation, titration and resourcing. Lumiere suggests that a therapist's awakened presence is an additional powerful resource that helps allow a client's nervous system to relax and surrender to *what is*. She presents a case study that blends inquiry and the felt-sensing of SE, resulting in a profound transformation. Lumiere suggests that trauma, endemic to modern life, is the source of most of the violence in the world and that both SE and the awakening of non-

dual wisdom provide a much needed healing path out of the cycle
of traumatic reenactment. She ends by proposing that:

> Trauma can be a catalyst for profound surrender and awak-
> ening. I see it as a wake up call for the human race. Trauma
> is a primary cause of human suffering and yet, it can only
> be truly resolved by coming home to the eternal now. In the
> healing of trauma, we must let go of the mind's illusion of
> control and discover the beingness that is always present.

Bryan Wittine accents some of the difficulties associated with
psychospiritual splitting in "Jungian Analysis and Nondual Wisdom." He suggests that authentic nondual awareness requires development of both the vertical path of transcendence, which focuses
on the awakening of the Self, and the horizontal path of individuation that involves embracing disowned parts of the personality and
actualizing the unique gifts of the individual self. Wittine presents a
detailed case study illustrating how his client Jenna used and identified with images of God to compensate for her childhood deficits,
leading to a grandiose sense of self and a turbulent work and relational life. The course of analysis involved a painful relinquishing of
grandiosity and the gradual uncovering, feeling, and seeing through
of the shadowed subpersonality constructs of a needy child and
invalidating mother. This personal work allowed his client to settle
into her silent depths as simple awareness and to live a more creative,
peaceful, and open life. Wittine writes,

> There is a seamless continuity between ego and Self. The
> paths of transcendence and individuation come together
> as we realize the Self in its formless radiance, prior to and
> beyond all images, expressed as and through our sacred in-
> dividuality, which becomes the lens through which compas-
> sion, wisdom, and power pour forth into our relationships
> and the world.

In the final chapter, entitled "Dancing with Form and Emptiness in Intimate Relationship," Jennifer Welwood explores relational dynamics in the light of one of Buddhism's best known nondual aphorisms from *The Heart Sutra*: form is emptiness; emptiness itself is form. Welwood writes:

> So in both the inner and outer worlds, whenever we look deeply into emptiness we discover form; and whenever we look deeply into form we discover emptiness. This is the sense in which form and emptiness are inseparable, indivisible, and nondual. In tantric language we could say that they are lovers joined in eternal embrace—distinct yet not separate; not one, not two."

When this is not recognized, we take ourselves only as a solid form and are continually threatened by emptiness that appears as anything that we don't want to be happening. In this samsaric process both form and emptiness become distorted versions of themselves—form is something we feel we must fabricate and emptiness becomes deficient. Welwood analyzes the "psychodynamics of samsara" where individuals lose touch with their basic ground of openness as they try to adapt to their psychological environments and then identify themselves with their adaptive strategies. A more conscious *compensatory* identity develops to cover up the loss of being, accompanied by a less conscious *deficient* identity associated with this same loss. Welwood hones in on how these polarized identities function in relationship where an initial contract is often made between compensatory identities that inevitably falters in the face of real intimacy. Using a case example to illustrate this dynamic, she encourages couples to recognize the deficient identities that each is triggering in the other, and to open to their vulnerability. Transparency allows intimacy and a reconnection with the ground of being—our native openness and presence.

Endnotes

1. I wish to thank my coeditors Peter Fenner, Ph.D., and Sheila Krystal, Ph.D., for their valuable suggestions and feedback for this chapter.

2. For three excellent examples of this phenomenon, see Eckhart Tolle's *The Power of Now*, Byron Katie's *Loving What Is*, and Tony Parson's *As It Is*. Also see Lynn Marie Lumiere and John Win's *The Awakening West: Conversations with Today's New Western Spiritual Leaders*.

3. See David Loy's *Nonduality: A Study in Comparative Philosophy*.

2

Nonduality and Therapy

Awakening the Unconditioned Mind

Peter Fenner

In order to arrive at what you do not know
  You must go by a way which is the way of ignorance.
In order to possess what you do not possess,
  You must go by the way of dispossession.
In order to arrive at what you are not,
  You must go through the way in which you are not.
And what you do not know is the only thing you know
And what you own is what you do not own
And where you are is where you are not.

                                              T. S. Eliot (1963)

Introduction

E ven though the exploration of the interface between traditional forms of nondual wisdom and contemporary psychotherapy is only a few years old, we are already in the midst of a principled debate about whether we should allow the notion of nondual wisdom and psychotherapy to contract into the concept of nondual therapy or nondual psychotherapy.[1]

My thinking is at odds with some of my collaborators in this volume who acknowledge that nondual wisdom can make a powerful contribution to psychotherapy, but are uncomfortable about introducing the concepts of nondual therapies and nondual therapists into the lexicon of psychotherapy. I understand their concern. Nonduality isn't a method. Nor can it be specified by a way of acting or functioning at a physical level. Nor is it a way of thinking. In the technical spiritual sense nonduality isn't even an experience. The nondual approach cannot be contained by any technique, concept, or idea. As Subhuti (Hixon, 1993), the famous bodhisattva disciple of the Buddha, said, "This radical teaching of truth is openly presented as a nonteaching…. It is a nonteaching without any path to its realization, because no separate mode of access is recognized to exist inherently." The radical teaching he is talking about is the teaching of nondual therapy. Subhuti uses the term Perfect Wisdom (*prajnaparamita*), but the nonteaching of his teaching is identical to the nonteaching of nondual therapy. They can't be different because nondual therapy is the nondual wisdom of *prajnaparamita*. It is the insight into the empty and insubstantial existence of every conventionality, and the insight that automatically empties itself of any substantial reality or function.

As a nontherapy, nondual therapy casually reveals itself on park benches when down and outs, with leisure time and nowhere to go, transcend all ambition and join each other in the pure, ecstatic recognition that nothing has any intrinsic value, and that there is nothing beyond the present moment. Nondual non-therapy also arises in clinics, peer support groups, and nondual therapy conferences when earnest, well-educated, and like-minded women and men come together for the specific purpose of cultivating nondual wisdom within a psychotherapeutic environment.

So, short of talking about nondual therapy as a non-nondual therapy, what can we do beyond acknowledge that nondual therapy unfolds in every culture, time, and era, and inside and outside of any formal therapeutic training. Is there a relationship between nonduality and psychotherapy, and more specifically, can we talk about nondual therapy?

I believe we can look to Buddhism for an answer. When the Buddha was teaching in India twenty-five hundred years ago, Buddhism did not exist. During his lifetime people undoubtedly spoke about the "teachings and example of the awakened one," but probably not about Buddhism. Buddhism most likely came into existence some time afterward when his followers and disciples wanted to refer in a generic way to the corpus of teachings and methods that the Buddha taught. The Buddha himself said that he taught 84,000 different dharmas. A dharma in this context is—a device, a teaching, a method, a key, an admonition, an advice, a reward, a reprimand—anything in fact that brings someone closer to experiencing nondual awareness.

In using the symbolic number of 84,000 the Buddha was inferring that the ways of Buddhism are limitless, but not limitless in the sense that Buddhism is anything and everything. What makes a method (or nonmethod) Buddhist is the fact that it promotes the final awakening that Buddha experienced—the awakening into the nature of consciousness as pure and unstructured. When we understand Buddhism in this way, two things become apparent. First, "Buddhism" exists outside of Buddhism, since many people have realized their real nature having never heard about the Buddha or Buddhism. Second, many of the teachings, methods, interactions, and institutions that are called Buddhist are not Buddhist, because they don't awaken people to their ultimate, unconditioned nature. Instead, they condition people's experience or leave them with a set of beliefs.

The term "nondual therapy" is like the term "Buddhadharma," which signifies that among the many different types of dharmas, or spiritual paths, there is one that has its origins in the awakened experience and teachings of the Buddha. Within the Buddhadharma there are, as the Buddha said, countless different dharmas—schools, traditions, approaches, etc. The term "nondual therapies" similarly indicates that within the vast range of therapeutic approaches there are approaches that are explicitly sourced in the nondual experience. And within this there are a countless number of possible approaches.

We can already discern differences between Buddhist- and Advaita-inspired approaches to nondual therapy. They use a different language and emphasize different methods. And undoubtedly this new development in therapy will quickly become varied and highly nuanced. We can see this already in the contributions to this volume. In the same way that we can talk about Buddhism, schools of Buddhism, Buddhist traditions, and the realization that Buddhism doesn't exist, similarly I believe we can talk about a nondual form of therapy. Within this we can discern a variety of approaches, emphases, and orientations. And at the same time we know that there is no such thing as "nondual therapy." What makes nondual therapy unique is that is doesn't exist!

This Chapter

This chapter is divided into four main sections. The first section identifies some of the general characteristics of therapies that are inspired by the nondual experience. The second section talks about some of the barriers that are typically encountered in accessing and stabilizing an experience of the unconditioned mind. The third section very briefly presents some practices that can support people in cultivating the unconditioned mind. The final section describes some of the important conversations that occur in the trainings and sessions that I offer in nondual wisdom and therapy.

The Inspiration for Nondual Approaches to Therapy

In its most essential form, nondual therapy is the unimpeded and uncontrived expression of a contentless wisdom that instantaneously and effortlessly reveals the free and open nature of all structures of existence. As the Perfect Wisdom tradition of Buddhism states (Hixon, 1993):

> When the universal panorama is clearly seen to manifest without any objective or subjective supports, viewless knowledge awakens spontaneously. Simply by not reviewing any appearing structures, one establishes the true view of what is. This viewless view is what constitutes the Buddha nature and acts dynamically as the mother of wisdom, revealing whatever is simply as what it is—empty of substantial self-existence, unchartable and uncharacterizable, calmly quiet and already blissfully awakened.

The nondual approach to therapy is inspired by the example of masters and sages from nondual spiritual traditions. These traditions are mainly found in India and Asia. They include various traditions of Mahayana Buddhism: Zen, Dzogchen, Mahamudra, and Madhyamika. Outside of Buddhism, nonduality is found in the Advaita form of Hinduism and Chinese Taoism. The most illustrious of the masters are well known: Buddha, Lao Tzu, Nagarjuna, Bodhidharma, Hui-neng, Saraha, Tilopa, Padmasambhava, Atisha, Shankara, Milarepa, Longchenpa, and many, many others. But there are also tens of thousands of masters about whom we know nothing. They lived their lives as "realized governors," "enlightened mothers," "illumined farmers," and "awakened artists." Though they differ enormously in their personalities and influence, these masters all share in an identical experience of the unconditioned mind.

Many terms have been used in nondual traditions to refer to the experience of the full evolution of consciousness. The names include self-knowledge, witness consciousness, no-mind, primordial mind, reality, openness, pure awareness, buddha-nature and the unconditioned mind. In this chapter I will generally use the term unconditioned mind.[2] But when I use this term I am just as much speaking about Zen no-mind, Advaita self-knowledge, and Buddha-nature.

As a result of their embodied experience of the unconditioned mind, nondual masters create an energy field that has a potency and immediacy that is rarely encountered in conventional forms of healing and therapy. Their presence produces a therapeutic perturbation on those around them. Their words can be especially powerful. Often just a sentence or two from a master can act as a key—opening up new possibilities that can extend for months or years into the future. In the space of a few seconds, certain nondual masters can accomplish what may take months or years of conventional therapy.

The nondual approach to therapy uses the teachings and embodied presence of nondual masters as a model for how to manage our own evolution and thus make a powerful healing contribution to others. This model is based on the healing capacity of the unconditioned mind. The common element in nondual approaches to therapy is a focus on awakening an experience of the unconditioned mind for the therapist and client, and the ongoing cultivation of this experience.

The Hallmarks of Nondual Therapies

The nondual approach to therapy and healing makes a radical departure from more conventional forms of psychotherapy. Nondual therapies are based in the possibility that we have everything we need, simply by virtue of being conscious. As Dan Berkow writes in this volume, therapy "proceeds as recognition of presentness as well-being." Other forms of therapy tend to assume that we need to be fixed because something is wrong with us. We suffer because we've had a dysfunctional upbringing, are genetically predisposed to mental illness, have suffered a traumatic experience, or simply don't have the resources to cope with life. In contrast, the nondual approach to therapy invests in the healing power of the unconditioned mind. This approach is designed to awaken us to, and root us in, the ever-present experience of pure-bliss-consciousness.

The Unconditioned Mind

Whether we realize it or not, the unconditioned mind is the ultimate goal of all human endeavors for one simple reason—when we rest in the unconditioned mind, there is nothing we need. We are complete. Nothing needs to change. We are fulfilled exactly as we are. In the nondual approach it isn't necessary to remove thoughts or emotions in order to become free. When we are present to the unconditioned mind, thoughts, feelings and perceptions arise, but they no longer condition us. Even though this sounds extraordinary, the unconditioned mind isn't something that is removed from our everyday life. It is an experience in which we discover total freedom in the midst of our conditioned existence.

It's a way of being in which our conditioning—our age, sex, history, education, physical condition, and financial situation—no longer limit us. We find ourselves intimately connected with everything within and around us, yet we're beyond being disturbed in any way. The nondual approach to therapy directs people to the experience of the unconditioned mind as a way of transcending suffering, and healing the psychological wounds of the past.

The experience of the unconditioned mind is a very precise experience. It's the only experience that is totally open and without any structure. This is why it is sometimes called "contentless wisdom." The experience can also be spoken about in terms of its purity, depth, and durability. By purity we mean the absence of objectifying structures. By the depth of the experience, we mean the extent to which the unconditioned pervades or infuses our conditioned existence. By duration, we mean how long we can rest in this state.

The function of nondual therapies is to introduce people to the unconditioned aspect of their existence, and then deepen and stabilize the experience. This very simple intention is identical with Garab Dorje's quintessential summation of the Dzogchen tradition. According to Garab Dorje (Reynolds, 1996), Dzogchen can be summarized through three vital keys. These are:

1. Direct introduction to one's own real nature;

2. Clearly recognizing this unique state;

3. Continuing to abide confidently in this state of freedom.

In the context of therapy:

1. We introduce people to a space of contentless awareness in which there is nothing that needs to be done and nothing that needs to be thought about or understood.

2. We identify this state when it is present by demonstrating that there is nothing to do and nothing to know, nothing that can be enhanced or degraded, etc. The authenticity of this state can be determined through questions that reveal whether people are resting in a structured or unstructured state.

3. Finally we assist people to remain in this experience by (1) observing how they move out of this experience by making it into "something—anything—which can then be lost and gained." This "making it into something" can occur in a number of ways, for example, by trying to work out what it is, wondering how to maintain it, wondering how to discover it, in other (future) situations.

The "Ultimate Medicine"

In Buddhism the experience of the unconditioned mind is called the "ultimate medicine."[3] Other types of medicine—that is, other types of therapy—have limitations. They work for some people and not for others, and even then only some of the time. The ultimate medicine is universally healing. Every mind touched by the experience of its unconditioned nature moves closer to the experience of real freedom and liberation. Sometimes the experience may gently encourage us to acknowledge our higher potential. In other instances it may produce a radical reorientation of our experience of reality.

Beyond Suffering

The unconditioned mind heals in different ways. First, when we rest in the unconditioned mind, we *are* healed. We're cured of whatever it is we've been suffering: an illness, our fears, losses, or thwarted ambitions. The unconditioned mind can't eliminate a fear, a virus, or abject poverty. That's true. But when we rest in the unconditioned mind it is impossible to worry about a fear. We don't need to find a miracle cure for an illness, and we are satisfied wherever we are. When we rest in the unconditioned mind, we are free of the need to be ill or healthy. We might still have a diseased body or experience confusing emotions in our lives, but we are no longer battling our condition. No matter what our physical and mental conditions might be, we aren't limited by them. This is not a state of denial. If anything, we are more aware of our circumstances. But we don't relate to them as "something that shouldn't be happening." When we rest in the unconditioned mind we are in total harmony with ourselves and the world. We are at home with ourselves in a totally effortless and uncontrived way.

In therapy, people arrive at a point where there is nothing left to do—not because they've reached the limit of their therapist's competence or exhausted the capacity of a therapeutic method, but simply because it is impossible to construct a problem. They have no energy or interest in creating deficiency. Even the knowledge that they may suffer in the future is meaningless, because in nondual awareness, *future* suffering is experienced simply as what it is—a thought.

Of course, it's also true that if we are in pain it can be difficult, even impossible, to connect with the unconditioned dimension of being. This is where there is a clear role for other forms of healing and therapy.

A Homing Instinct

When we spend time savoring and appreciating the unique quality of the unconditioned mind, we develop a homing instinct. The more time we spend resting in our ultimate nature, the more familiar we become with the experience. When opportunities arise to let go of our preoccupations and daily concerns, we find ourselves moving effortlessly and without resistance into a more open and accepting way of being.

We recognize the value of the unconditioned mind and head straight to it when conditions support this. We don't waste time in petty distractions or superficial intellectualizations. We value the deep peace and spiritual nutrition we gain from abiding in the unconditioned mind. Our values and priorities change naturally. We grow in our capacity to accept more freedom, love, and happiness in our lives.

The Unconditioned Mind Reconditions Thought Patterns and Emotions

The experience of the unconditioned mind also percolates through the layers of our conditioning long after people have been enjoying the experience itself. The experience changes the very structure of our habitual conditioning. We become less reactive and defensive—and hence better able to release our fears and insecurities.

The Yoga tradition of Buddhism[4] describes this process as the "transformation *(paravrtti)* of the structural foundations of our being *(asraya)*."[5] Through contact with an unstained stream of pure being, the energies and mechanisms that condition our present and future existence lose their power to distort our experience and cause us suffering. Other nondual traditions describe how the experience of the unconditioned mind infuses the conditioned mind like a sweet perfume or a soothing breeze.

We can't predict in advance how this deconditioning will unfold. It occurs at its own pace and rhythm. Sometimes it is smooth and gentle, at other times rough or abrupt. At times we might even think we are moving backward: returning to an earlier stage of our development that we felt was complete. Each of us is infinitely complex and our path to full evolution is unique and often mysterious.

Living in the Here and Now

Another characteristic of nondual approaches to therapy is a focus on what is happening in the here and now. This feature isn't unique to nondual therapy. Other therapies, for example, Gestalt and Eugene Gendlin's Focusing, bring attention to the felt quality of what is happening in our bodies and how our emotions are moving in the present moment. In addition to this awareness, nondual approaches to therapy also invite us to be aware of our attachment and aversion to the present moment. Are we holding onto our experience, wishing that it would continue, or are we pushing it away and seeking something different?

Nondual approaches to therapy focus on enhancing the quality of the present moment rather than on processing problems. They tend to cut through stories about what has happened, should have happened, or what might happen and identify what seems to be missing in the present moment rather than reactivating past memories or an anticipated future.

The reason nondual therapists don't get caught up in speculating about the future is because the future is only a theoretical possibility. It may not happen. Certainly the futures that we project often do not happen. The most direct way to create a more fulfilling future is by creating fulfillment in this moment. It's a matter of conditioning. The future evolves as a function of the present moment. We can't touch the past and can't touch the future. If we are attracted to processing the past or devising strategies for coping with the future, we predispose ourselves to repeat the same strategies in the future.

If the choice is one of continuing to rest in a state of complete fulfillment, or clearing our past, or wondering about how to sustain the experience in the future, the most responsible thing to do is to enjoy the present moment rather than degrade it with worries and anxieties. There is only the present anyway, so it's best to just be content and complete.

At the same time, nondual therapies also recognize the paradox that the here and now is all there ever is. We don't have to do anything to be in the here and now. We can never be anywhere else. Yet we keep struggling to be where we already are!

Embodied Transcendence: An Integrated Approach

The nondual approach to therapy takes a different shape in the hands of different practitioners. The form I will focus on shortly is inspired by Mahayana Buddhism. In this tradition the experience of the unconditioned mind is cultivated in the midst of our everyday existence. It isn't an experience of being "spaced-out," "up in the clouds," or disconnected from other people. The wisdom of Mahayana Buddhism fully engages the complexities of our human drama and permeates the structure of all of our relationships. Embodiment is integral to the bodhisattva ideal. The experience of the unconditioned mind lets us transcend the slightest traces of human suffering *and* expands our capacity to identify and release the suffering of other people. As Subhuti says in the Perfect Wisdom Teachings (1993), "The enlightened and enlightening art of the bodhisattva is to move in the transparent sphere of conventional characteristics and harmoniously functioning causality, while remaining totally merged in the signlessness and causelessness of sheer Reality."

In the Mahayana approach the conditioned and unconditioned dimensions of being are integrated throughout. The very structure of our personality reveals the transpersonal nature of being itself. In fact, any attempt to resist or escape our conditioning blocks us from experiencing our unconditioned nature. In the nondual approach there is absolutely no effort, struggle, or need to escape from who we are, since this is our unique expression of transcendence. Every aspect and dimension of our experience is an exquisite expression of freedom and transcendence. In this way, the nondual approach closes the traditional rift between physical embodiment and spiritual transcendence. As the Buddha says (1993), "The sublime purity of transcendent insight is identical with the natural spontaneous purity of the countless configurations that present themselves as the universe in all its multidimensionality. The intrinsic purity and peacefulness of all structures of relativity and the blissful purity of total awakeness are not two separate realities." This integrated approach removes the possibility of producing experiences that put people at risk. It automatically corrects any personal bias that might lead someone to disconnect from their physical, embodied, and social existence.

The Union of Love and Wisdom

Another way in which the unconditioned mind unites with conditioned existence is through the union of love and wisdom. In a nondual approach to therapy, a therapist simultaneously identifies and disidentifies with a client's experience. The capacity to identify is love. The capacity to disidentify is wisdom. Both arise simultaneously and without any conflict. Ideally, therapists experience their client's immediate reality—thoughts and feelings—as intimately as our own. As the Perfect Wisdom Teaching (1993) says, "Diamond beings are neither obsessively involved in the play of structures nor dispassionately distant from the evolutionary careers of living beings." They see that there is suffering and at the same time recognize that there is no suffering. This pure love is empty of any pity or sympathy.

There is an experience of profound connectedness in which there is no resistance at all to whatever someone is experiencing. As Prendergast (this volume) writes, "Therapists may experientially sense that they have entered into the core of their clients' 'wounds' or contractions, even as they retain a feeling of space around them." Therapists identify with their clients' suffering and let this dissolve into their own experience of nothingness. We could say that therapists offer a clearing for a client's suffering. From this experience of pure spaciousness therapists can authentically question the structure, the texture, the nature of someone's suffering in a way that begins to dissolve a contracted and self-serving interpretation of the present moment. If a client stays intimately connected with a therapist who is in this state, they have no choice but to observe the evaporation of their problem.

Obstacles to Experiencing the Unconditioned Mind

Because we are deeply identified with our conditioned way of being—our beliefs, values, and preferences and their related emotions—initial access to the unconditioned mind can be obscured and obstructed. The most common psychological phenomena that hinder access to the unconditioned mind are:

- Our attachment to suffering
- The habitual need to be doing something
- The need to know—what is happening and where we are
- The need to create meaning
- Fearful projections about the unconditioned mind

Attachment to Suffering

It might sound strange to say that we are attached to our pain and our problems, particularly given the amount of time and energy we spend complaining, privately and publicly, about our circumstances and dreaming about a "better life." But if we are *so* averse to suffering, why does it continue to plague us year after year? It seems we feel quite at home with our worries and concerns. Often it is easier to soak in miserable stories about how we are unloved and unappreciated than to live in a free space where praise and blame, loss and gain, simply can't touch us. Even psychotherapy—the very discipline that is meant to free us from our problems—can oblige us to have problems. Therapists and clients can cling to the known, fearing what might happen if their conversations and behavior are no longer directed by what they know. An important function of nondual therapies is to reveal attachment to problems, and through awareness create the possibility of releasing those attachments.

The Habitual Need to Be Doing Something

One of the characteristics of our modern Western culture is a need to be active and busy. There are strong cultural disincentives to simply being—in sheer unproductive fulfillment! We continually create projects: material projects, relationships projects, lifestyle projects, and of course the big one—the enlightenment project! Our actions don't even need to be productive. In the absence of interesting stimuli we doodle, sleep, even trace hairline cracks on a wall with our eyes just to keep busy. If we have a problem, the stock response is: "Well, we need to do something about it!"

The invitation in nondual approaches to healing is to let go of all effort and struggle and experience supernal peace in this very moment. As Longchenpa, the great Dzogchen yogi, writes (1998), "Since effort—which creates causes and effects, whether positive or negative—is unnecessary, immerse yourself in genuine being, resting naturally with nothing needing to be done. The expanse of spontaneous presence entails no deliberate effort, no acceptance or rejection. From now on make no effort, since phenomena already are what they are. Even the enlightenment of all victorious ones of the three times is spontaneously present as a supremely blissful state of natural rest."

The opposite to not needing to do anything isn't doing nothing. It doesn't mean that we freeze up and become inactive. It doesn't mean we resist the idea to pick up the phone and communicate with someone, or sit at home when we could invigorate ourselves with some fresh air. "Doing nothing" means that there is nothing we need to do, or not do. We are free of all compulsion. Nondual therapies reveal our predisposition to do, and open up the possibility of simply being.

Needing to Know

The need to know can also function as an obstacle to resting in the unconditioned mind. There are two types of "not knowing." There's the situation where we don't know what can be known, for example, a foreign language, tai chi, and so on. And there's the situation where we don't know because we're in a space where there is nothing to know—where we can just as well say, we *know* "nothing." This is the unconditioned mind. The first type of not knowing produces feelings of frustration and inadequacy. Of course, sometimes we can acquire the knowledge we are missing. But this still requires work and effort. The second type of not-knowing is liberating because it frees us from the need to know anything more, or less, than what we do. In the space of the unconditioned mind nothing needs to be worked out, thought through, or acted on. We are fulfilled, integrated, and complete without the need to know anything. Yet everything that we know remains immediately accessible. We continue to feel, talk, identify, and relate. However, simultaneously, we are also present to the fact that there is no object of knowledge. It is the simultaneous arising of form and pure openness. This type of "not knowing" is complete because there is nothing to know. As Subuti says, (Hixon 1993), "Dear friends, you cannot understand because there is absolutely nothing finite to understand. You are not lacking in refinement of intellect. There is simply nothing separate or substantial in Prajnaparamita to which the intellect can be applied, because perfect Wisdom does not present any graspable or thinkable doctrine and offers no describable method of contemplation."

Creating Meaning

Closely related to the need to know is the construction of meaning. Often it takes just the slightest encouragement to trigger a well-honed multichaptered lifestory or bring forth a virtual dissertation on spiritual metaphysics! We are spring-loaded to construct stories and interpretations. Often therapists join forces with their clients; analyzing, reconstructing, reframing their clients' stories. Ideally this produces a more wholesome and liberating understanding, but it is still a case of superimposing one story on another.

In nondual therapies the creation of meaning is just one possibility. We aren't compelled to make everything meaningful. It is also possible to just be with *what is*, without needing to understand it or make it significant. We can be present to *what is*, without creating somewhere we have come from and somewhere we are heading. Nondual therapies explicitly open up this possibility by giving us less encouragement to think and interpret.

Fearful Projections about the Unconditioned Mind

The concept of an unconditioned mind can trigger both positive and negative associations. In many ways it is attractive as a concept because it comes bundled with ideas of freedom and liberation. But it can also trigger fearful projections. People can think that by cultivating the unconditioned mind you will lose touch with the real world and become less interested or capable of fulfilling your daily commitments.

People can think that because the unconditioned mind is spoken about as having no structure or content, it might be like a vast, barren empty expanse of darkness without life or humanity in it. As Jennifer Welwood (this volume) writes, "Rather than recognizing emptiness as our own nature, we see it as an enemy that we have to avoid or defeat." People also become concerned that if they transcend their preferences and desires and just accept *what is*, life will become bland, boring, and uninteresting. "What motivation would I have to do anything?" "I might just sit on my chair and starve to death!"

These projections have nothing to do with the experience of the unconditioned mind. In the unconditioned mind nothing changes. At the empirical level nothing drops out of our experience and nothing unusual enters it. We continue to think, to feel, to see, and to touch. In fact, all of the senses are as active as they ever have been. Yet everything is totally different. The unconditioned mind is not what we think!

Preparatory and Supporting Practices

Before moving on to describe some of the practices that are central to the nondual approach I offer to mental health professionals, I will briefly mention some practices that prepare and support people in cultivating nondual awareness. These practices deserve a full description, but I am limited by space.

Observing Fixations

The most central insight of the Buddha was that we suffer because of our attachment or aversion to what we are experiencing. Nondual therapies take this core insight seriously. They *apply* it in the here-and-now. When we do this, the results are radical. In nondual therapy we observe and release our fixations as they arise, moment by moment. It is sufficient to simply observe and acknowledge their presence. A recognition of our reactions releases us from their influence. As this awareness grows, an uncalculated correction occurs. Feelings of attraction no longer magnetically grip our body, and feelings of aversion no longer repel us.

The nondual approach reveals our attachment to, or rejection of, different feelings and sensations, or to different thoughts, beliefs, and values. For example, in therapy clients are invited to recognize that every time they think "I want this to continue," it points to an attachment. And every time they would like their experience to change, they are rejecting what is happening. They see how fixations distort their thinking and cloud their perceptions. At a subsequent point this opens into the recognition that there is nothing to cloud or distort!

Fixations also manifest in our bodies and nervous systems. They determine where we move and how we hold our bodies. Our preferences draw us into some situations and hold us there, and repel us from others. Nondual therapists use their own body as a sensitive instrument for detecting the presence of cognitive, emotional, and/or behavioral reactions. They sense the presence of fixations by tuning into the movement of subtle energies in their body. They read the physical expression of moods and emotions such as embarrassment, pride, fear, excitement, and boredom.

Discovering a Desireless Way of Being

According to many spiritual traditions, real fulfillment can only be achieved when we are free of desire. This accords with the wisdom of the famous British psychiatrist Wilfred Bion, who said effective therapy unfolds from a state that is free from desire and memory. Nondual approaches to therapy encourage people to discover a place in their experience that is free of strong desire, learning to acknowledge and respect this place as the source of the most effective actions we take. Desirelessness is one of the most effective ways to decondition our experience. Far from being boring or bland, the experience of desirelessness opens us to far deeper levels of intimacy, trust, and confidence than can be built on attraction and aversion. From the therapist's point of view, desirelessness expresses itself as detached commitment to awakening the unconditioned mind.

Achieving Completion in the Moment

In order to awaken the unconditioned mind we need to live in a state of ongoing completion. We need to be complete with the past and fearless about the future. When we are complete we don't *need* to think about what we've done, or what we'll be doing. This allows us to fully encounter the next moment.

There are two ways in which we create incompletions. Either we don't do what needs to be done, or we do what doesn't need to be done. Often we find out only some seconds, minutes, hours, or days afterward, when we sense that we have been careless or unconscious with our words or deeds. When our actions come from the conditioned mind they're not optimally responsive to the needs of the moment. We're unable to read and respond to the uniqueness of each situation because we're operating from a model of what has worked in the past. But it's also possible to tune into the present moment with a subtlety and depth that lets us sense the potential of our speech and behavior to condition the future. In fact, this sensitivity and care arises naturally when we connect with the unconditioned mind.

Broadening the River of Life

In nondual traditions the nature of the spiritual path changes from one of avoiding suffering and pursuing pleasure to one of expanding our capacity to be present to everything that human life can produce—open to the full force and richness of our conditioned existence. We develop a capacity to receive all experiences without fear or addiction. In Buddhism this is called broadening our spiritual horizon to include the bliss of nirvana and the full range of samsaric experiences. Longchenpa (1998) says, "There is no better or worse, so there is no rejection of samsara or acceptance of nirvana." This is what differentiates the nondual liberation from the goal of dualistic spiritual paths.

In the nondual approach to therapy, suffering is not presented as something wrong—as something that shouldn't happen to us. Problems are natural. We all suffer, and will probably continue to until we die. It is a part of life. The nondual approach supports people in cutting through the fantasy that something is wrong when we suffer. We stop making a problem out of having problems! We accept the basic structure and patterns of our experience—our life circumstances, not in a defeatist way, but with dignity and grace. We *welcome what is* as a gateway to the unconditioned mind.

Developing Serenity

When we try to escape the burden of boring and limiting thoughts, it's difficult to be effortlessly present. This is why the time-honored wisdom of Asia's nondual traditions recommends that initial access to the unconditioned mind can be greatly enhanced by slowing our thinking down so that we feel peaceful and serene. In nondual therapy, if a person's thoughts are racy or disturbed, a crucial step is to help them slow down and discover a place where they are more composed and less urgent. We don't need to eliminate thoughts completely. We just need to arrive at the point where thoughts can float through awareness without producing disturbance. In Buddhism this is called the practice of serenity or *shamatha*.

The most direct and effective way to slow down our thinking is to give ourselves nothing to think about. This is logical. If we have nothing to think about we have fewer thoughts. And thinking about nothing also reveals the unconditioned mind. The two practices support each other. In Buddhism this is recognized as the interdependence of serenity (*shamatha*) and clear seeing (*vipashyana*).

In therapy, thoughts are thinned out by not feeding the interpretive process, by not digging for problems, by not offering anything to think about. Therapists stay in intimate communication and relationship without encouraging their clients' mental processes.

Resting in Healing-Bliss

In nondual traditions, experiences of bliss arise in the slipstream of the unconditioned mind. As Longchenpa says (1998), the "supremely blissful state of natural rest—is sublime meditative stability, spontaneously present without having to be cultivated." These experiences occur like clockwork when our thinking slows down and we move into more subtle states of consciousness. These experiences can be profoundly healing, especially for people who deprive themselves of pleasure. They are medicine for the mind and the soul. They soothe our minds and repair the damage done to our nervous system by pain and trauma. Therapists recognize their healing power and let people rest in these experiences for as long as they arise.

However, like all conditioned experiences, bliss comes and goes. From the nondual perspective, when people experience healing-bliss, there is still further to go. Therapists let these experiences do their work, and then gently ease people forward into the ultimate experience of the unconditioned mind.

Some Distinctive Features

The nondual approach to therapy is paradoxical. There are no methods in the nondual experience because there is no work to be done. Yet if this is introduced to a client as mere theoretical possibility, without any experiential recognition, there can be a disconnection in the relationship between a client and therapist that damages the capacity for dissolving suffering. For this reason alone, techniques, interpretations, practices, and observations can have a provisional role in nondual forms of therapy. In what follows I will outline some procedures that I feel are consistent with a nondual approach to therapy. In presenting these guidelines I fully acknowledge that a nondual approach to therapy can unfold without reference to anything I present here. The nondual approach is not confined, or defined, by these guidelines.

Pure Listening and Speaking

Pure listening is a quality of being that therapists with an affinity for the nondual may bring to their interpersonal relationships. It is a type of listening that neither adds to, nor takes away from, what is being communicated. There is no need to encourage or subvert the client's communication. This listening is pure because the therapist hears without any interference. There's no static. They "get things" exactly as they are. When someone listens with this degree of purity, they "listen from nothing." They are like a clear mirror, receiving exactly what is communicated—nothing more and nothing less.

Normally when people communicate with us, we listen through a filter of reactions and assessments. Whether or not we overtly express them, we constantly validate and invalidate what people are saying and doing. But validation and invalidation also have more subtle expressions. For example, simply thinking "I understand" is a form of agreement. Saying "Yes" or even just nodding can be interpreted as signaling agreement. In contrast, spacing out, looking restless, or just thinking "How much longer are they going to go on?" are forms of invalidation. They express some level of intolerance and nonacceptance.

When we listen through a screen of judgments and assessments we distort the natural flow of people's experience. A positive listening pumps energy into a construction. A negative listening takes energy away. Whenever we agree with someone, we tacitly encourage them to continue what they are doing. Our contribution prolongs an emotional or intellectual construction by giving it attention and positive energy. On the other hand, when we disagree we interrupt the flow of someone's experience. We undermine a construction.

When we listen from nothing, we hear everything! We are in an equal and intimate contact with ourselves and the people with whom we are in communication. There is no distinction between ourselves and others. The space of pure listening contains all speaking and listening without privileging either. Communication arises as a beautifully coordinated display of nonmanipulative speaking and listening. It is the only form of communication that respects the integrity of the speaker and the listener. And the only form of communication that can take us beyond our conditioned identities, into an experience of the unconditioned mind.

Natural Release: The Practice of Noninterference

In many Asian spiritual traditions, healing occurs through the practice of noninterference. This is a central method in Taoism, Dzogchen, and Mahamudra spirituality. When we let things be as they are, contracted emotions can often dissipate more quickly than if we meddle and interfere. The ability to let things be, without judgment or reflection, is an important component of the nondual approach to therapy. We simply create space around a problem, and let it run its course and dissipate of its own accord. As Longchenpa says (1987), "Do not condition your mind by [trying] to suppress your experience, apply an antidote, or mechanically transform it, but let your mind fall naturally into whatever [condition you find it]. This is the incontrovertible essence of what is ultimately meaningful."

Conventional therapies assume that the release of intense emotions involves work and effort, either through progressive change or cathartic release. The nondual approach to therapy opens up the possibility of liberating disturbing thoughts and feelings by doing nothing! In the nondual Dzogchen tradition this is called "self-liberation" or "natural release." It is based on the practice of "leaving what is, just as it is."

How does this work? Behind every experience of suffering is resistance. We're either resisting what is happening, or resisting losing it. When we identify what we're resisting and let go, we are immediately free and complete. For as long as we resist, our suffering persists! Emotions and limiting beliefs liberate naturally from within themselves once they are experienced without resistance. When there's nothing to fight against, there is no fight. There's no struggle. Instead there is peace and freedom. This is a very gentle way to release suffering and conflict. It's a "stopping" rather than a "doing." We simply stop trying to confront or avoid what we're experiencing. We let go of the tremendous amount of energy we expend, each and every day, trying to control and manipulate our existence.

In the nondual approach to therapy, therapists facilitate the natural release of fixed beliefs and frozen emotions by creating a space that is free of all pressure to change or be the same. They offer people an open and nonjudgmental space that lets things be, just as they are. This is an extremely respectful way of working with people because we don't judge where they are, or how they *should* be. They give permission for things to be exactly as they are. With this we experience freedom and release. Giving permission for things to be as they are doesn't mean that a therapist endorses who we are. They are not telling us we are perfect. Rather they acknowledge who we are, as the starting point of our relationship. And once we recognize who we are, there is no one else we can be—nor any need or possibility to be anyone else—and hence the fulfillment of our path. At the real point of departure there is no where *else* we need to go.

But often we can't just let go of our resistance in one bold gesture. It feels too risky. But we can learn to recognize the point where problems naturally dissolve. Each time we energize a potentially stressful situation we also have the opportunity to let it return to a harmonious state. In a nondual approach, therapists tune into the points where problems and heavy emotions begin to dissolve by themselves. By recognizing this process they can assist us to return to a point of equilibrium and balance. They recognize the seed of harmony that lies at the heart of every conflict and anticipate the blending and dissolving of conflictual beliefs before they disturb us and throw us into alienating and painful situations.

Deconstructing Fixations: The Madhyamika Way

A feature that is found in many nondual approaches to therapy is the use of conversations that directly reveal the unconditioned mind. In many ways these are the same conversations that go by the name of "inquiry" *(vichara)* in nondual spiritual traditions. These conversations are rarely encountered in daily discourse. I call them deconstructive conversations. They can be spoken and silent. Deconstructive conversations dismantle the foundations of our conceptual constructions and thereby allow us to experience the unstructured mind. They penetrate the seeming reality of feelings, emotions, and sensations in a way that dissolves their existence. These conversations move in the opposite direction to most of our conversations, which unfold as a commentary on our experience. One thought follows the next as we elaborate, modify, develop, rework, add detail, change direction, validate, invalidate, approve, disapprove, etc. Deconstructive conversations reverse this process.

The most powerful technology for deconstructing fixations was developed in the second century by Nagarjuna, Buddhism's greatest philosopher and founder of the Madhyamika system (Fenner, 2002). The Madhyamika system offers a very comprehensive set of deconstructive tools. They are used by yogi-philosophers in their private meditation and transformational debate. The Madhyamika method for dissolving limiting constructions is called deconstructive analysis *(prasanga-vichara)* or unfindability analysis. This type of inquiry lies at the heart of Mahayana insight meditation *(vipashyana)*. These traditional methods are a form of cognitive surgery. They presuppose a level of concentration and thought-control that exceeds the capacity of most people. This makes them relatively inaccessible to most of us.

In therapy, suffering is deconstructed in a conversation, rather than through a meditative or debating routine. The final experience—that our problems can't be found—can be delivered with an informality that is consistent with the repartee of therapeutic conversations. The conversations may have an air of casualness about them, but they are also highly precise.

Normally when we listen to people talking, we assume that what they're actually telling us means something: that there is some truth or reality to what they are saying. There's a strong consensual pressure to listen in this way. When we don't understand what people are saying, we still assume it's meaningful. We typically try to work out what they mean by inviting them so say more.

When we listen to a "story" from the unconditioned mind, there's no intrinsic meaning. We no longer assume their suffering is real or fictitious. What seems to be happening may *not* be happening. This opens up the possibility of engaging with someone's constructions from a place of total innocence and freshness. We learn to speak and listen from the "beginner's mind." This is what Tilopa is describing when he poetically sings (Hixon, 1993), "Gazing with sheer awareness into sheer awareness, habitual, abstract structures melt into the fruitful springtime of buddhahood."

In therapy, therapists identify the core concept upon which a limiting story is constructed. They then inquire into the existence of the reality behind the concept and dissolve the painful feelings associated with fixed ways of thinking.

Another simple way to deconstruct a problem is to disidentify with it. We do this by shifting our perspective and seeing what we are doing from a more spacious and detached point of view. Some people call this "going meta." One way to effect this shift to a meta-perspective is to ask a question such as, "What am I doing right now?" If we were inviting a client to go meta, we could say, "What would you say you're doing now?" This is an invitation to see what we're doing, as though we were observing from the outside. Often, with no prompting or suggestion, people will say, "I see. I'm complaining." Or, "I'm indulging in self-pity." "I'm justifying my rage." "I'm invalidating an accomplishment." And so on. When we move to metaposition, we *see* what we're doing in contrast to just *doing* it. This produces detachment and peace.

In order to facilitate this change in perspective, a therapist appreciates the structure of someone's experience without being pulled into its significance. They listen with care and compassion, but without becoming involved. Therapists distinguish between the content and function of a story. Sometimes they focus on the content. They'll closely track the structure of a story and dismantle it from the inside. At other times they'll bring awareness to feelings and intentions, and invite a client to observe their behavior from a metaperspective. If clients can't see what they're doing, therapists may offer their own observation and encourage clients to see it for themselves.

From the viewpoint of nondual therapy, what is most significant is not the structure or the details of the problem because we're always creating problems. We have this never-ending set of circumstances and memories we can draw upon to construct problems. What is significant is the fact that we are doing it. We are using the energy available to us, using our mind and emotions, to construct a problem. We are constructing that something is happening that shouldn't be happening.

We share with the client that, from our own perspective, we have a very real experience that there is actually nothing wrong with what is happening. We are unperturbed. There is no problem.

The Perfect Wisdom teachings (Hixon, 1993) describe this as "the vision which simultaneously sees and sees through all subjective and objective structures without remaining to grasp or even encounter them." In therapy the therapist becomes a role model for that possibility—not because they create or invent that vision as therapeutic obligation or professional identity, but because it is real and true for them. They share this by staying connected and in relationship with the client through the simultaneous expression of empathy and noninvolvement.

Natural Koans

Koan practice is usually associated with Zen Buddhism. Koans pose questions that cannot be solved—at least conceptually. In Zen, koan practice has been formalized and institutionalized. The entire koan system of Rinzai Zen is a form of contemplative inquiry that deconstructs the conceptual mind in order to reveal unstructured awareness—an experience that in Zen is called "no mind." But koans are actually timeless. Koans arise naturally in our minds when our experience of the conditioned mind expands to include unconditioned awareness. When our familiar points of reference dissolve, questions arise such as: What is this? Where am I? Am I moving forward or backward? Am I moving at all? Is there something special I should be doing? Who am I? These questions are all koans because each one of them is a key that can unlock the conceptual mind and take us into the unknown.

In some forms of nondual therapy, these naturally arising koans are used as tools for deconstructing our habitual ways of thinking. The silences that punctuate nondual therapy often give birth to a gentle cascade of natural koans. By letting our thoughts ride on these koan-type questions, fixed ideas about who we are and what we are doing can dissolve into the infinite expanse of unconditioned awareness.

With skill, these questions can also be consciously introduced into therapeutic conversations. This is a delicate skill because the same questions that can be used to release us from our thinking, can also embed us further in our thoughts. Generally we need to be in a fairly unstructured state of mind before we invite someone to contemplate these koan-type questions. If they are introduced prior to a threshold point, the effect can be counterproductive. They produce *more* thinking rather than a disidentification with thoughts. However, if the questions are well-timed they lead directly into an unmediated experience of the present moment.

Checking the Purity of the Unconditioned Experience

Natural koans arise spontaneously in one's mind. Sometimes these same questions can be introduced by a therapist in order to check the quality and purity of the unconditioned experience. When they are used in this way I call them "checking questions." We can direct these questions to ourselves, and to clients. Normally we ask these questions only when someone is in a fairly open and spacious state of being. These questions reveal whether a person is resting in a structured or unstructured state. An example of a "checking question" is: Could you enhance this experience? If we discover the presence of conceptual residues within the experience of the unconditioned mind, we may choose to go one step further, into the fully unconditioned state, and enjoy the feelings of peace and serenity that arise when our thoughts dissolve.

For example, we can ask: "Is there anything we need to be doing at the moment?" This will give us direct feedback on where the client is. If they say yes, then they are still inside the construction that something is missing. If they don't say anything, or say no, then there isn't anything to do. There is no work to be done—we can talk, or we may not talk. Or, we might ask if the client's experience is pleasurable or peaceful. If it is either, then the state is still structured and different from the state of unstructured awareness, which is neither pleasurable nor painful, neither peaceful nor turbulent.

In asking these "checking questions" we also need to take care that they do not provide a trigger for a conceptual construction. If the client begins to think about our question in an elaborative way, then the question has missed its mark.

Dancing in the Paradoxes of Nondual Logic

In the West we have a long-standing habit of being very earnest and serious about our psychological and spiritual development. We feel compelled to communicate without any hint of inconsistency or inner contradiction. This habit comes from our Greek philosophical heritage. If we are "seen to be" saying one thing is one sentence and contradicting ourselves in the next, we fear that people will judge us negatively. They might think we are confused, superficial, or even crazy! Unfortunately, this is a very limiting way of thinking.

In contrast, Eastern sages move fluidly and confidently in the paradoxical domain without any trace of self-consciousness or distress. They know from their experience that paradox and contradiction are inevitable when we enter the space of unconditioned awareness. They welcome paradox because it points to the reality that cannot be captured by our thoughts.

In nondual approaches to therapy, paradoxes can arise in two ways. First, if we try to describe the unconditioned mind with real accuracy and precision, we are often led to use sentences that contain internal contradictions. The more rigor and clarity we bring to our descriptions, the more we are compelled to use paradoxical formulations.

Second, if we speak from *within* an experience of the unconditioned mind *about* the unconditioned mind, paradoxes can flow forth as a joyful and exuberant expression of mental energy that is usually trapped by the need to appear sane and sensible. In a group setting, an engagement with these paradoxes can also produce an explosion of hilarity and laughter that shatters our seriousness and releases the energy that gets tied up in maintaining a rigid image of ourselves and of others. If we let go of our need for conceptual consistency, these paradoxical thought-forms can lead us directly into the unconditioned mind. They also allow us to experience the unconditioned mind as a highly discerning and dynamic state of consciousness.

One of the most obvious paradoxes that emerges is a recognition that the unconditioned mind is simultaneously something and nothing. It *is* because it *isn't*. And it's the *only* thing that is because it isn't. Everything else is because *it* is. What are we doing now? We are playing in nondual thinking. We are letting our thoughts be shaped by the nondual experience. Instead of arising within the conditioned mind, our thoughts arise from a point where the conceptual touches the nonconceptual.

Further paradoxes arise with the realization that the experience of the unconditioned mind is neither conditioned nor unconditioned, and that it is neither one nor many. Another characteristic of the unconditioned mind is that it can't be lost or gained (because it isn't anything), yet we repeatedly enter it and then lose it!

One of the most delightful paradoxes is that at the end of the nondual path we realize that we haven't traveled any distance—that no path has been traversed and that we haven't attained "anything." But we also realize that if we hadn't believed that there was a path and made the effort we have made, we wouldn't have arrived at the point we are at. Even though we realize that our struggle and commitment has been pointless, in the absence of this effort we would still be drifting in the illusion that there actually *is* somewhere to go *and* something to achieve. Without doing what we didn't need to do, we wouldn't realize that we didn't need to do it.

Conclusion

The ultimate paradox for nondual approaches to therapy is that there is nothing to distinguish these approaches from any others. Or, to play with this a little, the only thing that distinguishes this approach is "nothing"—as an experience of the unstructured mind. As Berkow (this volume) says, this is a "psychology of nothingness." When therapists become trapped in the illusion that they are doing something, anything in fact, they betray that which can never be betrayed—the pure, localized experience of boundless awareness. For the most part, clients and therapists participate in the construction of having and fixing problems. To this extent, nondual approaches to therapy can have the appearance of a form and function, but if they are true to their worth they also reveal the utter futility of their own endeavor.

Endnotes

1.   I would like to thank Professor Barry Reed for reading through this essay and providing valuable comments, and John Prendergast, Ph.D., for very helpful feedback.

2.   Longchenpa, "The Treasury of Wish-Fulfilling Gems," In Robert A. F. Thurman (1996), *Essential Tibetan Buddhism*, New Delhi: HarperCollins India, p. 175, writes that, "This reality has names of many different kinds. It is 'the realm that transcends life and liberation.' And the primally present 'natural spontaneity,' As the 'essential realm' obscured by defilement, As the 'ultimate truth,' the condition of reality, As the originally pure 'stainless translucency,' As the 'central reality' that dispels extremisms, As the 'transcendent wisdom' beyond fabrications, As the 'indivisible reality' clear-void-purity, As the 'Suchness' reality free of death transitions. Such names are accepted by the clear-seeing wise."

3.   There is also a wonderful book of dialogues with the Advaita master Sri Nisargadatta Maharaj (edited by Robert Powell) titled *The Ultimate Medicine: Dialogues with a Realized Master—A Message and Example that Can Awaken Us To Our Original Nature* (Delhi: Motilal Barnarsidass Publishers, 1996), first published by Blue Dove Press, USA, 1994). The dialogues in this book clearly demonstrate the unrelenting way in which Nisargadatta's unconditioned mind interacts with the conditioned minds of his students.

4.   This tradition goes by various names: the Yogachara, Vijnanavada, and Chittamatra.

5.   The term *paravrtti* is sometimes translated as "revolution." The

energies and mechanisms that are purified are called *bijas*. The same idea is found in the Pali canon in the concept of the *alayasamugghata* or "uprooting of the *alaya*." Un-*alaya* or "no-*alaya*" is a synonym for nirvana.

3

Love Returning for Itself

An Interview with Adyashanti

(First interview by John Prendergast and Sheila Krystal at the Green Gulch Farm Zen Center Retreat for Psychotherapists in Muir Beach, California.)

JP—You have said that a real spiritual psychology is rooted in the Ground of Being—that without this there is psychology but no spirituality. What you mean by the Ground of Being?

Adya—The ground where we are right now, before we think our individual selves into existence. We could call it the Ground of Being or we could call it Silence. In that Silence, there's a great sense of presence and aliveness—something that we don't have to believe in, or not believe in. We don't have to be convinced or not convinced that it exists. With the willingness to simply be quiet, we very quickly start to come into a nonconceptual experience. We could call that nonconceptual experience the Ground of Being, or at least the beginning of experiencing the Ground of Being.

SK—Psychology is always looking for universal principles. Would you say there are others in addition to the Ground of Being?

Adya—No, there is no universal principle. Even the Ground of Being isn't really a universal principle. This is the world where true spirituality comes into being, where words and concepts fail. Eventually even what we think of as the experiences that we have through our five senses fail as well. All else fails. Even the principle of the Absolute is no longer there. If there's any universal principle at all, it's that there's nothing to grab hold of. As soon as we grab, whatever we have found is already dissolving.

SK—What is the best that we can do as therapists? Can we be contagious in our understanding? Is there such a thing as therapeutic resonance?

Adya—Of course there is therapeutic resonance. But the less that we're involved in the therapeutic resonance, the more of it there is. If we're sitting there thinking, "Wow! I'm really holding the space for what's happening," then actually the space is limited to something much smaller or less potent than it could be, because we have a concept that we're holding the space instead of just noticing that it's arising without an owner. Now there's not necessarily a therapist and a client. That doesn't mean that there's not therapy taking place. It's just like in my position, when we really come into something deeper than our conceptual environment, then there's no teacher and no student. But that doesn't mean there's not teaching. It could be nonconceptual, it could also be conceptual.

SK—How do we make ourselves attractive to grace?

Adya—Grace prone. That's my favorite phrase. The only way that we can truly do it in a way that is spirituality powerful is to realize our own self. We realize our own inherent emptiness or insubstantiality. There's nothing about us that we can find that's substantial. Only awareness waking up to itself seems to release or open something very powerful, not only individually, but when we meet together. There's an old Zen saying that everything is inherently enlightened. But if you don't know it, a fat lot of good that does you. When we're not aware of our own true being—this field, this presence—we don't experience it ourselves individually. Also, the field cannot come into conscious awareness nearly as powerfully unless there's real awakeness to our own nature. Otherwise, we're always getting in the way, without even knowing it.

JP—This raises the issue of facing emptiness. Is the avoidance of this emptiness the root of human suffering?

Adya—I like to call it the dirty little secret of humanity. It's the emptiness, the abyss, that's right in the middle of every human being. Its right there—that Silence that is always there, just waiting for some recognition of it. We tend to do everything in our power to dance around it.

JP—As therapists, it seems that allowing that Silence in others requires that we do so within ourselves. It can't be done inauthentically.

Adya—I don't think it can, no. One could have some conceptual understanding and maybe get someone close to that experience. They may even fall into it themselves. But what if they do? All they have is a conceptual understanding, but somebody really lets go into that abyss. Now the therapist is no longer of any use to them. They still may need some guidance there. They still may need somebody who has fallen in themselves. On one level we could say that it's true that, as a therapist or spiritual teacher, it is necessary to be totally authentic to what we're doing. I don't see how we could even introduce it, whether it's a spiritual environment or therapeutic environment in any way that's honest, if we haven't ourselves really experienced it. If we do, we get ourselves in way above our head, if the client makes a great big leap ahead of us and all of a sudden, we don't know the lay of the land anymore. In that sense—I don't want to make it too strong—it can even be a bit dangerous.

SK—Richard Alpert, also known as Ram Das, said in a lecture at the Menninger Foundation many years ago that you can only get as high as your therapist! Could you comment on the role of countertransference in psychotherapy?

Adya—If we're really speaking about the Ground of Being, where we started from, what we really deeply awaken to, and to the extent that we're actually embodying that and living that knowingly, then quite naturally we're not going to have a bunch of countertransference going on. Because we're actually in a state of openness. We can know all this. But our knowledge doesn't save us. We can think, "Uh oh. I'm involved in countertransference, and I've got to watch it." Too late! What are you going to do? Try to stop it? That's another form of countertransference. Even if it's a good idea not to just go with it, the process isn't stopped. Either we are being in transparency, or we're not. At least as far as I see, it's very black-and-white. I think that's where our own individual integrity lies.

To the extent that we're able to be with that, to be transparent, so many of the inherent problems of relationship—therapist/client or student/teacher—have a whole different way of working themselves through. They actually do work themselves through, if we're not invested in them. Even to the extent that we're not invested in stopping them. Does that make sense? You want to project? Go ahead! Have at it, you know? Just go go go go go go go go. You'll get tired, unless I'm feeding it. If I'm feeding it, it can go on forever, indefinitely. We see this constantly in the spiritual world, where the projections of the teacher are often manufactured and fed by the environment the teacher is moving in. The teacher sits on a throne, six feet taller than everyone else. There's a place for respect and appreciation, but there's a very definite line between respect, appreciation, even a very deep embodying love, and what

I call worship. Worship is when we put the head above our own. Devotion is heart to heart.

JP—You emphasize "embodiment" in your teaching. You have said that after an initial awakening happens, there is still quite a bit of transformational work most people must undergo in order to be fully embodied. Could speak more about this process?

Adya—It's probably the most subtle and confusing thing I talk about. As soon as a word falls out of my lips and into someone's ears, it tends to be received as, "Okay, now I'm going to do it. I've had my spiritual experience and my spiritual awakening, and now I'm going to go about the process of embodiment." It's quite natural to hear it this way, but that's not really it. Neither is it, "Embodiment is just going to happen as it happens, and there's nothing I can do, so I'll crack a beer and watch TV for awhile." These are the two sides of duality: that I'm going to do it, or there's absolutely nothing I can do. In the context in which this duality takes place, of doing something willful and doing nothing, is something that's much more inclusive. It's back to a deep honesty and integrity with what is.

Certainly, when we have had some deep realization of our true nature, we have an intuitive or innate sense of what's arising within us that's not in accord with that true nature and is the product of some element of divided mind or divided emotional body. We have this sense of it because we had a direct awakening to that which is undivided. Our own divisions tend to stand out much more clearly and vividly than they did before. In some ways they often hurt much more than they did before. They're much more painful because they have this backdrop of wholeness. A lot of the embodiment is simply remaining completely real and completely honest to our own experience in a very deep and authentic way, without necessarily trying to change it. Our conditioned tendencies are allowed to unfold into the field of awareness. It's the true spiritual alchemy that takes place almost by itself, if we can just get out of the way enough.

JP—You have used the phrase, "The heart witnesses from the inside," which is a very beautiful and intriguing description. It seems to be different than how witnessing is normally described.

Adya—I say it that way, John, because to me there's the witness that's often talked about in spirituality, the witness that is transcendent of and inherently different from the object which it witnesses. This kind of witness is, at least in part, a creation of mind. To witness in this independent way is not really the movement of our true nature. In relation to this whole idea of embodiment and the unwinding of one's own conditioning, this distant witness has very little effect on the most powerful elements of our conditioned self. Witnessing certain parts of our own conditioning from the outside is enough for relatively minor or not so deeply entrenched parts of separateness to melt away. Yet that simply doesn't work for the deep, really core remaining pieces. There needs to be a deeper death into what is—a yielding to being awake. Otherwise we're using our own awakeness to distance ourselves, rather than yielding to what it really means to be fully awake.

What it means to be fully awake is to be not only fully conscious but to be fully feeling, to be fully experiencing. On the level of our body-mind we literally feel that we are "watching-experiencing." This is the true nature of the self: watching-experiencing. Even when we're watching, there is always experience. If we don't try to play the watcher in our mind, there's this very natural and effortless watching-experiencing. One doesn't even have to try to do it. On the level of experience, when we're watching, we now feel that we're watching from inside our experience, or in the midst of it. The paradox is that the watching, even though it's inside experience and all around experience, it is not caught by experience. It's not identified even though it's so mixed in there that you can't distinguish it. The touching of awareness with experience enables this. It is a spontaneous act of love when we're watching from the inside with a willingness to yield back into our own experience.

JP—It's simultaneously completely intimate and completely spacious.

Adya—This is true nonduality. Everything else is another form of duality. To go to the impersonal is just to have switched allegiances in duality to the other side. But this is an embrace—something that the intellectual mind can't put together. On the level of experience, we can experience it actually from this place, witnessing from the inside, or witnessing-experiencing as all one movement.

On the level of experience, this intellectual paradox is beautiful. When we really get this, we feel very objective, unaffected, and even distant in our observing. At the same time we are deeply experiencing in a way that is much more intimate than when we are totally identified with our experience. This is very paradoxical to the mind. The more detached you become in this way, the more intimate you become with your experience. They seem to play off of each other, but only in the realm of experience. If this is happening in the mind, then they're always separate: either I'm watching or I'm experiencing deeply. I'm caught in one side of the duality.

SK—Is this integration?

Adya—I guess you could say that. It's not my favorite word. It's just a concept. It's not inherently a rotten concept, but it tends to mean, "I've had some sort of spiritual experience and spiritual practice. I've meditated and feel peaceful and good, and I want to bring that feeling into my workspace, my relationships, or into me." As soon as we're trying to integrate on this level, we're actually missing the whole transformative element and the truth that you cannot take something that's infinite and stuff it into a small box called "my life."

It's actually the reverse. We take "my life" and we release it into the infinite emptiness and space of true being. This is inherent, so we could say this is integrating, but it's integrating opposite, or upside down of the way it's usually done. Usually when we hear about integration, there's still a personal self that's controlling, that's integrating, that's trying desperately to bring their deepest experiences into their everyday lives. The impulse to do so is totally understandable. But this really, deeply misses the point. The point is actually something that is much more frightening to the personal self, where I'm releasing my life into something vast, into something unknown, into something unknowable, and I'm basically releasing my personal control. If you can pull that off, you've got integration. But you don't have integration that you have control of.

JP—You have also talked about "love returning for itself." Can you elaborate?

Adya—I got that phrase from my own experience. In my whole spiritual search I put very little energy into conceptual understanding. When this awakeness happened, it hung out for awhile in its own rarefied place of emptiness, divorced from human experience. That was a nice place, and it's often a very useful part of one's unfolding to experience this and hang out there. There's a lot of deep rest—what psychologists call dissociation—total, absolute spiritual dissociation. I don't know if it's dissociation in the clinical sense of the word, but in a certain sense it's a profound dissociation. Awareness wakes up from form and experiences itself totally independent of form. Of course, it *is* independent of form. When I noticed that it had this momentum when it seemed that it would forever have very little to do with form, and was very pleased to do so, all of a sudden it was like going around in a circle. You get farther and farther away as you travel around.

When you get halfway around the circle, all of a sudden the rest of the way you're going back, back, back. There was no coming back in a linear sense, but almost in a circular sense. There is a movement of inherent love for everything in the body-mind that had any amount of conflict, of suffering. This beingness or awakeness inherently had a tendency to move toward unawakeness or suffering—to welcome it back into its true nature. It was nothing that was intended, but I just noticed it happening. It welcomed back and welcomed back and it would touch everything that was untouched. It inherently seemed not to be satisfied with a grand exit from the world of time and space. It was satisfied with that for a while, but then its deeper nature brought it back in. This was real deep love, because in one sense it was a dangerous thing to do. As our birth shows, it's dangerous for this whole thing to come into form. It welcomed all within this particular body-mind and myself, until there seemed to be very little left to welcome in the sense of contraction or inner contradiction.

Then there was another surprise. Its inherent tendency wasn't to go, "Well, I crossed the nonexistent finish line. Look at me, I'm an enlightened guy." It didn't seem to be satisfied with that either, because it saw all beings as itself. It also wasn't, "I'm going to go out and help other beings." It was, "Oh. This is endless, apparently, because I look around and there's only six-and-a half billion to go," while at the same time realizing that everything is perfectly complete as it is. There's nothing to do. Everything's fine. Everything is an expression of the self as it is. Awake or not, it doesn't matter. This movement was just delighting in spending eternity welcoming itself. Even when it was done in one body-mind, it just seemed to get along with the business of welcoming itself in all the others, which to me was an act of totally unintended love. That's what our nature seems to do in this particular realm that we call the human being.

JP—You have said that the role of the spiritual teacher is mainly a demolition job—primarily deconstructive with maybe a little reconstructive work.

Adya—As it's played out in me. Not with all spiritual teachers, certainly. They have different roles.

JP—You have also said that the psychotherapist's primary role is reconstructive.

Adya—As it has commonly been held. Commonly probably doesn't necessarily apply to the people that would find your book interesting.

JP—That was my question then: Is there some overlapping of these functions or roles that may be evolving now?

Adya—Oh, sure. I don't believe in any rules, because I've seen too many exceptions. Like the rule that you've got to be somebody before you can be nobody. Like you've got to be a healthy ego before you can be no ego. It's a nice idea, it sounds cute, but it's not really true all the time. It's true sometimes and sometimes it's not true. All the rules fall away. I've seen that there is a place for what I call ego health—learning how to dream well, because it's a dream. Some people know how to dream well, and some people don't know how to dream well. Some people who have had spiritual awakenings still don't know how to dream well. It just tends to make life easier if you know how to dream well.

SK—What does "dream well" mean? Could you elaborate on that?

Adya—To be as healthy as an illusionary ego can possibly be. That's why I call it a dream. In this culture it's still very helpful that we know how to dream well. Just because we're enlightened doesn't mean we know how to communicate well, be in relationships well, or know how to communicate with our boss well. It doesn't mean that we necessarily automatically get a "bye," like you've found enlightenment and you're automatically greater. It would be the equivalent of Ramana being able to play quarterback for the 49ers and being great at it. I imagine he would not do too well, nor last too long. He wouldn't know how to do that particular dream well.
I think you have to have an intuitive sense of when it's time to build the dream better, to function better in the world—the dream

world, or when it's time to deconstruct. If I sense that somebody needs a tremendous amount of support to dream better, I often tell them it's not going to happen here. That's not the function I provide. I don't have the time. I suggest you go somewhere where you can get more of that. You can put the shoe on the therapist's foot, too. If somebody starts going to a place spiritually where the therapist isn't at or doesn't have a level of expertise, I would hope the therapist would feel very comfortable referring them over. Just like I would hope spiritual teachers could refer a student to whatever they may need. Awakening isn't the answer for everything. I found out early that it could be absolutely the worst thing that could happen for some people.

SK—In that context, can you talk about addiction? Carl Jung said to Bill W., who started Alcoholics Anonymous, that addiction could only be ended with a spiritual awakening. Yet addiction continues after a spiritual awakening. Could you speak about even the subtlest sense of addiction to sugar, stimulation, or the mind, and not just drugs and alcohol.

Adya—Our primary addiction is to our mind and to our particular emotional state at the time. A lot of people frantically feed themselves mental or emotional activity. It's like an addict—they literally don't know what to do. That's the ego, feeding itself on drama.

JP—What is the relationship of thought to feeling, and what is authentic feeling?

Adya—For the majority of average human beings, probably 95 percent of what they experience is the outcome of what they are thinking, of their own judgments. If we look outside and our mind says it's beautiful, then we have a beautiful feeling. But if we say, "Uh! Cloudy!" then we have that experience. Our emotion just translates our thoughts into an emotional domain. It's actually fairly rare that a human being has a true emotion—an emotion that's not born of a thought. It stands out in some way. It's very telling when we see how much of our emotional life is simply thought translated into feeling. In our culture, we go, "What I'm thinking may not be true, but what have I got left? Feeling. If I feel it, it's real. It's true." But of course, most human beings' feelings have nothing to do with truth. Nothing at all.

This is the tragedy of most human beings' lives. They're having very real experiences based on 95 percent unreal interpretations of what's happening.

JP—I wanted to just list a few emotions and see how this would apply: anger—is it 95 percent from thinking, and sometimes authentic?

Adya—Yeah! Usually from thought, but doesn't have to be.

SK—Hatred?

Adya—Always from thought.

JP—Fear?

Adya—Could be either.

SK—Jealousy?

Adya—Always thought.

JP—Grief?

Adya—Not always thought. Sometimes pure.

JP—Could you say something about that?

Adya—If we're yielding to being fully awake, we're in love with what is. Let's take something that causes a lot of people grief: a loved one dies or is dying. When most people get down to the heart of their grief, they sense that death is a disaster, the ending of something essential. This kind of grief is a product of a belief structure about life and death, about who and what people are. Death takes it all away. Every concept we could have about somebody goes when they die.

At least in spiritual circles, there's this idea that, "If I was really enlightened, I'd never be touched by certain emotions. I'd never get angry, I would never feel grief, because I would know that everything is eternal." This misses the whole point that nothing is separate from the truth, not even grief. But the grief that's based on an illusion doesn't necessarily need to be experienced, once we see through the illusion of it. Then there's what's left.

JP—Do you have any advice for therapists?

Adya—This just came up in the moment, and I think this is a tip for anybody who is interested in truth or transformation: endeavor to be as honest yourself and with yourself as you would ask whoever you're with to be. To me, this is the true field of transformation.

*****

(*Second interview, at Adyashanti's home in San Jose, California.*)

JP—What happens to the ego upon "awakening"? Different teachers talk about the ego dissolving, becoming transparent, or transforming in some way. What is your understanding about what the ego is and what happens to it?

Adya—Good question. It is important to understand what we mean when we talk about ego, because for ten people in a room it's going to mean ten different things. I wouldn't say that the ego dissolves upon "awakening." That just seems obviously true. Of all the people who have "awakened", even if you could say that a few of them seemed to be without what most people would call ego or very little of it, most have quite a bit of ego left. So I don't think awakening has anything to do with dissolving ego, at least as we define it in our modern psychological culture. Perhaps in the past, in spiritual cultures, they defined ego in a different way.

SK—So how would you define ego for the purpose of this book?

Adya—If we define ego as that sense of self which takes itself to be separate and essentially self-existing or independently existing in and of itself, and all the commotion and internal chaos and division that that causes, then we can say that when the awakening becomes very mature, full, or complete, then that ego is seen through or dissolves. One could take ego to mean aspects of the personality structure, the uniqueness of every human being that walks on the face of this earth whether totally liberated or not, that have certain amounts of cultural and genetic conditioning. When I use ego, or the falling away of ego, I mean that movement of inner division—that movement inside of contradictory, psychological elements that causes conflict and suffering. That is the part that falls away. The part that remains is a certain personality structure that often gets changed or altered, but remains in some form. Also, just enough of a sense of self remains that allows your body and personality to operate, but not so much that goes around creating chaos.

JP—Ramana uses the metaphor of the moon in the daytime sky to describe what's left after awakening.

Adya—I like to call it a perfume of self—just enough of it to orient consciousness to a particular body-mind so that it turns its head when it is called. It has a certain operational function that in my experience is about the order of 95 to 98 percent less than what we normally think of ego as, because we need so little of it to operate for consciousness to orient itself and move through the world. I would prefer to say it becomes very transparent, and only apparent when necessary, and not apparent when unnecessary.

SK—So it is called forth by the circumstances?

Adya—By the circumstances. It ends up psychologically where it is not supposed to. My sense is that when you lose yourself or your ego, the only place to find it is the outside. When you look inside, there is nothing there. If you want to find any semblance of it, it comes from the outside. It's not really true. It's not that you are finding yourself in the old sense. If there is any self-reflection, it's the only bit you are going to have. Another aspect of ego or self is the movement of interior self-reflection, which is almost like looking over your shoulder to see how you are doing, how you are being perceived, how you feel, if you've got it, or if you've lost it. It's a movement of energy that is always turning around to look at itself. My sense is that's the piece that stood out and that fell away the most—that movement of energy that would reference itself and be self-reflective. The only place I could find it is in the outside now, because it won't turn around.

JP—This raises an interesting question because depth psychology in particular emphasizes the development of an interior self, an inner life. People tend to be strongly outer directed and may not be in touch with their feelings, needs, or bodies. It seems to be a very natural movement to develop what we might call the interior, and yet there is this understanding in nondual teaching that there is ultimately no inner or outer. Is the development of an interior life a necessary phase?

Adya—I don't know. I say that because the only rule I've seen is that there are no rules. That to me is a rule. Some people who have very little interior sense of self sometimes can have a very powerful awakening. They never go through this phase of finding an interior life. Others can have a spiritual awakening and never had that phase developed, which can be very problematic indeed. If the majority of people have never developed an interior sense of self that is relatively positive, as positive as one can be, it's going to hold them back at some point, even if they have a very deep, transcendent experience.

SK—That brings up a question about how to facilitate this discrimination in people who haven't had a taste of the Ground of Being. How does one facilitate the discrimination between thought and Reality? Some people who come in have no clue that their thoughts are not the Truth.

Adya—By just starting to point it out in a very gentle, simple way. If people can tell you about their thoughts and their stories, you can start to inquire about the storytelling and the storyteller. There are 101 different ways. Both of you have discovered that there are an infinite number of ways to discriminate between the movement of thought or feeling, and the space or context in which thought or feeling is moving in or through. I found that if you get somebody that is in a very psychologically divided and difficult ego state in the right moment, they can see through it. But over-all, sometimes they are going to need some stabilization in their egoic state because they are too intellectually and psychologically fractured to even slow down. If someone is not in the place where they can psychologically slow down, which means that they have to have some ability, at least for some moments, to let the interior division settle, then it's going to be very difficult to point that out. I've also seen it's not always the healthiest thing for someone to see through the story, to see through the whole psychological self, and to see that it's essentially empty. If they're extremely divided inside and you catch them on the right day or the right moment and they see the ultimate emptiness of that, it can be tremendously destabilizing, and not in the positive sense. Healthy egos have a hard enough time when they start to really see the emptiness of the self. I've seen some people with a really fractured ego have a tremendously tough time.

JP—It seems that there is a very fundamental human need to be accurately mirrored. I have observed that you meet people right where they are and very accurately mirror back to them what their experience is. What is your experience of this process?

Adya—Well, for me it's unconscious. I'm not intending to mirror. I think what you said is what does happen—I tend to meet people right where they are. The effect of meeting someone right where they are is "right where they are" gets mirrored. It allows them to actually be right where they are. That's a big part of it. People are there, but they're not really consciously there. They're trying to get away from where they are.

SK—Pointing out is part of the mirroring, too.

Adya—Pointing out can be a powerful part of the mirroring as well, I suppose. Yes. I think sometimes it's just holding someone to their experience, either in a nice, open space or sometimes almost forcibly by bringing their attention back to what's actually happening. So, in that sense, I guess the process of mirroring is useful. Ultimately, the deepest mirroring is that somebody sees their own true nature in the mirror, because they start to see something that's outside of their own story about themselves. If they have a spiritual teacher or maybe a psychologist who is coming from that place that is not casting reflections, they will tend to see that that is what's looking at them and engaging them. They can also start to see that within themselves.

JP—Sacred mirroring, one could say.

Adya—Yeah, I think it could be a sacred mirroring.

SK—You mentioned that things happen unconsciously, and I'd like to come back to the question of the unconscious for a moment and the role of dreams. Is dreaming an expression of the unconscious?

Adya—When I use the term unconscious, I'm referring to something that comes about unconsciously or spontaneously. Spontaneously means that I don't have any conscious intention for it to happen and I don't particularly know where it came from. So when John said that I was mirroring, I thought, "Oh really? Okay." I can see how one could call that mirroring, but there's no intention to mirror. So if it happens, you could say it happens unconsciously, spontaneously, or automatically. As it relates to dreams, I really don't know because I've never been particularly interested in my own, although there have been a few that I've enjoyed. To me it's all of the same quality, whether I'm sleeping at night or awake during the day. It's all just new forms of the same thing. To me that's the chuckle—what happens at night is a dream and what happens in the day is awake, and actually in some way what happens during the day is more of a dream than at night, because people walk around thinking that it's all very real.

SK—What about the spiritual archetype you have referred to that it is tapped into?

Adya—When I talked about the archetype, it's a way of explaining something that is very mysterious and surprising for me. We actually are living archetypes much more than we are living human beings. The more realized we become, not as a body-mind but as something that transcends the body-mind completely, the more a living archetype gets out there and works. For instance, going back to dreams, I've had people who have dreamed about Adyashanti when they've never had any access to me. They've never heard the name and they've gone to the computer and done a search and, lo and behold, they're really surprised to find that there's actually somebody there, because they had a dream and we were sitting next to each other, and then they see my picture and they go "Wow, that's the guy!" Something is clearly functioning that's in a different realm. That happens so often. It's interesting, isn't it? My pet theory is that when we are not containing ourselves to a particular location, to a particular body-mind personality, then quite naturally it's not going to be confining itself to that location. Not being owned, it's freed-up to do whatever it wants. Of course, people think that Adya, Ramana, or Nisargadatta know about it. I don't know about anybody else, but for me, nine times out of ten, it's just as much news to me as it is to them. That archetypal thing is functioning totally independently yet with an incredible precision, timing, and intelligence.

JP—I wanted to come back to a point that you and Sheila were touching on that had to do with discerning thought from reality—seeing one's core story and also knowing who the storyteller is. Can you say something about the importance of being able to identify the core story and how you approach this?

Adya—When I talk about the core story, I really do mean the *core* story, which isn't really so much a story as a belief. I've never met anybody that couldn't put the core belief in a sentence of eight words or less. It's a very simple core belief. It's a statement that usually sums up a view of the self or the world. You can just find everything in it. I've suggested that people write down all their beliefs so they don't go there too quickly and to limit their beliefs to one sentence, so it doesn't become a dissertation or something highly intellectual. If it's one sentence per belief it stays very practical. When people actually do that, they start to see that there are these connections. These disparate beliefs actually start to be seen to form something that's very, very similar. It's almost like one voice that's ultimately taking on a thousand voices, but actually they're all coming from one voice.

JP—Spokes radiating from…

Adya—From the central hub. So I find that once someone finds really that core story, that core belief…

SK—It's like a linchpin.

Adya—It's a linchpin, if you ultimately get there. It's a process for most people to get there because it's a really deep thing. Usually people think they've found it and then they find something that's underneath it. When someone really pulls a linchpin on the core story, everything falls apart. Often people have had some sort of spiritual awakening and then find out that it's not true that just because you've had a spiritual awakening to the truth of your Being, that your core story isn't still functioning. Many parts of the exterior of the core story, many of the old stories, start to become transparent when we really awaken. A lot of them just fall away. But it's pretty rare that the core story falls away. It seems to be able to survive a very deep infusion of the spiritual truth. Often people who've had these kinds of experiences are still finding the core story operational and distorting what they know to be true. Part of them knows it's not real, but the core story is still operating and thinks it is real and the center of their own universe. It is very, very compelling.

JP—There seems to be a grandmother and a grandfather core story. One seems to be a sense of lack, of missing something, and the other seems to be that something is wrong with what I am—I'm bad. These two actually seem to be quite related to each other.

Adya—Well, I think they are.

JP—They are like two sides of the same coin: what I am is either not enough or bad.

Adya—There is a core story that I like to call the dirty little secret of humanity: when we look inside to the truth of our being, there's nothing there. There's a void. There's emptiness. There's zero. I think that this truth is the number one thing that everybody's scurrying from, racing around madly to try to not really see, to not feel, to not come to grips with. Its first manifestation is, "I'm not good enough. Essentially I'm lacking." Part of that is just not useful, but part is. If you think you're just a personality structure or ego, since that's not really who a human being is, our own egoic structure in one sense is telling us the truth. It's telling us, "I'm not enough, I'll never be enough, I'm not worthy, and I'll never be worthy." It is usually taken as a moral judgment, when its ultimate genesis is telling a truth that as long as I take myself as separate, it's never enough, I'm never good enough, and I always feel lacking.

There's something strangely appropriate in that because it's true. That's why you can't fill it up with enough self-esteem. Even with people who have great self-esteem, there's still some sort of nagging suspicion that this whole thing could collapse. It's a very delicate area. Of course I wouldn't necessarily point that out to somebody at the wrong moment, but I find when I talk to people, a lot of the time instead of it being horrendous there's a great relief. A lot of them have been to spiritual teachers, psychologists, or self-help books that are really trying to fill the hole and make it bigger. They often see me as somebody who's finally told them the truth that they know. Maybe they don't like it, but at least someone has said, "Yeah, we both know this. We both know that of course there's a sense of lack because the thing that's trying to sustain itself is never good enough, is it?" They know all of this (clicks fingers) just like that. Then there's a door.

JP—So here is where therapists may spontaneously reflect and invite inquiry with their clients: "It's not enough, is it? Explore this lack fully. What do you discover?"

Adya—Inviting most people into their experience is very frightening. It's more than painful, it's taboo. You're not supposed to find out that this is in the center of yourself. It's not okay. It will kill you. It's a void. It will render your life meaningless. Don't go there.

JP—You'll be annihilated.

SK—Or the ego will be annihilated, and that's exactly what we want. That's the paradox.

Adya—It is a paradox. You know, I find, Sheila, that the language that we couch this stuff in often transmits a much more painful experience than necessary. So many people come to me, and usually because of their spiritual conditioning they're waiting for ego annihilation. They're at the edge of the cliff, they're ready to take a leap, or they're ready to walk into the fires of the divine. They can barely stay in their own skin because they feel they're so close to something very profound. Oftentimes I'll just say, "Did it ever occur to you that you're making all this up in your mind, this whole carnival show?" Often they can just see it. The only thing that makes a big production out of ego death is the ego. What if ego death was actually more seeing through the whole production called My Own Death? The scene is just a projection of mind. That itself is actually the ego death.

SK—A fog burning off.

Adya—A fog burning off. It's just no big deal. The terms that have been used are pointers, but they also often create images in the mind that become a new barrier, "I have to go through ego annihilation."

SK—A woman recently asked you at a public meeting whether you thought therapy would help her awaken, and you answered, "No." Why is that?

Adya—In its traditional sense, therapy is trying to put a nicer looking tutu or lipstick on the pig, which is great. It makes the story better and enables one to dream better, which means to function as an ego better. I'm not saying that it has no practical value, because it is highly advantageous to be able to dream well, whether you are spiritually awake or not. But the mere fact that we can dream very well doesn't make us any more awakened. Some people are highly functional dreamers. They can make money easily; they can get along with human beings; they can be in satisfying relationships; they can raise their kid well; they can treat their dog well and mow their lawn on the weekends. They're actually highly functional. In spiritual circles, it's almost like a no-no to say that someone could be relatively happy without being enlightened. We can get the dream state to that quality. That doesn't mean that that person is any closer to really being awake.

SK—What can we do as therapists, if anything, to help people awaken?

Adya—That's a hell of a question, a loaded question. Well, be awakened yourself. That's the biggest thing. If one isn't to some extent awake, there's nothing you can do, and you're better off leaving the whole subject alone, because you'll probably do more damage than good.

SK—Could you elaborate?

Adya—When some people go through their process of awakening, it's very smooth, joyous, and a great relief. Other people's unfolding can be a very rocky journey indeed. It can be a lot of blood and guts as their whole world and sense of self is collapsing onto the floor. They're frightened and terrified. I've had more than one person that just got really spooked halfway through, as everything was crumbling and they realized they couldn't put it back together. Then they really get scared. If someone isn't very familiar with that landscape, they can trigger a process with that person that they don't know how to deal with it. Most spiritual communities don't know how to deal with it, because every time somebody goes through a spiritual emergency, they get rid of the person. Sometimes people are really going to be on the edge, between sanity and insanity, and you better know what you're dealing with.

JP—I wanted to read a quote from the sage Eckhart Tolle and get your response: "When a log that has only just started to burn is placed next to one that is burning fiercely, and after a while they are separated again, the first log will be burning with much greater intensity. After all it is the same fire. To be such a fire, is one of the functions of a spiritual teacher. Some therapists may also be able to fulfill that function, provided they have gone beyond the level of mind and create and sustain a state of intense, conscious presence, while they're working with you." What are the preconditions for the transmission of this light to occur, and do you agree with Tolle that therapists can fulfill that function?

Adya—I'll go to the last part first. I think anybody can fill that function. I think neighbors, grandmothers, mothers, friends, lovers, and anybody who's really on fire with the presence of Truth can fulfill that function. I don't think it's meant for anybody who even has a role, so of course a therapist can fulfill it. When I was younger I had a friend who was a street person and also a disgusting alcoholic when he was drinking. When he wasn't drinking he was so on fire with this presence that I was damn near nonfunctional for hours. I would meet with him because he would just take me into this dimension that was incredible and authentic. He also had this whole other problem. Anybody who's burning with the truth does that naturally. We all transmit where we are spiritually and psychologically all of the time. There's nobody who is not. A depressed person is transmitting depression; you can feel it when you walk in the room. A spiritually awake person is transmitting awakeness; you can feel it.

JP—Then the first question—what are the preconditions for that flame to ignite? Is there a readiness on the part of a client or student that allows a fuller transmission to occur?

Adya—Oh sure, I think there's definitely a readiness.

JP—What are the elements of that readiness?

Adya—Again, it's hard to qualify. I can sense it when somebody walks up to me. I can sense it if they're really ready. It's usually somebody who has a sense of quiet desperation to know what's real, what's true. I can feel it. I found it has nothing to do with how long they've been on the path or what they've gone through in life. Some people really don't know much about spirituality at all and out of nowhere they just had to know what was true. If they have to know, then that's the night for them every time. We could say they're very susceptible to the fire, they're very dry grass. Some people *think* they want to know—this is the difference. Some people look almost the same—they look very desperate, they're ready. I've had people say, "Okay Adya, I'm really ready to walk into the fire." But you can feel that there's an expectation. They've thought about it. They've gotten themselves spiritually ready and now, "Here I come."

JP—It's not spontaneous.

Adya—No. When I hear it, I just go, "Oh no." I just feel it because they're feeling something inside themselves. It's very innocent. It's real to them, but it's not spontaneous. A readiness isn't something we decide, but something that grabs us, doesn't it?

SK—It's authentic.

Adya—Yes, it's not something that we have control over. That is with a very obvious case. Other times, the therapist or the spiritual teacher doesn't give enough credit to people who really want to know what's true, who have something very deep, authentic, and spiritually significant happening. A lot of the time this is missed. We think we have to dummy it down or we can't speak directly. We actually can be direct much more often than one would think. What is intrinsic within me is by nature intrinsic within you. When I start to see that the truth is intrinsically inherent in everybody, not just theoretically but actually, then we're relating to that intrinsic truth.

SK—Our Self sitting with our Self.

Adya—Yes, with the deepest part of ourself. I think the energy of that is its own transmission, too—of what I see in you. Not only am I being a field of presence or awakeness—hopefully that's not even in our consciousness because then it's already being corrupted—but in addition I am really seeing the truth in you. That's different than, "I am being the impact. I am holding the space for you." There's something separating and hierarchical in that. That may actually be happening, that may be true, but I think there's this other part of really seeing God in the other, no matter what the exterior is. When we're really seeing that, there is a transmission. Even if we're dealing on a very relative level, we are connected to something else on the unspoken level of heart. That's very, very powerful.

SK—And respectful.

Adya—It's deeply respectful. If I know that you, no matter how you are sitting in front of me, are the manifestation of God, how am I going to be with you? Now maybe God is pretending over there in your part to be very confused and suffering, but if I really know that that's God but just maybe confused, now how am I going to be with you? Not only in my words but also in my energy, how am I going to approach you now? You see, it becomes holy, something very sacred. It doesn't mean I just skip by your suffering and tell you you're God and bypass and discount everything. But on the level of the heart it's a wholly different encounter.

In therapy you have to make the diagnosis, which is okay, but in that diagnosis there is that whole sense of: "What's wrong? What's the malfunction?" This is not only a diagnosis and a mental state, it's also a state now where we're energetically engaging with a problem. We're not engaging with God who's suffering or with the sacred who's having a difficult time. We're not even dealing with a human being anymore; we're dealing with a problem. We're trying to solve the problem.

JP—You have said, if I understood correctly, that the transformational process is different before and after awakening. I'm wondering if you could say more about that.

Adya—Before awakening we are identified with the very problems that we are trying to overcome. We're identified with the very limited self that's causing a tremendous amount of suffering in our lives and we're identified with a whole host of limiting ideas, beliefs, and experiences. I think when we've had some glimpse of real awakening, there is a fundamental shift of our sense of self away from all of that and into something else—you could call it awareness, consciousness, or presence. To the extent that this shift has taken place, we could say the conditioned self, the whole bundling of conditioning—thought, feeling, reaction, and history—is viewed impersonally rather than personally. It doesn't define me anymore; it's not telling me who I am. I'm not a rotten person, if it's still happening. Nor am I a great person, if it all of a sudden ceased. There's a very nonpersonal relationship to the extent that the identity has shifted. But that extent varies greatly from person to person. With some people it's a very clean severing of the old from the new, and for others it's very mixed where parts of their identity are still very caught up in the conditioned pattern. When that awakening has happened to whatever extent, then the relationship is much lighter. We can actually deal with the suffering itself, untainted by the struggle of our identity. Our identity is the glue that holds it all together.

JP—So conditioning would seem to undo more rapidly without this identification?

Adya—My experience is that it undoes much more rapidly. I often have people know in retrospect when pieces fell away. The whole process becomes a lot easier.

JP—There's a related question that I have about the subtle or energy body. Tantric traditions emphasize the importance of awakening the subtle body as part of the transformational process. How important do you think this is, and how does awakening impact the subtle or energy body?

Adya—When it's thorough, awakening ultimately has to do with all of it. Personally, I haven't found anything that's left out of the awakening. It has to do with the subtle body, the gross physical body, the nature and structure of thought, the way the brain literally operates, and with the emotional body. When it's thorough, everything is impacted and transformed. So I don't necessarily always work directly; I don't obviously work with subtle bodies or even with the physical body a whole lot. Although I do see a place for that, an appropriateness, it just doesn't seem to be what I do. I usually am working on the fullness of realization rather than on the particulars, because my experience is, the more full the realization is, the more is included. The subtle body and the gross physical body undergo a transformation. The way we hold our bodies becomes different. The quality of the experiences that we have is different.

In my case, the way the mind operated became very different. For months it literally felt as if there was a telephone operator in my brain reconnecting all the circuits. When it was done, the brain was capable of things it was never capable of before. It was capable of a subtlety of thought, a subtlety of perception in the brain, and an ability to follow a line of subtlety that I never could have possibly done before because I would have gotten lost in all the subtlety. There is a profound transformation on all these levels. In my case it was relatively natural. When the realization was full, all these aspects unfolded in and of themselves. Other people are going to have more knots in their subtle body, emotional body, and in their mind. Karmically they're going to be a little more heavily armored. They might really need to go into work with the subtle bodies. They might need to work consciously with the physical body. They might need to consciously work with their ability to dream well, so they might need to be with somebody in a standard therapeutic environment, although I think if they're doing spiritual work it behooves them to be with somebody that has some real presence. I think it's very individual.

But there needs to be a sensitivity, at least from my end. I have no qualms about sometimes referring people out to a few psychotherapists that I know well and who know what I'm doing. I've seen great benefits by doing so. I don't have the time and the energy to address some piece with some people. They might really need to be with somebody for an hour every week to really go in, and it just isn't going to happen with me. They're not going to go through that piece on their own. I think it's important to know that. Or if I see people who are physically really bottled up, where they really have knots, I can help some of them on the level of realization. That often does a tremendous amount. Some people find help just going at it very directly.

SK—This is a quote from the European sage Jean Klein. I'm interested in the threshold that he speaks of: "You can only understand what you are not. What you are, you can only be. When understanding dissolves in being, there is sudden awakening. The timeless nonstate cannot be achieved because the mind cannot evolve towards it. The mind can only bring you to the threshold. Awakening comes unexpectedly, when you do not wait for it. When you live in not knowing, only then are you available."

Adya—That is a beautiful description of what precipitates awakening and what awakening's really all about, the ultimate nonexperience. It's literally waking up, which is a whole other subject. But boy, what constitutes awakening and a spiritual experience are in my mind night and day, yet they seem to be horrendously confused in our spiritual culture. He hits it right on the head about it not being an experience. It's a nonexperience—not being a product of mind, not even being prepared through the mind. The mind just gets one to the threshold of it. It's not any more of an experience than waking up in the morning is an experience and realizing that whatever you dreamed the night before was only existing between your ears. Real awakening is ultimately very similar in that sense.

SK—What is our role as spiritual therapists in bringing people to the threshold and maybe even facilitating that arrival?

Adya—That's a hard one for me, to be quite honest. My only job is to be myself. That's what I do. My job isn't to wake people up. I don't even feel that people need to be awake. It's none of my damn business whether they're awake or whether they want to be awake. If they come up to me and they say, "I really want to awaken," well, then we might have something to talk about. Ultimately it's none of my business what somebody else wants or what they don't want. So, my role for me is only to be myself. My role isn't to awaken people or take their suffering away. It's not really to do anything. A rose blooms. That's its dance. This is my dance. That's all there is to do. It's just the way life is dancing through me.

JP—Being who you are.

Adya—Right. I think things get weird when we start to take on our roles and the expectations of the roles. If I'm bringing a spiritual expectation in that someone's interested in awakening, it's just another phony thing. It's so easy to see the old as phony or unnecessary and then not to see the new as just another form of the old. We're going to have everyone sitting around being spiritual psychotherapists. What does that mean? Does it mean anything we could say it means? As soon as we start to do that, has it suddenly become not spiritual? Has it just become more of the same in different clothing? If it is spiritual, if it has that element, I think ultimately it's the element of our own awakeness, of our own presence, of being the fire of that, without even necessarily having any conscious recourse to it. It's just who we are. Then we go about our work.

If there is a spiritual psychotherapy, it's not really about the therapy. I don't think there is a spiritual psychotherapy, because as soon as it becomes that, it's not spiritual anymore, it's just more models. I think there can be a spiritual psychotherapist, which is a transformed, awakened psychotherapist. The therapist seems to me to be the most potent part of the therapy, wouldn't you agree? That therapist can use a hundred and one techniques, or just sit there and babble. Something else is going to be going on in that room. There's going to be a different presence available.

Psychotherapists have recourse to working at a wide latitude because of their training. People tell me that I have certain elements of being a trained therapist in the way I work with people. But as far as I'm concerned, I'm pretty narrow in what I do. Therapists potentially have a lot of things on their plate to play with when somebody comes in. If that fire is alive, it will be a real potent part. They'll see it in you. They'll start to wonder, "Gee, John, what do you have in your eyes? What's going on there?" There is an intrigue and then the door can open. I think that one of the nice things that I see happening in therapy, at least around this area (San Francisco Bay Area), is that a lot of the therapists still have their tools that they'll use when they need them. But there's a whole other facility that has to do with who and what they are, which is as potent or powerful as anything they might be doing as a human being.

Endnotes

1.   The editors wish to thank Sumitra (Roberta) Godbe for transcribing this interview.

4

The Sacred Mirror:
Being Together

John J. Prendergast

We are the mirror, as well as the face in it.

—*Rumi*

Introduction

When we look into an ordinary mirror, we see how we appear.[1] When we look into a sacred mirror, we see who we are. In the first kind of looking, we find an object—our face or body—and take it to be our self. In the second kind of looking, we see *through* a mental object (our self images and stories) and find no one. This is both unnerving and tremendously freeing. While the function of sacred mirroring has historically been assigned to a guru or spiritual preceptor, it has begun to appear during the ritual of modern psychotherapy as increasing numbers of therapists *and* clients, either spontaneously or through spiritual practice, have discovered a vast and open awareness within themselves. This essay describes this emergent phenomenon and explores ways that it may be included within, as well as expand, the theory and practice of transpersonal psychotherapy.

Over many years as a therapist and teacher, I have wondered how presence or unconditioned awareness may arise during the encounter between therapist and client so that it is directly felt by both parties. How does such a shared conscious encounter impact the therapeutic experience? When presence arises during therapy, both therapist and client have the felt-understanding that they are no thing in particular. Rather, they experience that they simply *are*. Personal identity fades into the background as unconditioned awareness comes into the foreground, much as the view of a landscape will change when we shift the lens of a camera. The conditioned sense of separation between a discrete self and other falls away and leaves the felt-sense of nonseparateness or nonduality. The great twentieth-century Indian sage Ramana Maharshi (1984) likened the mind at such times to a sliver of the moon in the daytime sky—its reflected light barely noticed amidst the direct light of the sun. Such openings into a vast shared spaciousness bring a sense of deep peace, great freedom, and quiet joy. Clients often report a sense of coming home and of being connected to the whole of life, at least temporarily.

While it does not appear that presence can be created, it can be attuned to, recognized, or welcomed. Over the years I have discovered that engaging clients in a relaxed, largely silent, nonintentional eye gazing tends to welcome presence into the foreground of awareness for both client and therapist. This quiet looking may emerge spontaneously, or by the therapist's informal invitation. In addition to inviting presence, this powerful contact inevitably brings up deeply entrenched defenses against intimacy and letting go that are usually directly related to the client's presenting problems. Compelling negative beliefs, powerful emotions, and intense somatic constrictions are frequently uncovered and gradually worked through. This transformative process is particularly important since it is of limited value to evoke presence in order to temporarily bypass difficult personal material. Instead, approaching the knots and veils of personal difficulties from a much larger shared space allows them to open or dissolve more easily, even as they are accepted as they are.

I call this nonintentional looking *being together* because it is a shared experience of Being by both therapist and client. During this quiet looking the therapist is open and transparent, attuning with and reflecting back the client's essence. At such times the therapist functions as a sacred mirror.

Therapeutic Mirroring

Therapeutic mirroring plays a well-recognized and valued role in many forms of modern psychotherapy. Heinz Kohut (1971), the founder of Self psychology, identified mirroring as one of three basic human psychological needs. In his view all children have a narcissistic-exhibitionist need to be seen as special, to feel welcomed, and to be delighted in. Kohut observed that "the gleam in the mother's eye...confirm(s) the child's self-esteem." He theorized that if a child receives sufficient mirroring early on, she will develop her own capacity for self-mirroring, which sustains a relatively cohesive sense of self even when subsequent external mirroring is inadequate or absent. Conversely, a deficiency of early mirroring leads to a precarious sense of self. Kohut believed that individuals need mirroring throughout their lives and seek it out from increasingly appropriate sources as they mature. Psychotherapy is one such source. For Kohut, the therapist's empathic understanding—the ability to enter into the client's inner world—addresses and in part fulfills the client's profound need for mirroring. He believed that empathic understanding was the most curative factor in psychoanalysis and equated empathic failure with the absence of mirroring.

Both Margaret Mahler (1975) and David Winnicott (1971) affirmed the importance of early maternal mirroring. Mahler recognized eye contact between mother and child as an essential component for creating the full development of symbiosis—the necessary stage of "dual-unity" where the child feels herself at one with her mother. Winnicott described the mother's face as "the precursor of the mirror" and observed that if a child first encounters a mother's chronically unresponsive face, then the subsequent experience of an actual physical mirror will be of "a thing to be looked at but not to be looked into." He saw psychotherapy as "a complex derivative of the face that reflects what is there to be seen."

Sigmund Freud (1913) directly prohibited any kind of visual mirroring by recommending that patients lie down on a couch and analysts sit out of view behind them. Obviously uncomfortable with direct eye contact, Freud acknowledged that he disliked "being stared at for eight hours a day." He rationalized this posture by explaining that face-to-face contact blocked the therapist's ability to attend to his own unconscious thoughts and interfered with the development of the patient's transference.

Freud explicitly encouraged psychoanalysts to be opaque rather than transparent. Wolman (1994) noted, "Much of the atmosphere in which analysis is conducted, with its stress on the analyst's relative neutrality and anonymity, can be traced back to [Freud's] barrier against mirroring." It is interesting to wonder how psychoanalysis might have evolved had Freud been more at ease looking directly into his patients' eyes.

Freed from Freudian orthodoxy, neoanalytic schools of psychotherapy, particularly Self psychology and Intersubjectivity (Stolorow, 1987), have come to value empathy and mirroring. Nonetheless, an important transpersonal dimension of mirroring remains largely undescribed and unexplored in conventional psychotherapy, with the notable exception of Carl Rogers.

Rogers (1980), founder of client-centered therapy and one of the twentieth century's most creative and insightful psychotherapists, identified three primary healing qualities provided by a therapist: genuineness (realness, congruence), unconditional positive regard (nonjudgmental acceptance, caring, prizing), and accurate empathy. By genuineness, Rogers meant the capacity for a therapist to be "transparent" to the client, free of a "professional front or *personal façade* [italics added]." He defined empathy as a process of being at home in the private perceptual world of the other. This ability to enter into another's reality, he noted, required "in some sense...that you lay aside your self." Toward the end of his remarkable career, which included a nomination for the Nobel Peace prize, Rogers acknowledged an increasingly spiritual dimension to his work with people:

> I find that when I am closest to my inner, intuitive self, when I am somehow in touch with the unknown in me...whatever I do seems to be full of healing. Then, simply my *presence* is releasing and helpful to the other. There is nothing I can do to force this experience, but when I can relax and be close to the transcendental core of me...it seems that my inner spirit has reached out and touched the inner spirit of the other. Our relationship transcends itself and becomes a part of something larger. Profound growth and healing and energy are present.

While he emphasized the importance of attending to a client's moment-by-moment "felt meanings," Rogers also clearly pointed to an inherent healing awareness that would sometimes spontaneously unfold between and transcend therapist and client. This awareness or presence is the core of sacred mirroring.

Discovering Sacred Mirroring

I first discovered this function of *being together* or sacred mirroring in 1988 while working with a very sensitive client with whom I shared an intimate rapport. There were several moments in our work together when there was a natural stop to our conventional thinking and feeling and we simultaneously dropped into a shared space of Being. There was a spontaneous feeling and understanding of common ground beyond and before the roles we were playing as therapist and client and whatever individual identities we were attached to at the time. It felt like a holy meeting and a truly sacred space.

While I had experienced this with my spiritual mentor, the European sage Jean Klein (1989), on a number of occasions before this, it was the first time this happened with someone in therapy. I was a bit disoriented. "Should this be happening in therapy?" I wondered, as if it could be otherwise! "Where do we go from here?" I was not fully at ease with doing nothing and just being together. I thought that something more was required of me in my role as a therapist. My client also felt some mental injunction to be doing more—to be working on her issues. So we again entered into our familiar roles.

Over the years, as I have felt more at home in the unknown, I have noticed that this space arises more frequently as a shared experience with different clients. In 1996 on occasion I began to casually invite clients to settle into a soft gaze with me while we are both silent. I now encourage clients to feel free to remain silent or to verbalize anything that needs to be expressed while we sustain our intimate contact with the eyes either open or closed.

Sacred Mirroring Distinguished

Unlike various descriptions of psychological mirroring that focus on the importance of therapists accurately and empathically reflecting back their clients' thoughts, feelings, and sensations, sacred mirroring involves Being mirroring itself. This is not to devalue other levels of mirroring or to suggest that they are unimportant or profane. Ordinary mirroring is also vital for full human functioning. Sacred mirroring, however, is of a different order. It includes an essential dimension of the human experience that often is completely overlooked or only dimly intuited during therapy. While conventional mirroring reflects a client's personal experience, sacred mirroring reflects back the impersonal Ground of Being shared by client and therapist.

Although all of life's expressions are ultimately sacred, clients often use words like "sacred" or "essential" to describe the extraordinary wholeness and intimacy that arises while *being together*. During the gazing they sometimes report contacting an unknown sense of wholeness beneath or behind their sense of lacking something. Some report that what they fear as groundlessness or emptiness shows itself to be an authentic ground or core as they participate in the quiet looking. Over time, many clients' feelings of isolation, alienation, and disconnection gradually transform into an intimate connection with life. When clients let go into the imagined terrors of abandonment, engulfment, or fragmentation while sustaining this intimate contact with their therapist, they often eventually discover a greater sense of freedom and authenticity.

Functioning as a Sacred Mirror

When we, as therapists, deepen into Being, we begin to spontaneously take on the function of a sacred mirror. As the opening quote by Rumi suggests, we come to know ourselves as the mirror *and* the face that is reflected in it. We have the growing intuition that we are not essentially separate from those whom we mirror.

When sacred mirroring is happening, it feels as though no one is mirroring. We experience it as an impersonal event. The line between subject and object at first blurs and then eventually dissolves. The apparent subject (me) is seen to be no different than the apparent object (you) at an essential level. However, if we begin to identify with this function and take our self as special mirroring somebody, we impose duality upon what is an essentially nondual relationship with our clients. From this perspective, no one can be a sacred mirror or be sacredly mirrored! Being itself is the mirror. Being knows itself as the apparent other and communicates this understanding in silence and through words to the "client" who also is none other than that. It is an impersonal understanding, which is communicated with the unique flavor and qualities of an individual human being.

Naturally, sacred mirroring requires a high degree of maturity. If we have residual needs to be admired or idealized in any way (which most of us have), the function of sacred mirroring will be partially undermined. The crosscurrents of the self-image or ego will distort the clear mirroring of Being. Realistically, this distortion is bound to happen to some extent with most therapists, as we learn to relax into Being. It is important to be aware of any feelings of inflation or needs to be idealized, and to honestly investigate what may feel unloved, unaccepted, devalued, or lacking within our self. The ego will tend to appropriate the sacred mirroring function as a special skill. It is humbling to discover that this capacity is inherent in all individuals. Not surprisingly, the less attached to and identified with sacred mirroring we are, the more freely it functions.

Sacred mirroring also enhances ordinary mirroring. Once therapists and clients are connected in an expansive space, they may approach the contents of awareness with much more clarity and intimacy. The conditioned body/mind is more easily seen to be what it is. Core beliefs are seen as thoughts instead of gospel truths. Shameful and frightening feelings are more readily accepted and allowed. Sensations are explored with less resistance. The contents of awareness—thoughts, feelings and sensations—come into clearer focus as therapists and clients consciously share the ground of Being. There is a greater sense of welcoming whatever arises in one's awareness.

Given the profound value of sacred mirroring, it is natural to want to know how to attain or achieve it. How do we become a sacred mirror? Paradoxically, the effort to become a sacred mirror takes one farther from it. Trying to be present, open, and available is like trying to make the sun rise (or the earth turn)—it happens of its own. Certain things are obviously not in our control. Being is one of them. Furthermore, we already *are*. Trying to be present or to be a sacred mirror is like standing in our house and asking how to get home. We are already there.

Attuning with Being or presence is a matter of nonmental understanding, which in turn allows a deep letting go. Efforts may be made to understand, to quiet the mind, to fix or purify something that we imagine is wrong or missing. In the end, however, effort is discarded. There is literally nothing to do to be present. It is enough to notice when we are not present. Eventually, we come to realize that what we are looking for is the one who is looking. The search comes to a natural stop and we simply recognize what we already are. We discover that we have always been the sacred mirror that we have been trying to become.

What is the inner felt-sense of functioning as a sacred mirror? Subjectively, there is an enhanced capacity to be with whatever arises within oneself or within another, including the resistance to what is arising. Therapists who are attuned with being are less likely to believe that anything is fundamentally wrong or missing in their clients. They may be aware that their clients misunderstand or overlook their own deepest natures, yet even this misunderstanding is not seen as a problem. Therapists who are deeply attuned with being engage much less in projecting or protecting some image or story of themselves, and they are less likely to collude with their clients who do this. Instead of being goal oriented, they tend to trust in the unfolding process of self-discovery. They may introduce a variety of skillful means to help their clients, but with much less attachment to an outcome. They are more frequently open, present, engaged, intimate, spacious, and compassionate. Their attention tends to be more innocent and affectionate. Naturally, therapists will also have a unique flavor and presentation depending upon their personality, gifts, and life experiences.

The function of a sacred mirror is different from the blank screen described by traditional psychoanalysis. There may be a superficial similarity of detached observation, but the awareness is worlds apart. Therapists who are attuned with being come from the heart, not the head. Rather than feeling themselves as being essentially separate from their clients, they feel joined on a fundamental level. They are moved by their clients' suffering in an intimate way because there is a natural flow of empathy and love between them. While a blank screen is designed to evoke transference, a sacred mirror will simply reflect back a client's multidimensional experience, which may include transferential phenomena when this is relevant. The broader purpose of sacred mirroring is to be with whatever arises rather than to analyze transference. Open acceptance stimulates authentic transformation.

Being Together Described

Broadly stated, *being together* is a shared *being with* what arises. It is not a staring contest, a power struggle, a form of analysis, or a method to get somewhere or accomplish something. It is not a hypnotic induction. It is shared presence.

One relaxes into the background silence prior to thinking, even as thoughts come and go. It can be described as an opened-eyes meditative space, but without a discrete identity as a meditator. Attention is nonintentional and open, alert but undirected, free of the need to accomplish or attain anything. It is a shared space rather than a private one. One could call it an interpersonal or intersubjective space, but such language may be too dualistic. Jean Klein (1989) has called it a nonstate of pure subjectivity, where there is no self and no other—effectively undermining our conventional understanding of what relationship is and can be.

Since therapists and clients are already *being together*, knowingly or unknowingly, this shared presence will sometimes come spontaneously to the foreground without any conscious invitation on the part of the therapist. At such times there may be the sensation of falling into a vast space together. While this can happen at any point in therapy, including the very first session, it generally arises after clients feel safe and have established a feeling of rapport with their therapists. There may be a natural pause in the dialogue or the quiet meeting of the eyes during or after a deep internal search. It is as if the space between thoughts shows itself and an openness to the unknown appears. Such openings often pass by unnoticed or unvalued by both clients and therapists. Pauses and periods of verbal silence are fairly common during the dialogue of conventional psychotherapy, however, they are usually not consciously engaged in the way that is being described here. If therapists are attuned with this silence within themselves, they will be receptive to it in their clients. Therapists and clients may meet in a completely new way.

Sometimes I will more directly invite clients to join me in this nonintentional looking. The invitation can take many creative forms. I may suggest that psychotherapy is an experimental laboratory where one may explore different ways of *being together* in a safe space. I may talk about the longing for connection that they have expressed and suggest that we explore a way to investigate what gets in the way of an authentic contact with another individual.

With some clients I will explain how words can be used to defend rather than to connect, and that talking can be a barrier to intimacy. Sometimes I continue to sit where I am and at other times I may ask if it is all right if I sit a little closer. If it is, I will pull up my chair another foot or two. While this change in position is not essential, it can signal the creation of a different and more intimate therapeutic space. I then invite them to stay in touch with themselves *and* with me as we are together in quiet contact. While this contact accents silence, it doesn't exclude words, since Being holds them both. In any case, verbal silence usually doesn't signify a corresponding inner silence.

As natural as this meeting is, it can be quite surprising and even unsettling for a client at first. Sometimes a little bit of orienting or educating can be helpful, allowing the mind to relax so that one may let the experience unfold by itself without conscious manipulation. Often only a few words of reassurance or explanation are enough. I may validate that the contact is surprising and that there is something about it that feels very natural, even if it is unusual. I may say that there is nothing to change or do; that it is enough to simply be together. I may ask what a client is experiencing and disclose that it is similar for me, if this is the case. I also may acknowledge the feeling of intimacy and how normal our resistance to such contact is. One client, described in detail later in this chapter, had lived in New York City. He said that if he looked at people in the subway this way, he could get into a lot of trouble! I laughed and agreed with him. At first his mind tried to discredit our quiet looking as a weird "Californian thing." In time he grew to love it, finding it to be a door to a profound connection within himself and with others.

Although there is an invitation to generally sustain a soft gaze, clients may close their eyes at times to rest, to facilitate an inner search, or to more fully let go. Naturally, attention will sometimes focus and other times wander, since this is what the mind does. Clients may or may not be motivated to explore a specific issue. Cooperation and resistance are both welcomed. This way of *being together* offers a huge arena for experience to spontaneously unfold. Every thought, feeling, and sensation is acceptable in the space of just *being together*. It is an open space to simply be with one's self and one's client without an agenda to fix or change anything.

Therapists may be drawn to inquire into some element of their client's experience. If there is resistance to being present and connected, they may explore it. If there is an opening into an expansive state of awareness, the therapist and client may rest in it together for a while. Therapists may also approach issues that are of concern to their clients from this broader shared awareness. There is an important and spontaneous weaving of dimensions when this happens. The ensuing creative dialogue and exploration is often punctuated by periods of intimate silence. This way of *being together* can continue as long as it feels fruitful to both parties.

As therapists sit in this quiet contact, they will be aware of various thoughts, feelings, and sensations. If they are relatively peaceful and clear within themselves, they may discover that these thoughts, feelings, and sensations often correspond to what their clients are experiencing at the same time. This is the surprising phenomenon of empathic resonance, which happens more frequently as the shared field between therapist and client deepens.

The Shared Field of Awareness: Empathic Resonance and Countertransferential Reaction

During the intimate and quiet contact of *being together*, therapists and clients usually quickly discover that they share a field of awareness. Usually there is a mutual sensation of dropping into a deeper place together. While this space may at first be more familiar to the therapist, clients can quickly acclimate. The openness of the client is an important variable, which contributes to the level of the shared contact. The depth and intimacy will change between different clients and between or within sessions with the same client. Therapists engage clients as deeply as they are able to go. At times it is the client's openness that induces the therapist to deepen. In any case, it is a collaborative exploration.

The intimacy of this shared field brings up clients' resistance to being present and letting go. Often they will report negative self-judgments, strong feelings such as fear, shame, anger, or grief as well as sensations of contraction in their bodies. Transferential phenomena are very common. Clients may project a critical, abusive, engulfing, or uncaring caretaker onto the therapist and fear attack, absorption, dependency, or abandonment. Alternatively, they may idealize the therapist as the loving, caring, and protective parent that they never had. The intimacy of the contact may also evoke strong erotic feelings when there are sensations of melting and merging.

This shared field also includes therapists' resonant responses and countertransferential reactions. It is critically important to distinguish empathic resonance from these reactions. Empathic resonance is a response where therapists are accurately attuned to their clients' inner experiences without being lost in them. Resonance is distinguishable from projective identification where the therapist is unconsciously acting out elements of the client's disowned psyche, such as rage. In the case of resonance, therapists will sense their clients' unexpressed rage, for example, but have a subjective feeling of space around it. (Prendergast, 2000) They will recognize it as their client's and not carry it beyond the session. Empathic resonance and countertransferential reactions can and do coexist. It can take some maturity and clinical experience to discern the two phenomena.

Therapeutic empathy can be greatly enhanced during the experience of *being together*. Mirroring occurs at increasingly subtle and profound levels. Depending on the openness of both therapist and client, it is possible to enter into the heart of the client's suffering. At times therapists may experientially sense that they have entered into the core of their clients' wounds or contractions, even as they retain a feeling of space around them. Such moments are very intense and poignant experiences for therapists, who may cry or even subtly shake. It feels as though love is entering hell. It is clearly a shared experience because most clients can directly sense that the therapist has joined them in their inner world. Over time this intimate yet spacious joining in the wound melts the client's feeling of separation that is the core of their suffering. It is as if compassionate awareness penetrates the contraction of the client's private world. These moments of shared suffering often prepare the ground for opening into a lighter and more transparent shared space.

Therapists' countertransference may arise while *being together*. Because this way of Being tends to evoke expansive states and intimate contact, therapists' own desires to be idealized or adored can emerge. Therapists who are less clear and grounded may be subject to inflation and grandiosity, imagining that they are the source of their clients' peak experiences. As discussed earlier, they may take themselves to be a special someone who can induce altered states of consciousness. This need for power compensates for a lack of love. None of this is inherently bad; however, it arises from a lack of clarity and obscures the openness of the shared field of awareness. Therapists' natural humility, simplicity, and clarity most support their clients' empowerment and attunement with Being.

Therapists' countertransferential self-devaluations can also arise. Therapists may feel extremely uncomfortable while apparently being the object of intense and intimate scrutiny by their clients, especially without the cover of words. *Being together* requires being at ease with oneself without the safety of the therapeutic identity. Some therapists will avoid being so transparently present and offer elaborate rationalizations why doing so isn't good for their clients. While there are legitimate reasons not to sit this way with certain clients, which I will discuss later, most objections will stem from a therapist's nonacceptance of self. Such undefended contact may be unbearable for them, evoking intense feelings such as fear, shame, or rage, and the belief that they are a failure as a therapist. Or they may simply fear the unknown. It requires a deep trust in oneself to be so open.

Common Client Experiences

This experience of *being together* or sacred mirroring often evokes the sensation of a vast space. Clients commonly will report sensations of dropping, opening, or deepening into a more expansive awareness. This experience of space can be very liberating for some clients as they touch a sense of wholeness and completeness they may have never known before. An unknown dimension of self begins to open that feels connected to a greater whole. Some clients will report a sense of homecoming.

As comforting as this space is, it may also be terrifying for those who fear loss of control if they relax into this unknown vastness. Resistance to letting go is extremely common and takes a variety of forms. Clients may report a fear of losing all ground and falling endlessly into an abyss or of floating away into outer space. Such imagery is often accompanied by feelings of anxiety or terror, sensations of intense contraction in the body, and the belief that they are going to be annihilated. If clients are able to tolerate these feelings and sensations, and can begin to question their core beliefs, their experience over time takes on a positive valence and the vastness is increasingly welcomed as one's true ground. It is not uncommon for clients to experience the vastness as alternatively terrifying and comforting, often in rapid succession.

The intimacy of this sacred mirroring also tends to evoke strong emotions including shame, fear, grief, and anger as well as awe, gratitude and love. These reactions and responses are to some extent standard therapeutic fare. Since shared presence is unusually strong with this contact, however, strong feelings are often elicited with greater speed and intensity than by more conventional therapeutic contact. Whatever is not welcomed within the client, what I sometimes call the "unloved self," tends to quickly surface in the face of this intimate, loving acceptance. The inner child often pops out with all of her or his strong feelings, primal needs, and sense of wonder. As the child's needs to be accurately mirrored and emotionally held are met or at least better understood, the client is gradually able to more fully relax into and embody the bigger space. All of this presumes that there is a bond of trust between client and therapist, a bond that is further strengthened by being together in this close and open way.

It is natural for clients to feel deeply grateful and loving when they are met, perhaps for the first time, at this level. Erotic feelings may also arise. The standard advice to therapists holds: stay open, don't shame, and keep your boundaries. Eros is just one stream in the larger current of life energy that is to be welcomed like everything else. An innocent love and feeling of mutual gratitude are the most common responses that arise out of *being together*. The therapist is as touched as the client by this sacred contact. These moments are the jewels of the art of psychotherapy.

Clients will also experience a range of beliefs while *being together*. Sometimes they will believe that they are being judged and that the therapist sees that something is either wrong or missing in them. Such projections are common to any form of psychotherapy, but may intensify given the closer contact of this process. Clients may think that they are supposed to be doing something special or making an effort in a particular way. As mentioned earlier, a bit of educating and reassurance can be helpful at such times. All of the client's core negative beliefs will become activated at some point. Clients can more easily deconstruct these beliefs through inquiry (i.e. "Who or what is aware of this belief?" "Is this belief true?" "Who am I without it?") when they approach them from the expansive space of being. They are much more attuned with their inner knowing and natural clarity. When looking from this open space, clients are much more likely to see their limiting beliefs as meaningless constructs. The personal narrative tends to spontaneously suspend and in time more easily deconstruct.

Being together can also evoke some very unusual visual phenomena. Clients will often report shifts in their visual field. They may see the therapist's face begin to dissolve so that only the eyes remain. Light may appear around the head or in the room. One of my clients from time to time experiences everything turning into white light. Light and dark fields may reverse so that it appears that one is looking at a photographic negative. More rarely, clients may report other faces being superimposed upon the therapist and wonder if they are viewing past life images or their own projected shadow selves. These shifts in the visual field are generally accompanied by kinesthetic shifts so that clients also report feeling like their own bodies are expanding or dissolving. More than once, clients have described these phenomena as "psychedelic." Interestingly, therapists will often have a parallel experience with their clients. While these experiences are unusual and at times unsettling, they are unimportant in themselves.

They may be viewed as by-products of the awareness that unfolds from the natural intimacy of *being together*.

Cautions and Contraindications

It is important not to approach *being together* as another method, technique, or exercise to try out on a client. In a way, it is best to simply be aware of it as it spontaneously arises. There may be times, however, when there is a natural and intuitive movement on the part of the therapist to casually or informally invite a client to sit together in a different way. Use it when it feels spontaneously appropriate. If it is imposed with some agenda or intention, it can easily degenerate into just another interesting technique that may disrupt a more natural therapeutic flow. It is helpful to think of *being together* as a description rather than a prescription—a shared way of Being that may naturally suggest itself when one is aware of its possibility. If therapists feel ill at ease, split within themselves, or attached to some result, it is best to not invite this contact.

The experience of sacred mirroring or *being together* is soft yet potentially provocative. It is important to rely on intuition as well as common sense as to when and with whom one introduces it. It should not be used with highly disturbed clients. Be particularly cautious with clients who have experienced narcissistic invasion or boundary violations of any kind by primary caretakers. Since this approach induces a remarkable level of intimacy, certain clients can easily misperceive it as a fearsome invasion.

Since my private practice does not include clients diagnosed with low or midlevel functioning personality disorders, I cannot draw any conclusions about working with these populations. Common sense would dictate being extremely cautious about introducing this process to them. However, there may be special potential in gradually and safely introducing this kind of contact with clients diagnosed with a schizoid personality disorder, since their issues center around their sense of isolation and difficulty making contact with others.

Above all, it is important that therapists be at ease within themselves and sensitive to their client's responses and reactions. It is generally best to begin with very short periods of quiet contact and then leave plenty of time to talk about what happened afterwards. As trust builds, longer periods of contact can be sustained. I have not had any damaging experiences with this process; however, a few clients have found it to be either too intense, temporarily unsettling, or unproductive.

Case Presentation: Armand

Armand, an artist in his early thirties, was a veteran of nearly ten years of therapy when we began to work together. He had spent the first eight years with a traditional psychoanalyst and the last two with a transpersonal psychotherapist. He was referred to me to try EMDR (eye movement desensitization and reprocessing)—a powerful uncovering and integrative method.

Armand reported feeling generally depressed, anxious, and tired. He said that he often felt like he was underwater and numb. "There's a lot of emotion in me that I can't relieve," he reported, adding that he often felt sad, angry, and fearful for unknown reasons. He was also burdened by many self-critical thoughts, including the beliefs that something was wrong with him, that he wasn't good enough, and that he didn't know how to relate to others. He mused whether he was trying to preserve imaginary ties to his family with his depression—a prescient insight. He had few friends and reported that it was hard to connect with others.

Armand was also bright, creative, and philosophically inquisitive with a wry sense of humor. His family of origin was deeply troubled: his mother had been very anxious, distracted, and unable to strongly bond. His father had been highly critical and verbally aggressive. His parents divorced when he was five years old, after which his father became hostile and devaluing toward his mother. In time, influenced by his father's relentlessly harsh criticism, Armand lost respect for her. While he loved her, he saw her as pathetic and incompetent. When he was twenty-one, she was murdered by her boyfriend. At the beginning of our therapy Armand was alienated from his father, in a tumultuous relationship with his fiancée, and struggling to get his career off the ground. We met for a total of eighty-two sessions over a little more than two years.

In the first few sessions we reviewed his family history, clarified the issues that he wanted to work on, and more precisely explored his felt sense of self. He shared an image of himself as a little boy reaching out and wanting to be picked up:

> He is wanting, leaning, reaching out to be part of something, but he feels separate. Others are not attending to or connecting to him enough, so he wants to pull back. He is walking around half alive. I sense a light in him that wasn't safe to share with his family.

This poignant description directly pointed to his central issue—his strong longing and deep fear to open up and connect with others and with something greater than his limited sense of self. The chasm of separation and aloneness seemed impassable to him.

We tried EMDR in our fourth and fifth sessions with unimpressive results, and Armand began to feel disappointed and frustrated. It became obvious to me that the therapy needed to focus on our relationship—our contact and connection and his resistance to it. As an experiment, I suggested that we try a few minutes of quietly *being together* and then talk about what happened. It was an unexpected shift of modalities, but Armand was willing to give it a try. Afterward, he reported feeling a fear of being judged, shame, doubts about the method, and several other strong emotions. He said that it had been hard, but it seemed that we were now on the right track.

The following eight months were marked by a gradual opening

to layers of repressed grief, anger, fear, and shame, an investigation of core negative beliefs, a continuing referral to our relationship, and a growing sense of trust. The practice of *being together*, sometimes for only a few minutes per session, almost always brought intense and painful feelings to the foreground. Armand would often cry intensely, grieving the loss of connection and the feeling of aloneness. Also, he gradually became better able to tolerate the anger he felt about his childhood. During this time he married his fiancée and, despite some rocky periods, began to feel more confident in their relationship. He described our therapy at this point as fostering a "second birth, with a long gestation."

After many months of beginning sessions by reporting that he was feeling sad, angry, afraid, or stuck, Armand began to report feeling clearer and better. He wanted to focus on more existential questions and deepen the intimacy of our contact: "I want to start putting my attention on serenity. I want to surrender to God and show you my fragile self." This statement of intent signaled an important shift in our work together.

We spent most of the following session quietly gazing and deeply exploring the connection. At first he feared that I was judging him as being boring or immature. As he stayed with his fear, it changed and we both felt a shift into a very different space that was both intimate and expansive. He reported having "a glimpse of some commonality beyond the ego." It was a moment of awe—a sense of something greater than, yet common to, each of us. We were both deeply moved. After this contact, he felt more trusting and natural during our nonintentional looking. Daily events in his relationship with his wife and his work continued to trigger his old conditioning, but the accent had begun to shift to the power of the present moment and our shared contact. A month later he spoke of "the remarkable power of this open presence." He reported that, although it was difficult, he was beginning to remember this presence outside of our sessions and wondered "what the world would look like if people lived from this openness?"

We continued with the long periods of quiet looking, and Armand reported "a deepening into the heart and a trust that you see me as O.K." He saw our heart contact as a referral point and reaffirmed his desire to be in touch with God. As we sat together, he began to feel a sense of joy from time to time, which often would be followed by self-doubt and the fear of losing control. He noticed that this joy began to arise as he opened to "the wall of pain" in his heart.

Armand also expressed love for what was beyond both of us, and a sense "of God's kindness" through my eyes. Around this time we had an interesting session of gazing where he encountered "the fear of being nothing and no one," which then shifted to feeling loved just as he was. As he opened to his inner emptiness, he began to discover a source of love within himself. Armand felt very nurtured by the quiet looking, as if something frozen inside was starting to thaw. He began to see others more as subjects than objects, and noted a spontaneous upwelling of greater compassion. All of these phenomena reflected the opening of his heart.

About a year and a half into our therapy we had several profound sessions of *being together*. During one, Armand felt a strong sense that he was okay and that nothing was broken. While gazing, he again felt something greater coming through me and expressed a desire to be cared for by God. "It is very frightening to let go into this," he said. "I am afraid of losing control and of being alone." In the following session he expressed a desire for greater connection to the mystery of life. As we quietly gazed, he first reported feeling room for both joy and grief, and then added:

> I have the same feeling as when I have looked into the starry sky, although I have never had this experience with another person as I am now. It is terrifying and it is what I most want. I have feelings of being home as a child, but bigger. I come to a precipice and shrink back. I have been drawn to this since I was a child.

Armand was directly encountering the vastness of unconditioned awareness or Being. In the subsequent session he reported, "It feels like I have bought a new home [the present] and sold the old one [the past], but there is still a lot of packing and moving to do." It was an apt metaphor for the profound shift in his sense of identity that was underway. A spontaneous inner commitment was in motion to live life from a very different space, yet there was still a lot of footwork to do to align with the new direction. In this same session he added, "When I look into your eyes, it is as if I am looking into all the eyes that I have ever seen. I guess this is what everyone wants—to be seen." It was a beautiful description of his need to be mirrored at all levels of his being.

The sacred mirroring also touched very early places of eye contact that he had with his mother, recalling Kohut's, Mahler's, and Winnicott's observations about the importance of maternal mirroring, noted earlier in this essay. "I now know the difference between a baby looking into released, calm, and peaceful eyes and my mother's fearful, distracted, and medicated eyes," Armand observed with deep feeling.

This very early level of disconnection was being addressed and healed through our present innocent and affectionate looking. Armand's grieving continued in subsequent sessions as he touched this early level of loss. Simultaneously he felt a deepening connection with me and with God. These plunges into the unknown and upwelling of feelings led Armand to liken the process to a shedding of a skin and a homecoming—metaphors reflecting the depths of transformation that he was experiencing.

The final six months of our time together continued his accelerating inner shift of identity. Armand was relating to his inner and outer experiences with a different quality of awareness. "I want to be heard and to hear myself and to have the space to see," he remarked. In the same session he reported a feeling of vast space. "I feel that I am everything," he innocently remarked, unknowingly echoing the *rishis* (seers) of ancient India who affirmed their oneness with all of life. A week later, while *being together*, he reported, "I'm leaving old family and coming into new family." Later in the same session he noted that:

> This big space or openness exists prior to the terror and anger that are like veils covering it. It feels like I've dropped into a radiant source like the sun when I'm here with you. It increasingly radiates into my daily life between sessions.

Armand was clearly becoming more at ease in this unknown and radiant spaciousness. He was also beginning to experience his highly charged emotional states as covers or veils to this underlying radiance. These emotional states did not stop, but Armand received them with greater kindness and clarity, knowing that they would pass in time, and that a deeper level of his self would emerge.

Armand's plans to move to the East Coast brought an end to our time together. He acknowledged that he could continue to fruitfully explore whatever arose by our *being together*, but he also felt equipped to live his life. He said that he could see the fruits of the therapy in his reduced fear around work, his improved ability to appropriately express anger in his relationship, his reduced self-judgments, and his greater sense of safety and inner freedom. Armand's depression had lifted and his anxiety had significantly reduced, replaced by a sense of excitement about his new life. He felt lighter, tired less easily, and experienced a stronger creative flow in his work. He also felt more open to others and to the divine. A quiet joy from an unknown origin was starting to appear in his daily life. The movement from the inner "old home" into his "new home" was still in transition, but well under way. We ended with an authentic feeling of mutual gratitude.

This case study realistically portrays the weaving of levels that occurs during the course of therapy, as Being is directly evoked through this process of nonintentional looking. The first stage of our work focused on building trust, uncovering painful feelings, and unpacking the conditioning of early childhood. These oppressive feelings and their related negative self and world beliefs were in the foreground of Armand's experience. It was the first layer that *being together* evoked. It took a number of months for Armand to feel through this layer before there was a shift to inviting a deeper contact between us and within himself.

This second phase continued to evoke intense feelings rooted in childhood, but also marked the first encounters with an unknown vastness. This contact was characterized by an initial opening, immediately followed by a strong contraction of fear—the fear of losing emotional control, experiencing repressed pain and grief, and losing his self-story. There was also great pain in realizing what he had been missing by avoiding "contact with God's boundless love." He also experienced strong feelings of love and the desire to be of service to others. Sharing this space with our quiet and steady eye contact allowed Armand to begin to relax into this openness.

The final phase of our work together involved an explicit focus on this present-centered and vast openness that began to actively transpose to Armand's daily life. Strong reactions and conditioning continued to appear, but they no longer thoroughly shadowed or veiled his inner sense of freedom and subtle, causeless joy.

Six months after we ended I sent Armand a draft of this essay for his feedback. In response, he wrote:

> When I "open to the vastness," I sometimes feel these feelings of homecoming and great release. There is something that feels very natural and true in this experience of vast space that has less to do with grief, or even love. It is perhaps something like a felt experience of the mystery of being. Experiences of opening give me a glimpse of what seems to be the truth of being. Against this experience, the activities of daily life lose their significance My life is being slowly reset with this new compass.

Conclusion

There is intrinsic value to Being. It is what we fundamentally are. Discovering and eventually resting in this Being brings a feeling of deep inner peace and freedom. As we become intimate with this still center within, we feel more connected to all of life. We experience our wholeness firsthand and become lovers of *what is*—of life as it appears. Our approach to life becomes increasingly less problematic as we accept what comes and allow what goes, grounded in something that feels unchanging in our core. The ups and downs of health, work, and relationships are held in a bigger and more connected space.

Recognizing and consciously welcoming Being into the conventional ritual of modern psychotherapy brings a feeling of shared spaciousness to the therapeutic exploration. Clients come to see that they are not problem-holders and gradually find a way to relate to their inner and outer lives with more compassionate acceptance and clarity. Therapists also discover that they are not problem-solvers but rather collaborative coexplorers. Their role identification falls away as the sense of common ground emerges with their clients. The function of the therapeutic relationship continues in a changed form. Therapy becomes less about fixing imagined problems and more of an exploration into experiential truth, a collaborative journey into wholeness.

Our greatest suffering stems from our sense of separation and the feeling of being alone and disconnected from life. One of the beauties of *being together* is that it directly addresses this core need. It also offers an intimate shared space for clients to explore their fears of opening to another being as well as to the whole of life. *Being together* covers the same ground as conventional psychotherapy (although perhaps at an accelerated rate) in the initial phase of work. As the old conditioning is gradually processed, integrated, and released, the transpersonal domains of the soul and spirit begin to unfold. *Being together* offers a simple and elegant way for the self to meet itself in the apparent other. In so doing, psychotherapy becomes a sacred mirror for both client and therapist.

Appendix

Sample approach for introducing *being together*.

1. Would you be interested in joining me for a period of quiet looking?

2. Let your gaze be very relaxed and soft. This is not a staring contest. Just notice your inner experience—your thoughts, feelings, and sensations—*and* stay with me.

3. There is no wrong way to do this and there is nothing to achieve. Welcome whatever arises. Feel free to be silent or to speak, to close your eyes at times, or to move so that you are comfortable. We can end anytime that you feel like it.

(Note to therapists: Please carefully review the sections entitled "*Being Together* Described," "The Shared Field of Awareness," and "Common Client Experiences.")

Endnotes

1. I want to thank Stephan Bodian for his valuable suggestions for the introductory sections of this chapter, and Richard Miller, Dorothy Hunt, and John Amodeo for their thoughtful comments.

2. Readers may send comments or inquiries to me at: 900 5th Ave., Suite 203, San Rafael, California, 94901 or call (415) 453-8832.

5

A Nondual Approach To EMDR

Psychotherapy as Satsang

Sheila Krystal

Introduction: Psychotherapy as Satsang

Tibetan Buddhist Dzogchen, Hindu Advaita, Taoism, Kabbalism, and mystical Christianity all suggest that the fulfillment of human potential and the liberation from suffering happen when attention rests peacefully in its source, prior to thought.[1] These traditional spiritual disciplines inform a nondual approach to psychotherapy that views form as a natural and temporary expression of a unified, omnipresent, nonlocatable, and pregnant emptiness. In time all forms—everything and everyone—dissolve back into this emptiness which is present now. In Hinduism this formlessness is described as truth-awareness-bliss (*satchitananda* in Sanskrit). In the Christian New Testament, the phrase "the peace that passeth understanding" hints at this nondual awareness.

Satsang in Sanskrit means association *(sanga)* with truth *(sat)*.

Satsang—the coming together in the company of God (as lovers of the truth)—supports the discovery of one's true nature. When Jesus said, "Whenever two or more are gathered together in my name, there shall I be," he was describing this sacred meeting. The nondual approach to psychotherapy is comparable to satsang when therapists and clients come together in the now to investigate the deepest truth of their shared experience.

In this meeting clients may discover that the root of suffering lies in their identification as a separate ego-self. Once clients begin to appreciate that they are actually not their distracting thoughts, emotions, or bodily sensations, but rather a dispassionate, observing Presence, a process of disidentification begins and peace of mind unfolds naturally. Clients learn that they have within a natural predisposition toward health and wholeness. Freedom from psychological suffering is often immediately available when clients know how to look or how to just *be*. Clients learn that simply being fully present now in a timeless moment of silence can reveal what is already and always free.

With a nondual approach, psychotherapy might begin dualistically by briefly identifying and describing clients' problems in the process of developing a personal history. However, in time, therapists and clients begin to deconstruct the "idea" of the problem. As they come together in the here and now, resting in Presence, the apparent problem is dismantled and clients' attention is unhooked from the idea of being a problem holder.

A nondual approach to therapy promotes no method, no theory, and, indeed, no mind. Therapists rest in empty awareness without holding any model, diagnosis, goal, or technique in mind. They reach for nothing and avoid nothing that arises. As they sit with their clients, therapists know that they are the student and the teacher as well as the projection of one another. The Self meets itself in the sacred mirror of satsang.

Therapists with a nondual perspective may have access to a repertoire of techniques such as meditation, visualization, and mandalas, quiet nonintentional mutual eye gazing, mantra, meta-phor, paradox, storytelling, and dream analysis. These techniques may arise spontaneously in the moment in a way that is naturally appropriate for the client, greatly assisting the therapeutic process. Various forms of bodywork and the integrative psychotherapy approach of EMDR (eye movement desensitization and reprocessing) can also be used with a nondual perspective. However, holding any orientation or goal or promoting any approach other than selfless, nonjudgmental compassion can trap therapists in their own thinking, binding them to the mind instead of enabling them to rest in Presence in which the deepest healing resonance occurs. Instead of trying to become more competent in some methodology, therapists become more quiet and empty, learning to listen for the flavor or gist of the client's story. The focus is on that which is more essential than facts or any point of view: the underlying Self that exists prior to thought, emotion, and sensation. As this reality is pointed out and focused on, clients' stories become transparent and gradually fall away.

Therapists who experience psychotherapy as satsang neither promote nor undermine any particular perspective or belief system. They model nonattachment and nonaversion to anything that comes up in a therapy session. Therapists realize that while the personality or body-mind complex is a phenomenal reality, it is not the ground of Being—the essential, undifferentiated Self. Therapists are challenged to hold the space for both dual and nondual experience, straddling the relative and absolute dimensions, and to speak about the unspeakable in a relentless yet effortless way.

As the therapist rests in nondual awareness with an empty mind, without attending to any inner commentary other than an intuitive impulse or direction, entrainment or therapeutic resonance can occur. The therapist's empty, peaceful and quiet mind is contagious, and clients begin to experience their own peace and truth. Clients are naturally invited into a deeper level of reality beyond their belief systems, concepts, conditioning, and tribal consciousness. Essence comes into the foreground from the background shadows, allowing healing and peaceful contentment to occur. As H.W.L. Poonja (1995) advises, "Call off the search!" since all that has been sought by the seeker (and the client) is found to be already present here and now.

Therapists in satsang rest in openness, free of right and wrong. Their presence facilitates the deconstruction of their clients' fixations—mental, emotional, and physical constructs—allowing them to recognize the underlying presence of awareness in themselves. Once this awareness is known directly, deep relaxation and contentment arise. Within it, unhealthy patterns and conditioning continue to dissolve.

The nondual approach to psychotherapy equalizes methodologies because nothing is given priority. Any next step in the therapeutic process becomes intuitively obvious. The practice of psychotherapy can become a *sadhana* or spiritual practice for therapists, encouraging mindfulness, full presence, and the dissolution of their own conceptual structures as they relentlessly focus on truth. This requires vigilance and integrity. The therapist is an impersonal vehicle for healing and education rather than a personal doer. Any pride in being the doer is seen to be illusory. The therapist does not do therapy or give an experience. Instead, Presence facilitates or evokes experience so that both therapist and client heal and awaken into ever deeper dimensions of nondual reality. Awakening is endless.

Psychotherapy as satsang reminds clients of what they may have already glimpsed: the flow, the Tao, the Divine, or the numinosity of their original nature. They may remember that they already know what a healing moment feels like and have tasted the nondual reality. The therapist's sacred trust is to be present with quiet, bare, and receptive attention, free of any agenda. Health and deep gratitude will then spontaneously emerge.

EMDR and Nondual Wisdom

EMDR is an integrative psychotherapeutic appproach first discovered and developed by Dr. Francine Shapiro (2001) in 1987, which is guided by an information processing model that has numerous protocols and procedures including the administration of bilateral stimulation to the client. The procedure was originally used to treat trauma, but it has now developed into a comprehensive approach used widely to ameliorate a variety of psychological symptoms and disorders including anxiety and depression, phobia, addiction and substance abuse, among others. In fact, EMDR is now used to target experiential contributors of all clinical complaints. The bilateral stimulation is thought to activate information processing in the brain in order to resolve both major trauma involving the symptoms of post-traumatic stress disorder (PTSD) diagnosis as well as any of the childhood experiences that can qualify as trauma, desensitize overly strong emotion, and facilitate inspiration. Please see Shapiro (2001 and 2002) for a complete description of this approach, its theory, rationale, guiding principles, and procedures, and its understanding of how experiences are dysfunctionally stored as memories, with the affects, sensations, and beliefs of earlier events, and how these arise in the body/mind in the present to create psychological symptoms.

EMDR is also useful in dissolving fixated attachments and in bringing to the surface unconscious distractions, often associated with trauma, from present awareness of Self. As clients' mindfulness develops, they begin to discern more clearly and quickly when awareness has become distracted from itself. Clients learn to come back from suffering and dysfunction to the eternally present, underlying peace. They learn that life takes care of itself effortlessly in the moment.

The classic EMDR protocol for use with trauma and limiting belief systems can be held very lightly in psychotherapy sessions with a nondual approach. After processing traumas, issues, and blocking beliefs with the traditional protocols, bilateral stimulation can ultimately process the subtlest of distractions to awareness resting peacefully in itself, from either this or past life memories (*samskaras*). In EMDR therapy, behavior modification and symptom removal are often the results of treatment. The mind is directly influenced, filtering out reactivity and intense emotions so that the client is more peaceful; and as more reflective work occurs, new structure is created through natural insight and inspiration and through therapists' use of "cognitive interweaves" (the therapist's intuitive suggestions to the client).

During EMDR therapy, reprocessing of traumatic experiences occurs and desensitization is a by-product of the reprocessing so that detachment from old emotional reactions to traumatic memories and core beliefs or interpretations (stories) about the Self is facilitated. Desensitization and reprocessing are not separate. As the target traumatic experience is reprocessed by bilateral stimulation and "cognitive interweaves" to break through high levels of disturbance, the associated memories, emotions, cognitions, and physical sensations simultaneously shift and a new sense of self and new behaviors emerge. Shifts in all the modalities (cognitions, emotions, sensations, and images) take place during reprocessing as the emotions shift, associational connections are made, and insights occur. Clients are retrained by their own self-regulating healing process and by "cognitive interweaves" gently supplied by the therapist along the lines of acceptance and forgiveness. Therapists using EMDR add virtually no interpretation to the events arising in the session, just allowing the process to flow or move. Clients are continually encouraged to "just allow anything to come up" and to report what they get now, permitting full autonomy and the free expression of experience without interference from a separate, relative reality. Clients feel in control of the session, not only choosing the issues they wish to address, but also, if they desire, by starting and stopping a "lapscan," "light bar," or "tac/audio scan," which are various devices designed to administer bilateral stimulation.

From the nondual perspective, EMDR reprocessing can invite entrainment via the interconnectedness of the therapist and client and can naturally recondition the client around the universal themes of impermanence, trust in Self, nonabidance in the mind, loving kindness, forgiveness, compassion, freedom, creativity, well-being, detachment, and the renunciation of habitual preoccupations of mind. Therapists seeing therapy as satsang are mindful of superstitious and habitual interpretations of what causes change and are scrupulous when using cognitive interweaves to simply point the client toward the acceptance of life, death, and perpetual change.

EMDR targets physical sensations in the body as well as emotions, memories, and interpretations of the distracting events or symptoms to be desensitized and reprocessed. It is seen by some as the ultimately sophisticated body work or body-based therapy. And it is often noted that practitioners of Wilhelm Reich's (1945) Orgone therapy used lateral eye movements created by having clients follow a moving pen light with their eyes to help break up the armor of the body's eye segment. In the Eastern traditions, the body/mind complex or bundle, as Nisargadatta Maharaj (1982) called it, is seen to be ephemeral, changing, and impermanent. EMDR gives clients the direct experience of emotions arising out of nothing, growing, peaking, subsiding, and disappearing into emptiness. Since they are constantly moving and changing as emotion in motion, they are untrustworthy as a source of security. Clients also experience the flexibility of thought when negative or self-limiting thoughts, attitudes, and beliefs are naturally replaced by positive cognitions during EMDR reprocessing. They learn to disidentify from the personality's vicissitudes of thought and emotion and to identify with a deeper stratum of Being. Although formless, it goes by all names and shows up as all forms, so call it awareness, openness, or Presence; it is eternal and provides the only true security.

In standard EMDR therapy, clients are instructed to visualize an inner safe place where they can return as needed. This procedure is a direct invitation for clients to go within, quiet down, and discover that safety is already available now. The practice of coming back to the safe place can enhance mindfulness and encourage reorientation to equipoise, and potentially, to the nondual, objective reality instead of the subjective, personal story about the client's suffering. Forgiveness spontaneously arises in many EMDR sessions, as do spiritual, empty, or numinous states. Loneliness and shame are often experienced as solitude and atonement. Bilateral stimulation may at times offer direct access to the unconditioned mind so that the contents of the conditioned mind can be seen to be ultimately illusory and the natural mind can have freer reign.

After EMDR processing, many people no longer hold so dearly to negative beliefs. In frequently instructing the client to "just notice," therapists become witness to the present moment so that they can discover together from their oneness a heretofore unimaginable and often surprising outcome to their meeting. EMDR directs therapists to not repeat what the client reports but to simply stay in the presence of whatever arises. How similar to mindfulness training this is! This vigilant focus tends to circumvent countertransference and the "personal." However, the cognitive interweave process of refocusing on the present and reeducation can bring the personal back into focus, if therapists are not careful to point only to absolute principles of safety, nonviolence, love, forgiveness, the formlessness of the absolute, and truth.

The positive treatment effects of EMDR support relaxation, contentment, and responsiveness rather than reactivity. They enhance detachment from strong negative emotions and compelling, distracting thoughts, the replacement of fear by a sense of inner safety in the here and now, and the substitution of anger with humor and the acceptance of *what is*. EMDR tends to bring core personality strategies and ego defense mechanisms to awareness and then deconstruct the habitual reactions of the personality. The possibility for the emergence of nondual awareness increases as clients are empowered to return again to peaceful calm from strong emotion-laden concepts, eventually learning to consciously rest in the Ground of Being.

A Transpersonal EMDR Protocol

EMDR facilitates the activation of the inner organizing principle in every individual that evolves naturally toward wholeness and health and allows the emergence of the unknown. EMDR can be used from the point of view of any psychological framework (Shapiro, 2002). From the nondual perspective, it opens a doorway to deeper consciousness, the archetypal Self, and the experience of "I am that I am," thus sidestepping the black box of conditioned thinking. It invites clients to reach their full potential and the awareness that they are already, and always have been, the Self. The self-regulating tendency to achieve balance and freedom can be unleashed in EMDR therapy sessions with a nondual perspective. Facilitation is the key here, as the deconstruction of the personal history and the ego defense system, and the arising of fresh insight, can often occur more easily, and frequently more quickly, with EMDR. More subtle deconstruction of packaged or fixed positive beliefs about spiritual awakening that rob it of its spontaneity can also be undertaken with EMDR. Any identifications of Self with persona, image, power, or safety, including reputation, status, relationship, beliefs, or standards, can be processed. Finally, even deconstruction of forms of worship, the concepts of meditation and spiritual path, and images of the Divine can occur if clients are so inclined, enabling them to become increasingly comfortable in the unknown.

From the perspective of satsang, EMDR can be likened to the alchemical container, the alembic, which contains or structures a therapeutic session without imposing form so that spontaneity can arise. Within this alembic, the "great work" can simmer as clients inquire into their concepts of who they are and what is possible in life as they ask "Who am I?" following the Delphic oracle's injunction to know thyself. EMDR can help facilitate the transcendence of all limitations to who one thinks one is, so that clients experience that they contain and are part of the Oneness. It encourages choiceless awareness in those clients who have lost faith or who have never experienced faith. It gives permission to relax, breathe, and just be, to allow to come to awareness whatever arises in the moment, to listen inside, and to "be still, and know that I am God."

As I realized the effectiveness of EMDR in my psychotherapy practice in these ways, I began to play with redefining the acronym EMDR as eye movement disidentification (from the self and its apparent problems) and recognition (of the one Self). Many of the people who enter my psychology practice come for what they think of as evolution, individuation, or to learn meditation, or to grow and fulfill their potential. Some come for satsang and freedom because several years ago in a meeting with H.W.L. Poonja in Lucknow, India, after a long discussion about the nature of psychotherapy, he told me to "go home and do satsang psychotherapy." I frequently find myself offering some clients, who have already desensitized their personal histories of traumas, negative cognitions, and symptoms, and are wondering what is next, a "transpersonal" EMDR protocol to inquire deeply into the Self (see appendix).

In spite of its name, this protocol is flexible and evolving and should not be limited to Transpersonal psychotherapy or become congealed and set as a method for doing "nondual EMDR." It is a suggested form to help discover and dissolve distractions from the formless. Accordingly, targets for EMDR are any thoughts, emotions, or sensations or conditioned responses that arise to distract attention from the quiet, peaceful emptiness and equanimity of who we all really are which I will call "constant contentment." Such distractions are often associated with incompletely processed trauma and early conditioning from childhood. For the purposes of the protocol, contentment is not an emotion as such, but the reality existing before thought arises that Sathya Sai Baba (1988) describes when he suggests that we cultivate constant contentment or bliss. The transpersonal protocol can be used very intuitively and it is not necessarily linear, although its steps are described sequentially.

The transpersonal protocol flexes to fit the client's deepening experience of nondual reality. The protocol also becomes a container that allows therapists and clients to access the different, deeper, impersonal Self. It promotes satsang and invites the client to join the therapist in the age-old *namaste*, where they are one and the same choiceless awareness. The bilateral stimulation used in EMDR can release the conditioned thinking of both clients and therapists.

Therapists may listen differently to their own habits of thought, feeling, and sensation. They may listen with an empty mind instead of to their inner commentary and hear, perhaps for the first time, what clients are saying from the client's frame of reference rather than from their own thought system. They may listen to what is not being said, to subtle psychic and intuitive cues as well as to the satsang space itself. There is room for experimentation with a different way of being, learning, and sensing. As therapists listen from emptiness, the next step in the EMDR process is self evident and often astonishing.

First, in the life review or preparation phase, clients review their entire life during long sets of bilateral stimulation. This step often provides an overall picture of the lessons and opportunities their lives offered. They can also discover during this step whether there is any emotional charge left unprocessed or unexperienced in any area of life. These targets are then processed with bilateral stimulation while clients invite the experience fully without trying to resist it or alter it in any way such as pushing it away, holding on to it, avoiding it, denying it, analyzing it, or jumping over it. When the emotional disturbance is desensitized and no longer experienced in the body, and clients are relaxed and peaceful, they can then review life lessons during eye movements or other bilateral stimulation and describe any distractions from peace and contentment.

Next the contentment experience is defined and discussed. If clients do not have a referent for contentment, they can be taught to meditate if they are interested and do not already meditate. Note, however, that meditation is only suggested, and described as the experience of the already present essence when being quiet or still and not as a technique to perform in order to achieve something that is not yet present. I sometimes suggest that these clients reference their prayer state if they pray, or I might teach them some of the centering images from *Cutting the Ties that Bind,* such as the Triangle, Hi C, and Figure Eight that my mother, Phyllis Krystal (1982), I, and others have developed over the last fifty years. Entrainment is facilitated during this satsang process as therapists rest in nondual awareness, joining clients and meditating together during this quieting phase of the protocol. The experience of becoming still replaces the traditional safe place in the standard EMDR protocol.

In the assessment phase of the protocol, a "contentment baseline" is established from clients' present levels of inner equilibrium. After quieting down for ten to fifteen minutes, clients are asked to rate their level of quiet or contentment on a scale of light, medium, and deep, where light is very distracted and deep is not distracted at all by thoughts, feelings, or sensations. Targets for eye movements then become any distractions that take awareness away from contentment or peaceful emptiness as established by the baseline, and any charged emotions or thoughts about or physical reactions to those distractions. Distractions are often persistent habits of mind, obsessive and intrusive thoughts, cravings, desires and addictions, memories, fantasies, self talk, sleepiness, numbing out, physical pains, itches, discomforts, noises, smells, or visual images, and the full gamut of emotions including strong, positive ones. More subtle distractions are those reference points by which awareness tends to ground and stabilize itself or identify and define itself as well as those concepts where awareness wants to land and stay, instead of abiding in the empty unknown of that which is the Ground of Being. It may be noted that, as distractions are processed and desensitized and their charge reduced or eliminated, the contentment baseline deepens.

Next, while the client is experiencing baseline contentment, the therapist can make the suggestion to let anything come up into awareness and to report it as a distraction to the quiet and rate it on a level of distraction (LOD) scale of 0 to 10, where 10 is very compelling or distracting and 0 is not distracting. In the processing phase, each target identified in the interview is brought to mind during saccades of eye movements, bilateral auditory tones, and/or bilateral vibrations. Later, when all previously identified targets have been processed to 0 on the LOD scale, clients are asked to return to the contentment baseline and any new distractions to contentment are processed with bilateral stimulation. During this processing, clients' meditative states deepen and distractions become less frequent and compelling. Clients also notice sooner and sooner that distractions arise from and disappear back into their source, the naturally quiet, peaceful, and empty Ground of Being. When clients realize that they are distracted, they can report this and therapists can begin the bilateral stimulation or the clients can control the stimulation device.

The bilateral stimulation can also dissolve any blocking beliefs to going deeper and can be used to install future templates for deep equipoise in difficult situations, relationships, and distracting environments. As clients meditate, if after some time they are not communicative and if intuition so instructs, therapists can ask, "Now, what distracts from contentment? Stay with that," and process with stimulation. I find that I use the LOD scale only in the initial sessions to help orient the client to the process of EMDR. I rarely ask the client to rate their level of contentment because this activity engages the relative mind to measure and judge, effectively reducing the depth of contentment and indeed distracting from the emptiness! In the final phase of the session, the client is grounded in the present through quiet sitting without bilateral stimulation and asked to log, if desired, any new distractions noted between sessions.

This protocol, if held lightly, can be instructive and give some minimal structure to an EMDR session in which the client wishes to become quieter and more contented. Clients often report experiencing not only a deeper and more abiding sense of contentment after these sessions, but also a greater sense of surprise, humor, and delight as they find themselves accepting whatever occurs as their lives unfold, welcoming what comes and letting go of what leaves as they experience life taking care of itself. The complete Transpersonal EMDR protocol is described elsewhere (Krystal, S., et al., 2002).

Case Study

A fifty-five-year-old professionally successful woman was referred to me for EMDR therapy by her life coach to deal with a freeway driving phobia and associated fear of getting lost on unfamiliar roads. The client was fairly psychologically sophisticated and had had "plenty of therapy" of various types over the years and felt that this was her only real problem. After the first few sessions of satsang we used the classic EMDR protocol to successfully resolve her phobia. In the fifth session we began by using the Transpersonal protocol to review her life, and during this process the client decided that she wanted to look at her tendency to hold grudges against her husband Mark and at her beliefs that he didn't love her enough, which were still charged. When asked about her grudges, she reported that although she had been brought up as an Orthodox Jew, she had stopped keeping kosher and never went into the temple after the death of her brother when she was eight. She reported, "I went to the door of the temple and no further." She was no longer religious and had rejected God and even a higher power. Yet, being agnostic and wanting to cover all her bases, she said, "Just in case you exist, God, I will pray to you even though you don't exist!"

As a child she had heard about her brother's death while "eavesdropping, crouched on the upstairs landing, up too late and being bad. I overheard my parents talking about it." She had a concept of a wrathful, unloving God who holds grudges, a God "who sees everything and will punish you." She believed, "I had to be a good girl or God would punish me." She choose to use EMDR to work next with resentment that her brother's death created, a traumatic event about which she had been holding a very old grudge against this wrathful God. As a child she felt that his death and her being bad by staying up late without permission and spying on her parents were somehow linked, and that God was punishing both her and her brother. Her resentment was mixed with feelings of fear at being mad at God and the belief that she is bad and unlovable. She mentioned that a girlfriend had recently told her that when she feels alone in the world she prays to God because she knows that God loves her. "I was dumbfounded!" my client replied. "I just remembered the story of Adam and Eve. God threw them out of Eden. So don't screw up because they never got back in!"

This trauma was then processed with the standard EMDR protocol for about forty minutes of the two-hour session until the client reported no more resentment and anger. We then switched back to the Transpersonal protocol, and the client was asked to deepen her peaceful feeling and report distractions to her contentment.

Ellipses (…) in the following end-of-the-session transcript denote sets of bilateral stimulation in the following verbatim session excerpt. My interventions are in parentheses and my explanations are in brackets.

"I feel very alone…This abandonment [by her brother] was God's fault. I thought then that God had taken his temperature and He tore him up…God is punishing me…God doesn't love me and Mark doesn't love me either…(What if you were love itself?)…Sheila! That is a really radical shift you know………I feel in an altered state and I can't tell if I was asleep or not (Just stay with yourself)…I AM love!…… oh!…… before, God was one more angry par-

ent who I couldn't please...I had to placate God rather
than pray.........God I want you to know that I am a good
girl and praying...I used to pray 'don't smite me,' I learned
this in Temple, that God is an angry God ... God is blank-
ness, not wrath; open, not empty like in 'bereft of'...a very
peaceful feeling...it's very different...open, empty, peaceful...It doesn't have characteristics...is there any end to
this? (Does it end with your body?)...No, not that I know
...it's infinite, I just can't conceptualize it...It feels really
good (Is there anywhere in you that this peace isn't?)...I
have threatening pressure in my chest (go with that)...it's
gone...enjoying this empty, peaceful openness is meditation
(Does it go away if you think thoughts?)...the peace is in
the background. It hasn't left...It's like residing in a medium, a nutrient-based medium like in a petri dish...I am not
the container. The agar is the experience...'foundation' isn't
quite the right word for it, there is no sense of position...it
has the quality of being surrounding but not engulfing...a
buoyant liquid medium...being in a liquid medium at room
temperature but not like wallpaper...(Tell me more)...there
is no separation between the fish and the water. As fish de-
rive oxygen from water, there is a flow between the medium and myself so there is nothing I have to do...there is
no experience of being separated into this and that but it is
not engulfing ...it's not being 'centered' because there is no
me and that...it has no energy about it...a different spectrum...I found God!.........I really got it...that was the experience, the epiphany...(What do you notice now?)...there
can be a sense of anxiety but it is not frenetic or panicked...
anxiety is reduced, it has no ability to stop me dead in my
tracks......... (What else do you notice?)...'I'm not good
enough' is still there but not strong...reprisals, self-recrimi-
nation and self-hatred are gone...(What happens when you
bring back the original memory? [of hiding at the top of

the stairs spying])...I can no longer get stuck in 'I'm doing something wrong'...this is a different environment to
dwell in...I am highly creative and visionary because it is
like breath, all about breath...breathing in air but not needing to do that consciously...things are transmitted between
the in and the out breath...breath is nourishing and whatever comes out is fine...it's very different, less quality of desperation and neediness...loving doesn't know what loving
feels like... I am used to a different pattern...I am no longer
looking for stuff from Mark, not needing approval as much,
gold stars everyday............ I'm enveloped in orangey red
light, it's not cloth it's gossamer, there is no smell to it...
beautifully colored light, it moves, transparent, bathing me
and crossing the physical boundary...it can wash in as well
as over........."

This numinous experience of her own essence was a first taste
for this woman who, until the end of this session, was agnostic. She
considered this as a life-changing epiphany in which she moved
from feeling unlovable to the experience of "I am love."

In the next session after the one described above, the client
came in with a continued profound shift in awareness. When asked
during the session about distractions from this peacefulness, she
remembered an event when her father died while she was away on
her honeymoon. She had wanted to pray for him when she learned
of his death upon returning, but a rabbi told her that she couldn't
pray for him until after he was buried. She experienced this as a
"slap in the face," which propelled her further away from her Self.
This memory as well as a few other related events such as the fact
that she was isolated from the family at the time of her brother's
death because she was too young and not allowed to take part in
the formal grieving, thus "breaking my belonging," were processed
with EMDR using first the standard and then Transpersonal protocol in ensuing sessions.

The client continued to find herself in love with God fairly continuously one month later and her relationship with her husband has continued to improve and deepen. She continued to drive on freeways and reported an incident in which she became lost and then found her way again without "freaking out." At this time she stated about herself: "I still do defense law. No, that's not quite right, it's more than that. I don't sue, I defend! I can now stand up in court and ask the judge for what I want easily, when a month ago I couldn't. I can do it now without any panic at all." Since this time, her experience of the nondual has continued to grow and expand with the occasional use of EMDR in therapy. She continued to see through her old conditioned thoughts more and more of the time as her experience of the nondual deepened. They are appearing as mirages now and she no longer trusts them.

These results of a nondual approach to EMDR-assisted therapy are holding up well longitudinally. Five months later the client reported in a session that,

> "I have had a radical alteration of consciousness which is not a small leap. My normal fear state is not what it used to be. I've lost it. I can't find anything to be afraid about. Fear just comes from images in my mind. There is a bigger opening. There are things in life for me to accept and I don't always prefer them and yet it's okay. My confidence level has gone up, my consulting practice has magically increased, and I haven't done anything different. What would ordinarily have thrown me and wiped out all the good is just one thing among many now, no big deal. It doesn't obliterate all the rest that's present. It's just one thing. There is a lot more self-trust and sense of my own ability to be present, especially with someone else like a client so that they become more powerful, and to be with people so they can see themselves more clearly and powerfully. I am now a Higher Power attorney!"

She again reported that she continued to have no trouble driving on freeways. We decided in this session to use the Transpersonal protocol to target her present awareness to see if any subtle distractions would arise for desensitization.

"There is a feeling of clarity and peace and a softness in my chest with no image or thought, just a little high (Go with that)...it [the picture] doesn't look the same...it's not the experience, it's just a memory now...Now is the experience...I didn't know how to access It [the nondual] before and it all felt like it used to be, it was devastating...It's [the Now] always been here but I expected it to look different...it is not like it was last time...I guess the experience of the Now doesn't happen again in the same way twice and what you remember is past...you experience it differently each time...what is present now is a sense of expanded consciousness...(Like a twelve-lane highway, not a two-lane one?)...exactly!...I'm suspended in a liquid medium of consciousness...no, not suspended, not stopped, as in banking not holding, being supported by breath...it's about being able to just have a sense of confidence that there is this consciousness that doesn't have a form or shape...there is an undercurrent of peacefulness where I am present to the consciousness...time is slowed down...when I am in overwhelm, I can come back to this instead of going with panicked thoughts and feelings...just talking about having the faith to get what I need to get on time without distracting myself by the immediate horizon...the old images of hiding behind my Mom's skirt have no energy, or of Mark and me yelling at each other...there is this huge vastness and a reservoir of capability which is not personalized as 'I can do this'...there is just peace about what is ...... nothing but peace...nothing!...ahhh .... mmm".........[silence].

We ended this session after enjoying the silence for some time without the bilateral stimulation. It is important that clients experience the nondual now as separate from the bilateral stimulation in the actual session so that peace does not become a conditioned response and in any way appear to depend upon the stimulation.

A year and a half later she is still enjoying her new awareness, which permeates her now full-time coaching and bodywork practice. She has given up the practice of law. Her awareness continues to expand and deepen as she rests more and more in the present.

Conclusion

This case study demonstrates that long-lasting healthful results can be obtained when nondual wisdom joins EMDR therapy. Psychotherapy as satsang is a coming together in conversation pointing toward the truth, which allows therapeutic resonance to occur. This joining in the company of truth can be assisted at times by skillful means such as EMDR. When therapists rest quietly in their own peaceful, empty awareness and clients are encouraged to notice any distractions to their own ability to be present to the Now, life experiences that hold charge or are still distracting can be targeted, experienced fully, and desensitized with bilateral stimulation. The remaining eternal truth of Awareness can be experienced more and more fully. This experience of nondual reality is, of course, not dependent on bilateral stimulation or on therapy. It generalizes outside of sessions and endures and deepens naturally in everyday life.

The above description of EMDR in psychotherapy as satsang is not intended to promote a set of techniques or a way to do "nondual EMDR therapy." Rather, I hope that this chapter shows that nondual wisdom enhances and transforms any form of psychotherapy. It describes many of the ways that EMDR can be useful in the service of healing and awakening. There is no formal nondual therapy, since that which is nondual is not an adjective, a belief, a domain, or even an object of awareness. It is the living Truth.

Appendix: Transpersonal EMDR Protocol

I. Preparation

  a. Life review, learning lessons

  b. Process new targets

  c. Review life lessons

  d. Define and discuss Contentment

II. Assessment

  a. Quieting down to Contentment

  b. Measure Contentment (light, medium, deep)

  c. Define and identify distractions to Contentment

  d. Measure distractions on LOD scale

III. Processing

  a. Process each target to zero with bilateral stimulation

  b. Return to Contentment baseline and note new distractions

  c. Process distractions

  d. Remeasure Contentment

  e. Process any new distractions

  f. Deepen Contentment with bilateral stimulation

  g. Process any new distractions

  h. Deepen Contentment again and remeasure Contentment

  i. Install future templates

IV. Completion

    a.   Ground in the Present

    b.   Explain log

Endnotes

1. I wish to thank our senior editor John Prendergast for his careful and painstaking editing of this chapter and all others comprising this book.

6

Double Vision

Duality and Nonduality in Human Experience

John Welwood

for Arnaud Desjardins

People living in modern cultures suffer an extreme degree of alienation that was unknown in earlier times—from society, community, family, older generations, nature, religion, tradition, their body, their feelings, and their humanity itself. In a dehumanizing techno-culture that has lost sight of the deepest potentials of human nature, we need a spirituality that can help us connect with the intrinsic power, beauty, and goodness of being human. For humanity to move forward in a positive direction, we need a guiding vision of all that it means to be human.

Even in the best of times, being human is challenging and confusing, for it involves living on different planes of reality at the same time. To be fully human, then, requires cultivating a taste for paradox—an appreciation of how very different truths can be true at the same time. Indeed it is this multi-dimensional quality of our experience that is the source of all human creativity and greatness.

Dualism and Nonduality

Most people's consciousness, however, remains restricted to a single plane of reality: dualistic perception, as fabricated by the conditioned egoic mind, which sets up a solid division between the separate self over here and everything else over there. All our main patterns of self-defense—repression, resistance, denial, avoidance, withdrawal, projection, judgment, rejection, dissociation, aggression—are ways of separating ourselves from reality, standing apart from it, and substituting a mind-created virtual reality in its place. This tendency to fabricate our own separate reality is a way of trying to protect ourselves against "other"—those elements of reality that appear alien or threatening.

The dualistic ego-mind is essentially a survival mechanism, on a par with the fangs, claws, stingers, scales, shells, and quills that other animals use to protect themselves. By maintaining a separate self-sense, it attempts to provide a haven of security in an impermanent world marked by continual change, unpredictability, and loss. Yet the very boundaries that create a sense of safety also leave us feeling cut off and disconnected. So unless we develop beyond the defensive ego-mind, we remain subject to endless inner conflict, alienation, and suffering—the hallmark of what the Eastern spiritual traditions call *samsara*.

Fortunately, as human beings we also have access to a larger dimension of consciousness that is intrinsically free of dualistic fixation. The Eastern spiritual traditions regard this egoless awareness as our true, essential nature, the very ground of our being. Tapping into this pure nondual presence, as in certain types of contemplative knowing, reveals a wide open field of awareness in which the separation between self and other, or perceiver and perceived, falls away.

By dissolving the cognitive filters that maintain the division between self and other, nondual awareness is the doorway to liberation from the conditioned mind and the narrow, conflictual world of samsara. It reveals absolute truth, the way things ultimately are: inseparable, undivided, interconnected. The Indian axiom, "Thou art That," expresses this discovery: our very being is not separate from the isness of all things. What I am is inseparable from the whole of reality as it appears and flows through me at every moment, in the flux of my ongoing experience.

If the dualistic egoic mind is prehuman, or subhuman, in that it is survival-oriented, nondual egoless awareness is transhuman, or suprapersonal, because it opens up a larger expanse of being or presence that is free from our ordinary, personal involvement in immediate existential situations. These two planes of existence—subhuman and transhuman, samsara and nirvana—are the main focus of many Eastern traditions, which lay out a path leading from the bondage of conditioned mind to the liberation of unconditioned awareness.[1]

The Human Realm

This potential to transcend the limitations of the human condition is certainly a most essential human capacity, as the East has demonstrated.[2] Yet in their focus on liberation from conditioned existence, the Eastern spiritual traditions often do not regard the human plane as particularly interesting or significant in its own right. In classical Buddhist thought, for example, the human realm is simply one of the six domains of samsara. It happens to be the most fortunate realm to be born into. But this is because being human is the best platform for liberation, rather than having any special significance in itself. It is the only realm in which it is possible to become enlightened.

While the East emphasizes liberation from the human condition, the Western spiritual traditions place special value on human incarnation in its own right, and are more interested in fulfilling the meaning of this incarnation than in going beyond it or finding release from it. The West appreciates the human realm proper, as a third, intermediate reality between unconditioned and conditio-end, transhuman and subhuman. Instead of liberation, the West focuses on humanness as an evolving vehicle through which the divine, or unconditioned being, can progressively manifest in conditioned, earthly existence. As Karlfried Graf Dürckheim (1992), an early pioneer in East/West psychology, sums up this difference between East and West:

"For us in the West, it is more important that a new worldly form should emerge *from* true nature and witness to Being...than that the ego should dissolve *in* true nature and *in* Being" (1992, p. 100).

The Western traditions also emphasize fully inhabiting our humanness, with all its precariousness and vulnerability. This means fully engaging in the relationships and existential situations we find ourselves in, and also giving ourselves to the evolutionary process of transforming this world. The Jewish teaching of *tikkun ha-olam,* "repairing the world," for instance, stresses the importance of fully engaging and transforming worldly existence. Similarly, Christ's willingness to submit to crucifixion points to the necessity of entering fully into the human condition in order to purify or redeem it.

Drawing on the wisdom of both West and East, then, we could say that to be human is to be vulnerable and indestructible at the same time. Fully inhabiting our humanness involves a willingness to open fully to the rawness of creaturely existence, and feel what it is like to be subject to hurt, limitation, conditioning, and death. Transcending our humanness means gaining access to the larger domain of pure being and limitless awareness that is not bound by conditioned existence at all.

Being fully human means honoring both these truths—immanence, or fully engaging with our humanness, and transcendence, or liberation—equally. If we try to deny our vulnerability, we lose touch with our heart; if we fail to realize our indestructibility, we lose access to enlightened mind. To be fully human means standing willingly and consciously in both dimensions. This makes human existence an extremely interesting crossroads.

Double Vision: Transcendent and Immanent Truth

A view that honors and appreciates the full range of human experience, then, must include three dimensions. First of all, there is samsara, the prehuman realm of conditioned existence, characterized by survival concerns and dualistic alienation. The *dualism* of the egoic mind sets up a strict divide between self and other, resulting in endless suffering and conflict. Then there is nirvana, transhuman liberation, characterized by a pure, open field of awareness that is not divided into subject and object. This awareness of *nonduality* is unconditioned, for it is not produced by any cause or condition. It does not arise and cease; it is always there, ready to reveal itself to the mind that knows how to tune into it. Nondual awareness is the doorway to liberation by revealing absolute truth: There is no separate self and no separate other, and thus dualistic alienation and conflict cease.

Third, there is the human domain proper, which comes to full measure through bringing the complete openness of suprapersonal awareness into personal responsiveness and vital engagement with the situations and people we encounter. On the human plane, our lives evolve and unfold through the relative *play of duality*—otherwise known as relationship. Indeed the central, defining feature of the human realm *is* relationship—the network of interactions with others that supports our life from the cradle to the grave.

Relationship only happens when there are two—who engage in a dance that continually moves back and forth between twoness and oneness. In this way, the human realm serves as a bridge linking samsara—the experience of separateness—and nirvana—nonseparateness. This is why being human is a living paradox, and also a field in which a vast range of feeling—from unbearable sorrow to unthinkable joy—is possible.

However, there is a one-sided perspective circulating in the contemporary spiritual scene that uses the absolute truth of nonduality to disparage or belittle the relative play of duality in human experience. This perspective casts nonduality in a primarily transcendental light, regarding only absolute truth—the nonexistence of separate entities—as real, while seeing phenomenal existence— the play of duality—as unreal, illusion, untruth. As one Indian teacher states this view, "Whenever there is duality, it is a dream state...a fraud." Yet in regarding the play of duality as only unreal, this one-sided transcendentalism verges on nihilism—negating the significance of relative experience altogether. In the name of nonduality, it creates its own form of dualism by setting up a divide between absolute truth and relative human experience.

Because human existence is a bridge spanning two worlds— absolute and relative, freedom and limitation, indestructibility and vulnerability—it requires a capacity for double vision, where we recognize how opposite truths can both be true at the same time. In the light of absolute truth, the play of duality is illusory because self and other are not truly separate. Even though two waves appear to be separate and distinct, they are but transient pulses of one and the same ocean. This is transcendent truth. Yet from the relative perspective, each wave is distinct, with its own unique characteristics. This is immanent truth. It is the perspective of a surfer out on the waves who must attend and respond to the particular quality of each wave if he is to ride it skillfully and not endanger his life.

While most spiritual teachings recognize the paradox of the human condition, few articulate an integrated perspective that equally embraces transcendent and immanent truth. One contemporary Jewish rabbi, Rami Shapiro, articulates such a balanced view by regarding separateness and nonseparateness, form and emptiness as two expressions of God's nature (or of the nature of mind or reality, if we use nontheistic terms):

> From the shore, the sea appears a vast field of waves, each separate and unique. From beneath the surface, the waves disappear into a sameness, a unity with diversity. Which view is right? Both are right. The waves are no less real for the ocean's oneness. Nor is the oneness less real for the waves.... The key is not to abandon one [truth] for the other, but to hold firmly to both (Shapiro, 1996, pp. 6–7).

The play of duality is real and unreal at the same time. Or we could say it is neither real nor unreal, and that is why it is a play. Transcendent truth—that separate waves are only an appearance—is what is true in the depths. Immanent truth—that each wave is different and unique—is what is true on the surface. A balanced spiritual perspective honors both these truths. Speaking of the equality of the two truths, Shapiro writes:

> There is no first and second, there is no primacy of one over the other. There is only co-arising and interdependence.... The temporal and fleeting world of *Yesh* [Hebrew for form, separateness] is needed to reveal the powerful and eternal presence of *Ayin* [emptiness, nonseparation]. And both are needed to express the completeness of God (Shapiro, 1996, pp. 10–11).

Dangers of Dehumanization

Seeing nonduality as the only truth, while regarding the trials and the playfulness of duality as simply illusory or unreal, makes it difficult to fully engage with our humanity, our existential predicaments, and our felt experiencing. It fosters spiritual bypassing, the tendency to use spiritual ideas to avoid dealing with basic human needs, feelings, and developmental tasks (Welwood, 2000a).

A one-sided transcendental perspective is especially problematic when it comes to helping people meet the difficult challenges of human relationship. It does not grant relationship much significance to begin with, because it does not recognize an "other" at all. As Advaita Vedanta teacher H. L. Poonja puts it, "Know that what appears to be love for an 'other' is really love of Self [unconditioned, impersonal being] because 'other' doesn't exist. All love is love of Self" (1995, p. 471).

Of course there is a certain truth here: Love does indeed come from beyond us, from pure being, from the absolute source that shines through us and those we love. And the essence of love does involve a dissolving of the boundaries of separation. Yet defining love purely as a mutual recognition of transpersonal being is incomplete and unsatisfying in human terms. On the human level, relationship is a dance of duality—a transformative encounter between two distinct beings, relative self and relative other in all their differences. And this dance has an integrity, reality, and value all its own.

Nondual teachings that mainly emphasize the illusory quality of human experience can, unfortunately, serve as just another dehumanizing force in a world where our basic humanity is already under siege at every turn. What is needed in these difficult times instead is a liberation spirituality that helps people recognize nondual presence as a basis for fully inhabiting their humanity, rather than as a rationale for disengaging from it. We need a spiritual vision that values and includes the central playing-field where our humanity expresses itself—relationship.

Relationship: The Play of Duality

Valuing the human domain per se, with its possibilities for creative expression, relational intimacy, and passionate aliveness, has been a major emphasis in the West. One of the great prophets of the human realm is Martin Buber. Buber's immanent perspective provides an interesting contrast to the transcendental emphasis found in many Eastern traditions. In his view, human beings cannot exactly reside in the rarefied air of absolute truth. Instead, where human life unfolds and find its meaning is in the play of duality. Human existence reaches its fullest expression in and through our capacity to enter into I/Thou relationship with reality in all its forms. The encounter and communion between I and Thou raises the dualistic perception of subject and object to a higher octave.

Egoic consciousness, which regards the other as an "it," is a form of monologue because it essentially involves talking only to oneself, seeing and reacting to reality through our own thought projections. At the other extreme, the realm of absolute being is essentially characterized by silence, since our essential nature cannot be realized or adequately described through words or concepts. The Buddha expressed this by holding up a flower when asked to speak about true nature. To fully inhabit the human realm, by contrast, is to live in dialogue, in Buber's view.

Dialogue is something much more profound than mere verbal exchange. Its essential characteristic is meeting and honoring the otherness of the other—as *sacred other*—which allows a mutual alchemy to take place. In his words, "The basic movement of the life of dialogue is the turning toward the other...accepting with one's essential being another person in his particularity" (1965, pp. 22–23). This is a far cry from *darshan* with a spiritual teacher who sees you as the absolute Self or nonself that you ultimately are. In Buber's perspective, trying to transcend duality shortcircuits the possibility of I/Thou communion.

Dialogue is not limited to person-to-person contact. Buber speaks of dialogue with God, and also describes encountering a tree in this spirit: "With all your strength receive the tree, give yourself up to it.... Then, indeed, you will be transformed" (quoted in Mannheim, 1974, p. 20). Even the great Indian mystic Ramakrishna seemed to recognize this sacred dimension of duality when he exclaimed, "I don't want to *be* sugar, I want to *taste* sugar."

The conditioned ego is immune to this kind of transformative exchange because it remains stuck in subject/object perceptions based on past conditioning. Absolute being also does not change and transform because it is timeless—"as it was in the beginning, is now and ever shall be." But the human realm, where the play of duality unfolds, is a theater of ceaseless change and evolution.

To Be Oneself

To encounter the otherness of the Thou is to appreciate another as not only different from you, but also unique, unlike any other you have ever encountered. Buber defines *uniqueness* not as individualism, but as the bearing of a particular gift that no one else can offer in quite the same way. Your presence in the world, your personal embodiment, the offering you make by manifesting as "you"—no one else can express this in the same way that you do. In Buber's words:

> Every person born into this world represents something new, something that never existed before, something original and unique. It is the duty of every person...to know and consider...that there has never been anyone like him in the world, for if there had been someone like him, there would have been no need for him to be in the world. Every single person is a new thing in the world and is called upon to fulfill his particularity in this world. Every person's foremost task is the actualization of his unique, unprecedented and never-recurring potentialities, and not the repetition of something that another, be it even the greatest, has already achieved.

The same idea was expressed by Rabbi Zusya when he said a short while before his death: "In the world to come I shall not be asked, 'Why were you not Moses?' I shall be asked, 'Why were you not Zusya?'" (1970, pp. 16–17).

What does it mean to be yourself in this sense, to "be Zusya"? It doesn't mean proudly proclaiming, "I am me"—the separate personality who has this set of traits, these preferences, this history. To be yourself in Buber's sense means to find the deepest laws of your being, to let your life find and carve out its true path, and to bring forth your innate gifts and qualities in time, through your interchange with life in all its aspects. Being yourself in this sense refers neither to the conditioned ego-self nor to the absolute no-self beyond all characteristics, the timeless Buddha nature that is the same in everyone. It involves appreciating yourself as a being-in-process, continually uncovering your true gifts and embodying them in the flowing current of time, relatedness, and action. We could also call this the *true person.*

Only the true person can be intimate, can relate in an intimate way to other people and to life itself. The conditioned ego, identified with roles and identities formed in the past, is incapable of true relationship. Similarly, in timeless, nondual awareness, there is also no relationship; there is only direct knowing, silent presence without involvement in the polarity of self and other. So to be fully engaged in relationship, we have to step into and inhabit our human form—the person.

Individuation

The true person is the self-in-process unfolding and ripening in time. This developmental process, through which the person evolves and blossoms, is the path of *individuation.* Dialogue—the creative, transformative interchange between self and other—is the flower of individuation. The rarity of true dialogue in our world indicates the rarity of individuation as well.

Psychotherapy can be instrumental in furthering individuation by helping people heal the wounds of relationship, develop their capacity for personal relatedness, and shed the conditioned identities that form the defensive shell of ego, preventing the seed of the person from blossoming forth. How fully the suchness of *you* shines through—in your face, your speech, your actions, your particular quality of presence, your expressions of love—is partly grace, but also partly a result of how much you have worked on polishing your vessel so that it becomes transparent to the pure being that is its ground.

Individuation as I am describing it here thus goes beyond the secular humanistic ideal of self-actualization—simply finding personal fulfillment or developing one's individual talents as an end in itself. The true person is a higher octave of the separate individual who remains confined within his individuality. According to Buber, the evolution from individual to person happens through fully engaging in the human relational field:

> Dialogue between mere *individuals* is only a sketch; only in dialogue between *persons* is the sketch filled in. But by what [means] could a man from being an *individual* so really become a *person* as by the strict and sweet experiences of dialogue, which teach him the boundless contents of the boundary? (1965, p. 21, my italics)

Appreciating the difference between self and other opens up a wider mode of being ("the boundless contents of the boundary"), an embodied, personal presence that can accept this difference without being confined by it.

While the true person evolves in the cauldron of human relationship, this evolution also requires a certain degree of spiritual transcendence—a capacity to recognize and open to our larger being, which lies beyond the person altogether. Indeed the true person is one of the potentials of our larger being—to find and express itself fully in the world, in a personal way, through the ineffable suchness of "you" and "I." Individuation is the forging of a transparent vessel—*the authentic person who brings through what is beyond the person in a uniquely personal way.*

We can thus distinguish absolute true nature—universal beingness, which is the same in everyone—from individuated true nature—how each person expresses absolute true nature through a unique path and a unique offering. Individuation is the process of bringing the absolute into human form—the "form" of our person, animated by our capacity for personal, interrelational presence, embodied in the world.

A Balanced Understanding

A nondual view that gives greater value to the transcendent than to the immanent is unable to recognize any significance in individuation, the dialogue between I and Thou, the appreciation of otherness, or intimate relationship. On the other hand, a purely immanent approach, such as Buber's, does not recognize the important role that transcendence—the capacity to step beyond the personal, dialogical realm into nondual, suprapersonal presence—can play in human development. We need a more comprehensive view that recognizes the nonduality of transcendent and immanent, absolute and relative, emptiness and form.

This is the understanding that can be found, to different degrees, in Buddhist and Hindu Tantra, Zen, Kashmir Shaivism, Sufism, and other traditions, which vary in the emphasis they place on the balance between the two truths. It is a view that can fully embrace paradox, for it recognizes that we live in form and beyond form at the same time. In terms of relationship, this paradox might be expressed as: "Through you I see beyond you to what expresses itself as the you I love."

One Indian teacher in the Advaita tradition, Swami Prajnanpad,[3] who also studied Western science and psychology, provides an interesting example of what such a balanced nondual view might sound like in modern terms. He builds a liberation teaching based not on transcending duality, but on attending more closely to the difference between self and other:

Ego makes you see only yourself and no one else. But it disappears as soon as you see that, along with you, there are others also. With this realization, the feeling comes that, like your own "I," others too have their similar "I." And when you accept the other's "I," you have also to include in it his ways of living, his customs and patterns of behavior, his ways of thinking—the whole of his being. Just as you have your own ways, he too has his own ways. As soon as this fact is accepted, the emphasis on your own self is lessened.

One has only to try to observe and see this: all are different, all are separate. This is only this. That is only that. You may call it good, or you may call it bad, but the fact remains: This is not that. That is not this. That is only that, what it is in itself. How then can you compare this and that, for they are each different and unique?

All things are different from one another. This one is simply this, nothing but itself, complete in itself, established in its own glory, unique. This is *brahman*, the Absolute.

To judge is to compare; but everything being distinct and singular, there is never anything to compare. Everything is incomparable, unique, and absolute. Nothing is absolutely good or bad. There are only differences. What is left then? The other is what he is. Try to know and understand him if you feel like doing so.

The course of life of someone else is different from yours. He will move forward according to his own circumstances. If I have something to do with him, then indeed I shall try to understand him. What sort of person he is, why does he say so, what is his attitude, how does he behave and speak? I shall try to know all that. Then only shall I be able to deal with him. As soon as you accept "that" as it is, your ego disappears then and there.

Unity with the other means to see, understand, and feel the other as he is. Understanding engenders empathy, empathy calls forth love and unity.

When you see the other, you are free from the other. Does there appear to be a contradiction here? When I see that he is just he, how do I get free from him? How can I keep him, as well as get free from him? You get free from him when you say, he is. Why? Because you have no expectations toward him!

Try simply to understand that he is he. This effort to understand, the feeling that I have understood, gives you freedom from him. When you have understood that this is this, that is that, you are free from the whole of the world.
Now do you get it? One is free from him by understanding what he is. Why? Freedom from whom? From my own mental creation, from the relationship that I have forged in my mind with him (in Prakash, 1986).

This perspective is interesting because it honors immanent truth within a nondual approach. It is also quite compatible with Buber's focus on relational duality. Swami Prajnanpad suggests that accepting each being as unique and different, and following its own laws, cuts through the narcissism of the self-enclosed ego. When we try to fit others into our standards or resist how they are, we actually contract and harden the boundaries of the separate self at the same time. We become smaller ourselves. But the act of appreciating the differentness of others, letting them be as they are, literally loosens and dissolves the boundaries that keep us separate at the same time. "The feeling of being not separate emerges in the heart only by accepting what is different," as the Swami puts it (1981a, p. 172).

In this way, we come to know others in their suchness, and are at-one with them. Unity, or nonseparateness, then, does not come about through transcending the difference between self and other, but through fully allowing the other's differentness—which naturally undermines self-centeredness.

Swami Prajnanpad recognizes the paradox involved here, asking: "How can I be one with the other by regarding him as another entity? ...This seems to make no sense at all....Well, it is only by accepting the other as another entity, that the other entity disappears. Contradiction indeed..." When I allow the other just to be what he, she, or it is, without imposing my preferences or offering any resistance, the other is no longer something separate over there, apart from me. I meet and mingle with the other in the open field of awareness, where separate selfhood and otherness dissolve and fade away. Then I discover what it really means to love—to open to others as they are, without imposing my judgments or agendas on them.[4]

Swami Prajnanpad asks: "What are 'you'? The perfect 'you' is always in contact. Always in contact." Here he comes very close to Buber's central dictum, "All real living is meeting." But Swami Prajnanpad takes one large step beyond Buber, by seeing the relative play of duality as an entry-point into absolute nonduality. Real contact, he says, "is always advaita, nondual." In fully accepting and opening to the other as the unique being he, she, or it is, "you are one with that. A paradox indeed." And "what finally comes about is that this acceptance becomes all-pervasive. Nothing indeed remains alien. Nothing different exists...Duality, which is the cause of all conflicts, of division, or disharmony—all that ceases to exist...(in Prakash, 1986)."

At One With Our Experience

This kind of balanced nondual perspective is not just a teaching for friends and lovers, but has implications for our whole orientation toward life. According to Swami Prajnanpad, letting each element, each being, each moment be just what it is at that moment, established in its own suchness, allows *brahman*—the essence of reality that is greater than any individual form—to be revealed. The absolute *is* how it is unfolding at this moment—in you and in the world. In classical Eastern terms, "emptiness *is* form," or "brahman *is* the world."

Since every element of reality—each being, each moment in time, each experience—is different from every other, this means that everything always arises freshly and uniquely as just what it is. The fact that all things arise freshly and uniquely in each moment means that they are inherently self-liberated, free of all the concepts we have about them—which are based on past conditioning. Similarly, the living, breathing process that we are is always free from all the concepts or beliefs we have about it. Letting our experience be helps us make an important shift—into that unbounded, all-encompassing space of pure being, which alone can let be. In the moment, the small, bounded, dualistic ego falls away.

Letting the relative be as it is, then, reveals the absolute. Thus there is no need to give absolute being a special status apart from the relative process of form evolving in time, for these are inseparable. Realizing this frees us up to move fluidly between engaging with our experience and discovering its spacious, indefinable nature, without regarding either side as more real than the other. There is no need to set up any divide between duality and nonduality.

So if you are angry and upset right now, any attempt to give up, change, or transcend that emotion only creates more dualistic separation. Your anger at this moment is also the absolute; it is how the absolute, the truth beyond all form, is manifesting. And if you can open to the anger and be one with it, then the flow of reality will continue to unfold and evolve without becoming frozen in a solid state. Just as each being unfolds according to its own laws, each state of mind naturally unfolds and evolves beyond the form it is presently taking, if we do not obstruct this process.

Swami Prajnanpad likens liberation to a ripe fruit letting go of its hold on the branch and falling to the ground. As the fruition of human development, liberation is not superior to individuation, any more than the fruit can be said to be superior to the flower from which it formed (1981b, p. 356). Every element of reality and every stage of development, unique in what it is and different from all others, has equal value. In this way, duality *(dvaita)* provides the vehicle that allows us to realize nonduality *(Advaita)* :

> Life is *dvaita*, everything has two aspects.... All activities are in *dvaita*: you are *dvaita* now and here! Start from this *dvaita*, see this *dvaita*, know this *dvaita*, fulfill this *dvaita*, let this *dvaita* wither away. And that is *Advaita*: don't forget the secret and mystery of action: be where you are, overgrow yourself, and the consummation will automatically manifest itself. Be what you are, now and here: that is to be *Advaita* now and here....
>
> Be true to yourself, be true intellectually, emotionally, and in action! That is to be the Absolute now and here. Don't divide yourself into: (1) what you are now and here (relatively) and (2) what you should be (absolutely). This division or this duality is the root of all misery. You are what you are now and here—that is the only 'you' that you know...And move on and on, simply because you are a dynamic process only. A bud is a bud now and here...The bud will flower and fulfill its existence—how? By fulfilling the condition in which it is...You can start only as you are now—as an individual and as a person. (1981b, p. 8, 11, 12)

This kind of perspective avoids two major pitfalls on the spiritual path—spiritual bypassing and the spiritual superego (Welwood, 2000b)—which are ways of imposing on oneself a higher spiritual perspective that lies far beyond one's actual state, thus creating further inner division. When people try to bypass, or prematurely transcend, their current psychological condition by trying to live up to some noble spiritual ideal, this does violence to where they are. And it strengthens the spiritual superego, the inner voice that tells them they should be something other than they are, thereby reinforcing their disconnection from themselves.

Psychotherapy in a Spiritual Framework

Interestingly, Swami Prajnanpad studied and appreciated Freud in the 1920s in India, developing his own version of psychotherapy, which he practiced with his students. This would be possible only for a nondual teacher holding a balanced perspective, with its understanding that the absolute—in the form of you and your experience—is naturally revealing and actualizing itself in and through where you are at each moment.

This understanding also provides a nondual framework for working with emotions and psychological blockages, an approach I describe as "psychotherapy in a spiritual framework" (Welwood, 2000c). The heart of this approach, as I practice it in my own work, is what I call "unconditional presence"—learning to be present with your experience just as it is. If you are suffering, you must suffer (which literally means "undergo") that experience fully. If you can acknowledge and be one with your pain, your confusion, your emotions, your reactions to pleasure and pain, and your resistance, if you can enter into these experiences fully, directly, intimately, they can move through you freely and fluidly. This fosters a natural unfolding in the direction of truth, compassion, and liberation (Welwood, 2000d).

Relating directly to *what is* fosters unfolding along two different lines: affective and cognitive.

Affective Work

The most basic problem people have is that they are afraid of their experience. Because feelings and emotions often seem overwhelming and threatening, they become suppressed, avoided, or denied—which reinforces inner division between the flow of experiencing and the ego-mind trying to control or manipulate that experience. If we can learn to acknowledge, allow, open to, and be one with what we are feeling, our experience naturally unfolds and releases its knots, revealing larger, egoless qualities of being—such as compassion, strength, clarity, peace, balance, groundedness—that those emotional knots normally cover and obscure.

Cognitive Work

The second problem people generally have is that they do not recognize what is actually happening, but are instead blinded and misled by their thoughts—the stories and movies their mind projects onto reality, based on scripts and identities formed in the past. Psychotherapy can address this problem by helping people recognize the difference between "things as they are" and their mental overlay.

For example, a wife reacts to her husband's neglect with anger and blame that only pushes him farther away. First of all she may need to work with her emotional reaction, by learning to open to the anger instead of trying to get rid of it by discharging it on her husband. Then she can begin to look at what is really happening, apart from her emotionally laden interpretations of what is going on.

For herself, she might see that her anger is driven by a movie playing in her mind—"I don't matter to him"—which in turn triggers an even more intense horror movie, dating back to childhood—"I don't matter at all." Looking into her sense of not mattering, she sees that she has a hard time feeling it is all right to have her emotional needs or clearly expressing them.

Out of this lack of entitlement she creates situations where people tend to neglect her, leaving her feeling frustrated, empty, and desperate. This pattern of frustration is what makes her hyperreactive to her husband's inattention. Her work, then, involves freeing up the belief that she is not worthy of receiving what she needs, so that she can let herself acknowledge her emotional needs and then communicate them clearly and directly.

This work on herself allows her to see that her husband tends to withdraw because he has a hard time standing up to her anger without collapsing into self-blame. He is afraid of her intensity, her emotional reactivity, and her tendency to criticize. Seeing that this is why he withdraws, not because she doesn't matter, further frees her up, allowing her to find new ways of dealing with the situation.

Finding Absolute Truth in Relative Experience

Those who hold a strictly transcendental view of nonduality often find it hard to understand the value of working with experience in this psychological way. Why engage or inquire into the emotionality of ordinary life, they argue, since it is only a symptom of egocentricity, ignorance, dualistic fixation?

While there is a certain logic to this argument, it can lead to spiritual bypassing—avoidance of the chaos and uncertainty of one's existential situation—rather than genuine "wisdom gone beyond." How is it possible to truly go beyond a state that one has not yet fully met? When a nondual perspective is used to rationalize spiritual bypassing, it can become an instrument that reinforces disconnection.

Swami Prajnanpad's teaching provides an example of how one can work directly with emotional turbulence within a larger perspective of transcendent truth. In the light of absolute nonduality:

> Emotional reaction is a warning that you are not in Truth... Emotion is an illusion because it is created by thought [which] wants to have something which is not...

Yet from the immanent perspective:

> Once the emotion arises, it *is* Truth for the time being. Why? Because it is there. So I can't deny it...Let it come. Allow it to express. Be with that emotion and then be that emotion.... Then you will see that very soon it will disappear...(in Roumanoff, 1989).

Bringing these two views together, Swami Prajnanpad articulates the paradox of double vision:

> Emotion is an illusion, no doubt, but this emotion is real [even] though it is an illusion. It is Truth because it is here. How contradictory! (in Roumanoff, 1989).

To avoid spiritual bypassing, transcendent truth needs to be grounded in a willingness to wade in and immerse ourselves in the stormy waves of immanence. We need to broaden the terms of the equation that offers only a choice between samsaric, dualistic mind and enlightened, nondual awareness. We need to include a third, intermediate term in the equation—the relational play of human experience, where evolution takes place as heaven manifests on earth, infinity infuses finitude, and eternity embodies itself in time.

Opening to the full play of human experience allows for the possibility of a sudden dawning of wakefulness, known in Tibet's Mahamudra tradition as "coemergent wisdom" or "wisdom born within." This is a sudden dropping away of dualistic fixation, allowing a direct and often abrupt entry into nondual presence. It arises right on the razor's edge where ignorance and clarity, appearance and emptiness, stuckness and freedom rub up against each other, and where their striking contrast triggers a moment of vivid awakeness right in the midst of worldly entanglement. When we recognize that unconditioned awareness can infuse each and every moment, regardless of how much we are suffering, then the play of being a person, being in relationship, facing our neurosis, and honoring the experiential process as it unfolds in time can all become vehicles for arousing a clarity of presence that is born right within the heart of duality.

Our alienation and neurosis itself, then, when fully met, are the seeds of wisdom. Trying to transcend our human shortcomings and imperfections, our "sins and defilements," does not liberate them. Only entering into them and suffering them consciously allows us to exhaust their momentum, move through them, and be done with them. Swami Prajnanpad calls this process of full conscious experiencing *bhoga*, stating: "It is *bhoga* that liberates (in Prakash, 1986)." Or as Chogyam Trungpa put it: "If you don't...actually have faith in your neurosis, literally have faith, there's no coemergent wisdom" (n.d.).

The faith that is needed here is the recognition that whatever we are experiencing is truth, for the moment; it is all that we have to work with because at that moment, it is "what is." Since the struggle and neurosis of the samsaric ego is also what is, experiencing it fully and directly *is* awakening. For wakefulness comes about through entering into *what is* rather than moving away from it. So when we can remain open and present with the experience that is arising, neurotic as it may seem, we discover—either gradually, through psychological inquiry, or abruptly, through coemergent wisdom—that this experience is not solid, fixed, or definite in the way it first appeared to be. As it starts to flow, unfold, ripen, or release, it reveals its true nature as the play of original wakefulness, embodied in human form.

Relationship as Evolutionary Task

Even though many great yogis, saints, and sages have for thousands of years realized the wisdom gone beyond that transcends all form, all strife, all duality, this level of realization has not penetrated very deeply into the fabric of worldly life on this planet. Why has it been so difficult for the Kingdom of Heaven or at least a relatively enlightened society to manifest on earth?

No doubt there are many reasons for this. But perhaps in part it is because we have not yet learned to fully stand in our humanness while also being able to step beyond it, to be true persons, with one foot in the absolute and the other foot planted in the transformative process of interpersonal relationship. If our focus is purely on liberation from samsara, and we have no interest in its embodiment in the true person—through relationship, dialogue, and individuation—then where will the Kingdom of Heaven put down its roots on earth?

The greatest ills on the planet—war, poverty, economic exploitation, ecological devastation—all stem from our inability to tolerate differences, engage in intelligent dialogue, and reach mutual understanding with one another. Social organizations and institutions at every level—marriages, families, schools, corporations, nations—are in disarray. And spiritual communities are hardly exempt from the internecine wars, schisms, and political intrigue that beset most secular organizations.

All the great attainments in the area of spiritual practice and realization, wonderful as they are, have hardly begun to transform the overall quality of human relationships on this planet, which are still driven by the most primitive of motivations and emotions. As the poet Rilke wrote, "For one human being to love another, this is the most difficult of all our tasks."

In itself, loving is certainly not difficult, for open, loving presence is an intrinsic, essential quality of our very nature. Why then is it so hard to embody this open presence in relation to other people in all circumstances? The source of this problem lies partly in early wounding around loving connectedness suffered in childhood—which is especially prevalent in modern societies. Out of this wounding, unhealthy relational patterns develop and perpetuate themselves unconsciously, despite our best intentions.

The hard truth is that spiritual realizations often do not heal our deep wounding in the area of love, or translate readily into skillful communication or interpersonal understanding. As a result, many spiritual practitioners—teachers and students alike—either choose not to engage in personally intimate relationships at all, or else wind up having the same relational difficulties and problems that everyone else has. Even though they may have a loving, compassionate intention toward all beings, most modern spiritual practitioners nonetheless continue to act out unconscious relational patterns developed in childhood. Often what is needed here is psychological work that allows us to bring the underlying psychodynamics that maintain these patterns into consciousness.

Swami Prājnanpad recognized the significance of this discrepancy between people's spiritual practice and their ability to embody it in their relationships, often telling students who wanted to study with him to "bring a certificate from your wife." He saw marriage as a particularly powerful litmus test of one's development, because in it one is "fully exposed…All one's peculiarities, all of one's so-called weaknesses are there in their naked form. This is why it is the testing ground." In solitary spiritual practice, the spiritual aspirant "may accomplish perfection and feel: 'Oh! I am at ease, oh, I can feel oneness.'" But in marriage "everything gets confounded." Yogis discover that their so-called realization "was only on the superficial level. It had not percolated deep within. It simply appeared to have gone deep. Unless you are tested on the ground where you are fully exposed, all those outward achievements are false. This is the point, and you have to grasp this completely" (in Prakash, 1986).

So instead of attributing the difficulties of human relationship to the nastiness of samsara, perhaps we need to accord relationship its rightful significance—by recognizing the major evolutionary challenge that it represents. It is a great wilderness in which humanity has hardly begun to find its way. Developing more conscious relationships is an important next frontier in human evolution (Welwood, 1990). And this will require a capacity to marry nondual realization—which dissolves fixation on the separate self—with careful attention to personal relational patterns that block or distort the free flow of loving presence.

To accord relationship its proper significance and welcome its challenges as an integral part of the spiritual path requires double vision: honoring engagement in the human condition and liberation from it as coequal, coemergent, cocreative truths. In accordance with that recognition, nondual awareness could then serve as the basis for entering more consciously into the human incarnation. This is the uncharted territory still waiting to be explored.

Endnotes

1. As the spiritual practitioner progressively stabilizes and integrates nondual awareness into his or her life, even the division between samsara and nirvana is worn away. At the higher levels of realization, the sense of moving from samsara toward liberation collapses altogether. Finally there is realization that samsara *is* nirvana, that dualistic perception is only a play of awareness, whose very nature is open and free.

2. I recognize that this discussion of the East is highly generalized, and applies more to the traditions of India and Tibet than to those of China and Japan. Yet the West has developed an appreciation for individual development and personal experience that has been mostly unknown in the East. As Karlfried Graf Dürckheim, speaking of the Zen masters he studied with in Japan, notes:

"As masters, they appear in a supreme form in which every personal element has been converted into something suprapersonal, almost remote from the world, or at least not involved in it. One rarely, if ever, meets the happy or suffering individual, through whose joy-filled, sorrow-filled eye the otherworldly glimmers in a unique personal sense...Is such a master a person in our sense of the term?" (p. 101).

Indeed, psychotherapy could develop only in a culture where human experience is regarded as interesting and important in its own right.

3. Swami Prajnanpad had a small ashram in Bengal and died in 1974. He did not write or give general talks or satsangs, but only met individually with his students. His work is preserved in his letters and some conversations that his French students recorded.

4. This perspective also provides a spiritual base for an approach to couples therapy based on recognizing that intimacy grows out of differentiation, the capacity of two partners to fully honor themselves and each other in all their differences.

7

Being Intimate with What Is

Healing the Pain of Separation

Dorothy Hunt

Recently, one of my clients gave one of the best descriptions I have heard for the *felt-sense* of Awakeness awake to itself. She had been upset talking about an issue she was having with her boyfriend when she suddenly fell silent. Our eyes had met, and the looking itself, that is neither hers nor mine, seemed to be spontaneously inviting itself to meet itself, to be aware of itself. We sat quietly together for some time, just softly gazing at one another. After a while I asked, "So, what is here now?" She began to talk about the situation with her boyfriend again. I said, "No, I mean what is *here*?" She sat silently a few more moments, looking a bit stunned, then answered, "It seems like a bare nothingness that feels very intimate."

I nodded in agreement, saying, "Yes." Then I asked if this intimate nothingness she was experiencing now was concerned about the issue with her boyfriend. Did it have a point of view? She said, "No, not at all." In this moment, nothing had changed in the situation with her boyfriend, and yet she was no longer suffering. She was visibly calm and seemed deeply touched. Nothing was analyzed, solved, fixed, or changed in any way about life as it was, and yet she sat transformed in the experience of simply *being* this *"bare nothingness that feels very intimate."* The invitation came spontaneously to meet her own *being,* and in this particular moment, suffering ceased.

Another client came in one afternoon saying she felt very depressed about how heavy her thighs were. She hated that they looked heavy and felt heavy to her. I invited her to just let herself experience fully the heaviness she felt for a few moments without judging it or needing it to be different. She sat quietly with her eyes closed for a very long time. When she finally began to speak, she told me that she had begun to feel the heaviness of her thighs as a kind of strength. She had visualized herself sitting cross-legged by a river, feeling solid and still, like a mountain. From this still seat, she loved watching the river flow.

The client was willing to be intimate with her own experience, to experience it directly. Awareness had deeply touched the heaviness she had hated and transformed her experience of it. She later reflected that from that moment on, her life began to transform in many ways. In those moments, she began to experience a deep strength within her and also an acceptance of the flow of life. She soon quit her job to fulfill a long-held dream to became a yoga instructor. Many years after therapy had finished, we spoke on the phone, and she still referred back to this particular moment as a turning point. She reflected, "You taught me how to welcome what feels unwelcome, and that has made all the difference in my life."

When what is awake *directly* touches its own experience of *anything,* there is a deep intimacy with *what is.* By *directly,* I mean when the thinking mind is not engaged in its usual efforts to separate, label, understand, categorize, judge, dampen, exaggerate, deny, change, manipulate, or create stories about the experience of the moment. To experience something *directly* is not to discharge it, deny it, act it out, redirect it, repress it, represent it, judge it, analyze it, make commentary about it, or "understand" it with the mind. It is to be one with it, to experience it fully. This direct experiencing is always transformative.

In this intimacy we find ourselves undivided. When we experience *being* our wholeness, we are not afraid to experience the truth of the moment, regardless of how things look to the judging mind. This realization of our undivided *being* feels very holy, because it is whole. The words heal, whole, and holiness all share the same root, but our own awakeness is actually neither sacred nor profane. It is simply awake. It is what draws our clients and ourselves together. It is experienced by some as Presence, but there is no one to "become" present. It is unfailingly healing because it experiences itself as whole. It is who or what we are when we are not busy creating our identities out of ideas. It is spacious, without boundaries of any kind, and yet expresses itself in the human experience of our lives. What is awake is never a concept and never separate from the moment as it is.

Direct experiencing is intimate experiencing. The conceptual mind cannot be intimate because it is always moving away from experience by naming it, representing it with words, thoughts, interpretations, judging it, comparing it to the past, deciding whether it is good or bad, whether it "should" or "should not" be here, etc. The concept "water," no matter how thoroughly we understand it, will not quench our thirst. The thought of "I" is not the *experience* of "I," and the concept "nondual wisdom" is not the *experience* or *nonexperience* of *being* undivided. When we experience ourselves ("I" without the concept of "I") and the moment *as it is,* without division, we experience healing into our essential wholeness, into the truth of our *being.*

The direct experience of anything automatically engages our *nonseparate being.* Because it does not happen in the thinking mind, *direct* experience usually comes from below the neck. It is healing because it is not separating. What is aware of our experience is not the thinking, judging mind, but awareness itself—the same thing that is aware of our thoughts and judgments, the same thing (or no-thing) that is looking through our eyes, listening through our ears.

What is awake in us has never been absent from a single experience. It does not require our life to change or our experience to be positive in order for awareness to be present to itself. What is awake and aware does not require years on the meditation cushion or the mind's learning anything or analyzing anything in order to be present. In fact, it cannot be acquired and it cannot be lost. It does not come and go with states of mind. It is here in the most mundane experience of tying our shoelaces, in the most overwhelming experience of terror, and in the blissful state of unity consciousness. It does not leave us in our suffering or in our joy. It is aware of life as it is without comment, without refusal, without claiming anything as its own. It is a total mystery yet experienced by all beings.

Being truth, it lives as truth, the authentic truth of each moment. The mind that is desperately trying to make things look or be a certain way cannot experience such truth, and thus is frequently frustrated in its attempt to find healing. Healing happens when we are not separating ourselves from the authentic truth of the moment.

One client recently had a recurrence of pain in her neck, arm, and leg, which in the past had been diagnosed as perhaps a neurological problem. She told me she had become anxious about this, that her doctor once told her if these symptoms recurred, it might be an indication that surgery should be considered. She was clearly anxious, but trying very hard to reassure herself. She said several times, "But this pain has appeared before and gone away. It's probably nothing."

I did not speak about what I knew nothing about, that is, whether it was something or nothing. (The mind's attempts to get or give "reassurance" will never produce true peace; it is only the truth that brings peace.) Instead I wondered what would happen if she just let herself experience the anxiety that was here now instead of creating stories in her mind about it—that she would either need surgery, possibly end up paralyzed, or that it was all probably nothing and she was just overreacting. Would it be possible to just let the anxiety be here?

She returned to her story that it was "probably nothing." I said to her, "The truth is, neither of us know right now, do we, whether it is something serious or nothing serious. You are trying to diminish the anxiety created by one story ('I'll have to have surgery') by creating another story ('It's probably nothing'), but what if you just let your anxiety be itself? What might happen if you brought the anxiety close to you? What if you just told the truth that you don't know? What would it be like for you just to *not* know?"

She seemed jolted for a moment and then sat quietly for quite awhile, becoming more and more relaxed. After a time, I asked her what she was experiencing. She replied that she no longer felt anxious. It was a relief to just tell the truth, that she *didn't* know. It was a relief to let the anxiety just be what it was. In fact, by the end of the hour, she said the pain in her body had disappeared as well.

When we do not separate ourselves from the mystery of our own *essential awake being*, or separate ourselves from experiencing the truth of the moment as it is—the felt sense of the *body of being*—we do not suffer. Physical bodies may experience pain; thinking minds may be confused; emotions may present themselves as intensely positive or negative; but we are not suffering. We are living from the truth of our wholeness, *being* who/what we truly are, and this is never divided, never in conflict, even when conflict is being played out.

We are not trying to transcend the moment, or change our thoughts about the moment; we are simply being intimate *with* the moment exactly as it is. Nothing needs to change. What was rejected is welcomed; what was divided is whole; what was "out there" comes close. Such living experiencing of the truth of our being and the authentic truth of the moment is *always* healing. Conversely, it is our separation from the moment and our separation from the truth of our being that create suffering.

When we have realized from our own direct, experiential, knowing that there is no one and no thing separate from the vast Mystery that unfolds itself seamlessly as a whole every moment, and that *we are That*, we no longer imagine or identify with an "I" who is separate. How can our client be separate either? How can this feeling or that experience that either one of us may be having be separate? How can this or that behavior be separate? Wholeness sees itself already whole, already healed. If we hold that one of us is healed and one of us unhealed, we cannot function as an instrument of true healing; for to heal is to realize our wholeness, our nonseparation from our essential nature, from one another, and our nonseparation from the moment as it is. What imagines it is separate (the mind or the intellect) cannot invite an experience of nonseparation. Only what is undivided invites a taste of or the ultimate realization of itself.

If we have not experienced the truth of our own being, or known what it is to experience the touch of this intimate awakeness on our own experience, we will not be able to invite our clients to do the same. There is nothing wrong with where we are working; this is Totality functioning exactly in this way. We each work in the realms that we know, in the ways we are called to function. But there may be a danger in a book such as this if one imagines that there is something that can be taught or learned about "enlightened" psychotherapy.

No matter how hard the mind wants to "try on" what it thinks it means to be awakened, we cannot pretend our experience is undivided when it is not. Whether we function as "therapist" or "client," to directly experience our authentic truth of the moment, whatever it is, and tell ourselves the truth of what it is, is actually to begin to live undivided. Neither can we pretend to be loving if we do not love. We cannot "try" to be present. What is trying is our obstacle to what is always already present. Wanting to "awaken" is what keeps us from noticing what is always already awake. Imagining there is a someone to be loving is what separates us from Love itself.

It also seems important to say that in my understanding there really is no such thing as "nondual psychotherapy." It would be just as accurate or just as ridiculous to speak of "nondual dreaming," or "nondual wars." What we try to point to by the term "nondual awareness" or "wisdom," in its awakening to itself, is not an adjective that one adds on to something else. *There is no something else.* Likewise, we do not "integrate" spirituality into our work or our life. To do that, there is a separate "I" who feels he or she has the challenge or the responsibility to try to integrate "truth" into life. Life as-it-is *is* Truth. What imagines it is "integrating" is the mind's thoughts. What is Whole has no need of integration, for it is never separated from Itself.

Appearances and interpretations of appearances can deceive. In my experience, which is all I can speak truthfully about, there really is no separate "I" to "learn" nondual principles and then apply them to his or her work. This is a play of mind—perhaps fascinating, perhaps perceived by some minds as "meaningful"—but ultimately, in the realization of who/what we are, one is surrendered into nondoing. Doing happens but there is no doer. Psychotherapy happens, but there is no separate psychotherapist and client. Flavors of work, flavors of personality differ, but what is "Same" always sees "Same." It also sees its own separations, its own identifications, its own delusions, its own sufferings, its own infinite faces, but from the place where there is no separation, identification, delusion, suffering, or multiple faces.

The total paradox and mystery of this cannot be untangled by the mind. The mind must live in openness and unknowing, without an agenda, without efforting to "get" something, for the Unknown and Unborn to present Itself. The mind that is eventually surrendered to Silence and Stillness receives the truth of its own identity, a truth that has never been anywhere else than right here, right now. But the mind does not know how to surrender. Surrender happens.

Awakeness, when it is deeply moving in its human experiencing, is incredibly free to move however it does in its sheer love, clarity, and intimacy with the moment. This is not to say there is a separate "I" who becomes free or learns how to be intimate with life. The idea of a separate "I" has to do with fiction, not freedom. This point seems particularly relevant to the mind that would like to imagine there are techniques for deconstructing identity or ways of being with experience or people that are somehow "nondual" and others that are not. It is only the separate mind that tries to divide what is seamless. What is awake and undivided can and does use anything and everything for its functioning. There is nothing else functioning! And its functioning, its manifestation, is always in duality. Time and space are constructs for *This!* to experience itself.

Awakeness is not a *state* of Consciousness. It is prior to all states, all conditions. It is not a point of view. Consciousness may take *on* an Absolute point of view or a relative point of view, but what I am describing has *no* point of view, and it does not depend on maintaining any state. It cannot be defined with words or known by the conceptual mind. It cannot be taught, approximated, imitated, or integrated into something else. It cannot be given or taken away. It is what we are, and it is present in every one of our therapy sessions.

In the Mystery that seems to move itself, there are two main ways that healing seems to continually invite itself as my client and I sit together. One is simply *being* together without an agenda, without a place to arrive, without needing to refuse, get rid of, or change anything. The other is the continual invitation to the direct experience of the moment as it is. *Whatever* is arising—be it feeling, belief, story, body sensation, energy, suffering itself—is an opening into the mystery of our nonseparate *being.*

Every moment holds that potential because every moment is exactly *That* which is our wholeness. As *The Heart Sutra* described so beautifully: "Form is *exactly* emptiness, emptiness *exactly* form"[1] (*italics* are mine). What is awake is exactly what is arising. It cannot be separated except in the mind of ideas. As a sweet friend once remarked, "In the Vastness that we are, where would we send something we wanted to get rid of?"

When we allow ourselves to fully experience what is here now, we are being intimate with *what is*. *What is* is described so poetically by Rumi (and his translator) in the following:

> *We are the mirror as well as the face in it.*
> *We are tasting the taste this minute of eternity.*
> *We are pain and what cures pain, both.*
> *We are the sweet cold water and the jar that pours.*

> —*Jalal al-Din Rumi,* The Essential Rumi
> *translations by Coleman Barks[2]*

We are the mirror of awakeness and our own face in it. *What is* is the mystery that is infinitely aware and all that is in awareness. Our *nonseparate being* is the Nothing that excludes nothing. When we are not separating ourselves from what we *are* by our thoughts of being separate, this "bare nothingness" feels very intimate, as my client noted.

No matter what type of work we do in our functioning as psychotherapists, simply *being* together is always the backdrop of our work with clients. When Silence has drenched our being, that Silence seems to invite itself to itself. The way of silently *being* together, which occurs fairly frequently in my work, always happens spontaneously. I do not invite sitting together in silence or use it as a technique. It simply happens, and it does not necessarily happen more or less with clients who come as spiritual seekers. How the Mystery meets itself in silence remains mysterious.

However, when awakeness is awake to itself, directly seeing itself, identifications fall away; we drop into the heart space together. We share the experiencing of the love, compassion, and clarity of our essential being. This seeing is not aware of seer or seen. Its vision is natural, automatic, and cannot be efforted to achieve. It occurs in openness without trying to *be* open, in *presence* without trying to *be* present. It occurs in *unknowing*.

This seeing focuses like an automatic zoom lens, moving in deeper and deeper to the truth of the moment. Without denying or refusing anything, it moves through the words, through the story, through the thoughts, through the feelings, through the energy body to the pure innocence of what we truly are. From here, nothing is separate, and everything that is arising is wholeheartedly welcomed. Sometimes both client and therapist seem to disappear in transparency or light. It is always Silent at these points.

Comments from clients in response to moments of such silent meeting include:

> *I feel such compassion right now*
> *I feel like my heart has been fed.*
> *I feel so peaceful right now.*
> *I usually have lots of thoughts all the time, but right now*
> *   most of them seem to be gone.*
> *I've never felt seen in this way before.*
> *It feels hard to let in such love.*
> *I want to run away, but yet I don't want to.*
> *I feel squirmy, like I am free-falling.*
> *What happened to my sadness?*
> *I wish I could do this all the time.*
> *Wow, this feels psychedelic!*
> *I guess I don't really have to close my eyes to love, do I?*
> *Your face sometimes looks really old and sometimes young.*
> *I had to look away because I felt I was disappearing.*
> *There's an equality here that isn't supposed to be here, is it?*
> *I feel vulnerable; it's like your gaze sees right through me.*
> *I really don't know how people do the kind of work we do*
> *   (uncovering early childhood sexual abuse and trauma)*
> *   without knowing This!*
> *I couldn't let in the pain if I didn't experience This here too.*

In therapy, there is no agenda to "wake someone up" to the truth of their intimate being because awakeness does not see anyone as other than itself. There is literally no "one" to wake up! The moment simply appears in this way. Many other moments happen in therapy as well, some of which look much more traditional, and what is awake is aware of them all.

However, when awakeness is meeting itself in the apparent "other," it knows itself consciously. The Mystery simply engages with itself directly, without words, without story, without obstruction. We do not have to call it by any name. It is actually more easily felt if we do not try to name it. If the Mystery wants to direct attention to itself, it will simply do so, as in the example where I asked my client, "What is here now?" At other times, it may simply present a strong "hit" of its innocence and purity without moving to invite attention to itself.

As the client comments above indicate, some clients will experience great peace and a sense of deep love in the face of such experience of nonseparation; others become fearful. Either way, the direct experience of the client is something we can meet together. When the experience is fear, the client will often quickly change to some other topic, even when the original experience was peaceful.

A typical comment when this observation is mirrored back to the client comes from a client who responded, "I was afraid. In this calm 'I am,' everything dissolved." In the presence of this welcoming silence, whatever wants or needs to be met begins to present itself. Love leaves nothing out, so whatever feels unloved in the client will move more quickly to consciousness in this nonseparate Presence, which does not engage the mind of separation. Many clients are quite surprised by the depth of feeling that presents itself after even a few moments of this quiet, spontaneous, and intimate meeting.

Because in the role of psychotherapist, we are not necessarily functioning to help awaken someone out of their dream of separation, it may or may not seem obvious to move in the direction of exploring the contraction of fear that is known as a "me." But in some clients, this exploration will happen automatically. The knot of identity that becomes a felt fear or felt contraction in the body will present itself as a topic of investigation and a focus of meeting. We do not invite the client to transcend this knot of fear but to experience it directly.

When the "lens" of attention automatically moves to the energy body, or the emotional body, it is not a "seen" experience but a "felt" experience. The energy in the client's body vibrates in your body. Then the client has a companion to meet fear, groundlessness, sexual wounding, rage, love, expression, clarity. If our work includes attunement with energy, we can actually feel in our own bodies the pain, nausea, terror, sadness, etc., that is in the room with us. All of us, whether we experience it consciously or not, live in a sort of "energy soup." The most powerful flavors are felt by everyone—extreme rage, for example, or powerful love. Some individuals may naturally attune to much more subtle energies or emotions as well. This type of attunement often deepens the quieter we are inside. We cannot help but experience what is here on many levels because we are not separate; everything is connected.

A couple I used to see for therapy had suffered the loss of a child. It created great stress in their lives and in their relationship. They were sitting one morning with me talking about issues in their relationship with one another—"he did–she did" sorts of things—when I found myself nearly in tears. I stopped them and inquired, "It feels to me that there is something powerful in the room that no one is talking about; do either of you know what I'm referring to?" *Immediately*, he said, "Sadness," and his wife started to cry. When we work from openness, we feel what is here in the body of our *being*. Can we say that the sadness that was coming to me as the experience of being near tears was really mine or theirs? It was in the room. Sadness was moving.

What is mine, what is yours, in the experience of nonseparation? Sometimes, of course, as therapists we project what the client is *not* experiencing, because we are *imagining* or *remembering* with our minds what it was, or would be, like for us to be in the situation we are hearing about rather than actually being attuned to the *client's* authentic experience. Sometimes we may be attuned to a particular sensation or energy but misinterpreting it. It is wise to inquire whether what is resonant in your being is also resonant in the client's experience. (For example, the energy of anxiety and the energy of excitement can feel similar.) Being attuned is not being identified with. Listening with our whole being *now* is not a remembering of *then*.

When we are working from the intimate openness we truly are, we may feel intensely the energy or the feelings of the moment, but when the client walks out of the room or something shifts within the client, the resonant feelings disappear. The openness is impersonal, which is why it can be intimate with any moment, any feeling. Whatever is going on in the client's experience moves right through this openness. It does not "stick." When something "sticks" in our own experiencing, then it is helpful to inquire about what has been touched in ourselves. We may be invited by that experience to meet something still unmet or unloved within our own experience.

In sitting with a client, when the energy of the moment feels particularly strong in my body, I might ask the client what they are experiencing, if anything, right now in their body (or specifically, in the heart, the belly, etc.—wherever the energy feels prominent). Some clients are familiar with chakras and experience consciously the movement of energy in these energy centers; some do not. It doesn't matter, except the vocabulary may change. The invitation is always toward direct experience of what is here now, however, and not toward any theory or system of cataloging experience conceptually.

When the "lens" focuses on, or we could say attention moves to, the physical sensations in the body, there are often accompanying stories, interpretations, and conflicts that can be investigated and invited to be experienced more directly. Directly and fully experiencing anything will transform it. Welcoming whatever is here, particularly what has been unwelcome, is what heals the pain of separation.

Another client described a different experience of "heaviness" than the one described previously. In her diary, she wrote and shared the following:

> *August 31*
> *From a Dorothy session: went in feeling very weighed down with work. She had me lie on the floor and truly BE heavy, supported by the floor. What a relief (once again) to let myself just experience what IS rather than fighting against it. "Heaviness is very underrated," she said.*

Even when the mind is very engaged in trying to figure something out, there is always an experience. What is the truth of our *experience?* Here is another journal entry from this same client:

> *March 8*
> *From a session with Dorothy Hunt, the reminding that the experience in the moment is all that is, e.g., entertaining ideas about why I find X so attractive—does he remind me of my father? did I know him in a past life? Southern cultural similarities? Perhaps some or all or none of those explanations hold. But the EXPERIENCE of attraction is present. Period. It's settling. It's clarity.*

The direct, intimate, and full experiencing of anything, from a lovely wildflower blooming on a hillside to intense hatred, childhood memories of pain, a bird song, or the fear of death, can and eventually will take us to what is always "right inside" the moment, or "behind" the mask. All forms of thoughts, emotions, energies, breath, and bodies are actually arising and returning to the Stillness or Emptiness out of which the movement comes. Here is another example from my work with another client to illustrate the point. This client was experiencing deep sadness over the breakup of a relationship.

> *Client—I haven't felt very good this week. I've just been really sad. I miss X so much, but I know I need a break. I know it's best for both of us. I was so unhappy in that relationship, but when I don't hear from him, I miss him. (She becomes tearful.) So I've just been feeling a lot of sadness, deep sadness.*

> *D—Where do you feel this sadness?*

> *Here. (Puts her hand on her heart.)*

> Can you feel the sadness right now?

> *Yes.*

> Would you be willing to work with that sadness for a bit?

> *(Nods)*

> Okay. What I'm going to invite you to do is to close your eyes and to BE the sadness. Just let yourself dive right into the sadness and experience it fully. And for right now, just be the sadness without any story. Just for a moment, simply become the sadness.

> *(Client sits quietly for some time, visibly relaxing.)*

> Can you tell me what you're experiencing?

> *Well, I feel much calmer now, not so sad.*

> *(We sit for a while longer.)*

And now what seems to be happening?

Now I feel a little anxious.

Where do you feel anxious? *(Hand lowers a bit from heart.)*
Well, just let yourself be the anxiety—just experience anxiety.

Now I don't feel it.

(A long time passes in silence.)

Is there anything else you're experiencing?

Well, I'm seeing colors—blue and yellow. It's pleasant.

Where is the sadness?

It's gone. I should do this more often—maybe get back to meditation.

The moment can just be what it is without any "shoulds" required.

(She smiles, nods. We sit quietly together.)

When we awaken to the truth of our own being, which can happen in a single instant, we see that whatever arises in life or in these body/minds is the impersonal Totality-Consciousness unfolding Itself moment to moment. This is usually an awakening *out* of form, which feels very free and impersonal. But when this awakening becomes *embodied,* which can take many years and never stops deepening, there is a felt intimacy with *what is.* We do not separate the moment, the body, the mind, the conflict, or the pain in life from this deep intimacy. This deep intimacy is none other than Love, but it is not an emotional love; it is love infused with wisdom, a clarity infused with compassion. If we prefer religious terms: our mind's separateness has been surrendered to God, and we are, without thinking, *living* "Thy will be done."

It is not only the mind that wakes up to its true nature, but the heart, the emotions, the core stories and energy patterns of our incarnation, and even the organs, muscles, and cells in the body that are eventually all invited to wake up to experience the truth. In the aftermath of an awakening experience, often people will say, "I know this is just a feeling," or "This is just a story" about some division that is arising in themselves. Often this is the mind's way to stay separate from what is here now, rather than being intimate with it. What we begin to see, however, is that the mind may know the truth, but our heart is not yet awake. Or, our emotions may know the truth, but our body still does not know. This awake, intimate love does not bypass anything. It returns for everything. Sometimes this process of truth returning for all of itself can be quite surprising and very intense.

When we realize that whatever arises in our own experience is actually coming to be met, or to be loved, we naturally welcome whatever our clients are judging in themselves that "should not" be here as well. When a client timidly admits she has worked for years and years on issues with her mother, and they really all ought to have been resolved by now, but she's feeling angry all over again, I say, "Let's welcome this anger! How wonderful that we have an opportunity to meet it right now. Tell me, what is your experience?" If the client begins to move away from her experience by judgment, intellectualizing (spiritual or otherwise), or by other means, I might say, "I wonder if you'd be willing to just see what would happen if you brought this anger closer."

Surprising as it may sound, people know how to do this. They do not require any so-called spiritual interest or background. What is important is that when we are speaking *from* what is awake *to* what is awake, we are not inviting the mind to try to figure out "how" to heal, or how to bring something closer. We know from our own direct experience that the mind does not know how to be intimate, yet something does know. The question is where our work is coming from, not what techniques "work."

It seems very important to reiterate that there are no "nondual" techniques for the mind to learn and apply. Obviously, methods and techniques may be used in psychotherapeutic work, but our effectiveness depends on how much we can *unlearn*, how much our minds can rest in unknowing. Intuitive speaking and listening is immediate, resonant with the moment, spontaneous, and intimate. Truth seems to directly touch itself. This movement is totally in the moment's unfolding. It could contain the application of learned techniques, but it is not coming from some intention to use them to effect a change. Preconceived ideas about how the moment *should be* limit our availability for the movement of truth or awakening or healing. Often what comes is quite surprising, yet right on the mark, when we are working from Openness and not from ideas.

The tendency of the mind is to imagine if one thing worked for one person in one moment, then one should make a technique out of it and use it for someone else in a totally different moment. Totality may or may not use anything that was used before, but if it does, it will be fresh and new in the moment. There is a sense of flow, of intuitive openness. Can we be open to what is actually here now—both in the client and in ourselves? Are we present to what is actually here now?

When I sit with my clients, I find my questions tend to be more about present experience and less about past history. I find myself interested in what is here now, in this moment, rather than trying to piece together a "story" the mind can cling to. Most people, of course, would prefer a "positive" self-image to a "negative" self-image," a "good" story to a "bad" story of who they are, and what their lives are about. But from the compassion of Awakeness, suffering ends when we are free from taking the mind's story to be truth. Stories may need to be spoken or experienced fully, but their reality is based on the mind's memory and projection. It is helpful to see that ideas are just ideas. Although some hold great power, they are ultimately insubstantial.

Our attachment to the idea of being a separate self, and the fear that this idea engenders, are what maintain the structure of our separate identity. It is not particularly useful to tell people that this is so; but it can be tremendously helpful to invite our clients to inquire whether or not they can know that their story is true, or to inquire what their defenses are trying to protect. Can we know our mother *should* have been different, for example, or can we know that this feeling, that is here right now, *should not* be here? Here it is! This is what is. This is Reality. When questions come spontaneously, intuitively, and not from fixed ideas, they may plant seeds of truth. There are many ways to invite the inquiry, "Who am I?"

When we work without judgment, however, we work without an agenda. We do not need to fix anyone, change anyone, or "improve" anything. This does not mean transformation does not happen; it means there is no one with an agenda of what *should* happen. I don't know what needs to happen. When we deeply and completely trust the unfolding of Life as Itself; when we know that whatever keeps the planets in their orbits is also keeping us in ours; when we are not afraid of suffering, silence, life, or death; when we know that we do NOT know how anything *should* look, only that it manifests as it does; then there is freedom to completely *be* with the reflection of yourself sitting in front of you, thinking or feeling whatever is there. Then it is possible to love what is here even when the apparent other hates it. This love lets everything be exactly what it is. Its *action* may need to stop one thing (harm, for example) in a given moment, or encourage something else, but not because it is refusing to see what is here. Its action is wise because it does *not* refuse the moment as it actually is.

Even in the case of serious clinical depression, when it might be very appropriate to evaluate someone for the use of anti-depressants, what is authentic in that person's experience is quite relieved to be seen, accepted, and met as what it truly is. Often when we are fully experiencing our sadness, anger, stuckness, and helplessness, we will not actually be feeling depressed. When there is no refusal of the moment, there is usually considerable relief.

We know immediately if we are in the presence of an agenda to change us or not. For people who believe peace or happiness is not here now, and that something must change in order to experience it, there will be a strong draw to take up an agenda. Actually it is our insistence that this difficult moment should not be here, or this sublime moment should last forever, that continually moves us away from the peace that is always already here.

There is nothing wrong with our clients' agendas, and we may find ourselves being quite helpful to our clients toward their own goals; but when we work from a place of *intimate being,* we no longer collude with the idea that changing something is what brings the happiness we seek. We know from our own experience that the love we have deeply longed for has always been right here, that peace does not depend on the world looking peaceful, that everything we wanted to be rid of is an expression of the wholeness we are, and that transformation can happen when our minds stop trying to control everything and we let in what is actually here now.

To experience this very moment *directly*, authentically, intimately, is to experience our being, our awakeness, our love, our truth. To do so heals the pain of separation. To allow things, moments, people, feelings, *to be* is felt as deeply loving. Grief, anger, boredom, fear, deeply appreciate being able to just be what they are. Sadness is very happy when it can just be sad. We do not have to create stories to sustain, or stories to deny our experience. Neither do we or our clients have to "try" to be compassionate, or "learn" to be loving. Compassion arises *naturally* in the presence of direct, *authentic* experience and the silence of our true being.

When "bare *nothingness*" intimately touches itself as *something;* when what is radiantly clear meets is own confusions; when what is looking through our own eyes sees itself looking back—this awakeness we *are* is awake to itself. When what is unconditionally loving meets the places in itself that have felt unloved; when what is innocent embraces fully what has been shamed; when what is infinitely open meets its own finite contractions—we experience healing.

When we discover that the very "entity" who imagined he or she needed to improve in order to find happiness was itself that which stood in the way of the happiness we sought, we realize what is most healing is not "working" on ourself, but simply *being* ourself.

Endnotes

1.   *Prajnaparamita Hridaya Sutra (The Heart Sutra)*, a condensation of *Astasahasrika Prajnaparamita (The Perfection of Wisdom in Eight Thousand Lines)*, is regarded as the essence of Buddhist teaching and is chanted daily in Buddhist communities throughout the world.

2.   Rumi, Jalal al-Din, *The Essential Rumi*, trans. Coleman Barks with John Moyne. San Francisco: HarperSan Francisco, 1995, p. 106. Printed with permission from Coleman Barks.

8

A Psychology of No-thingness

Seeing Through the Projected Self

Dan Berkow

A Psychology of No-thingness

A psychology of no-thingness studies the human being as that which is not-a-thing, not an object of
perception. Knowing the human being as object leaves out the
subject, and knowing the human being as subject leaves out the
form. That the object and subject require one another, and arise
together, implies that knowing doesn't reside in subject or object.
The human being who knows humanness as subject and object
is neither. That which is neither subject nor object is the actual
and present nature of the human being. Thus, a psychology of
no-thingness knows subject/object relatedness, without postulat-
ing an independently existing doer, knower, or subjectivity with
defined location (Balsekar, 1989). Thus, the nature of a human
being is not split into inside and outside, isn't ultimately quantifi-
able, and is not the thinker or doer constructed by thought (Krishnamurti, 1987).

From the framework of a psychology of no-thingness, we can

understand human psychological problems as the mistaking of a dependently constructed self-object for the real situation of an independent observer, doer, and experiencer. To see all constructions of self and other as dependent reveals oneself as no-thing, dissolving illusions of an owner of an autonomous body moving in space and time, a continuing residue of personal qualities (Nisargadatta, 1996). The result of mistaking self-conceptualization as one's true being is that an image is construed as an authentic existence in the world. Not only have I become an image to be projected to the world and within the world, I have come to live in a world where human beings know each other as objects, with each other in turn knowing self as the owner and knower of the self-object, and others as objects.

The projections that I make of you and me as images become the basis for what we know as relationships (Krishnamurti, 1987). As the result of this process, we don't know what relationship is, we only know how constructed self-objects can be imagined as if relating to one another. Psychological problems such as self-protection, control of experience, and defense against threats to self-image result from taking these imaged and projected realities as truth. Projection makes both me and you into objects existing out there in a space apart from an observer who is imagined as existing in here.

The appearance of a continuing constructed self-image, and the emotional investment in and focus on such image-objects, can be understood as an activity that requires human thought (Krishnamurti, 1987). Because we know locations and qualities through cognizing, it is inevitable that we will attempt to cognize a located self as knower and experiencer. The anxiety that arises as an attempt to maintain and keep secure this invented image is minimized by projecting that image as a real existing independent being in time and space. Projection, then, is the activity that results from an attempt to control the anxiety of having no ground, no secure located structure for one's self. Understanding oneself therefore requires a break from assumptions that tend to generate a sense of security associated with self-definition, self-structure, and predictable continuity. Psychology tends to define breaking from self-structure as psychotic, yet one can break from one's previous self-structure in a nonpsychotic manner when relatedness and functioning in day-to-day life is enhanced (Watts, 1989).

The projected self and other give a conventionally determined construction a sense of continuity in a perceptual space (Balsekar, 1989). The anxiety of situationlessness can only be temporarily contained by this strategy of taking a position "out there," as that self will inevitably experience friction, conflicts, intrusions of groundlessness, and a sense of lacking any ultimate security. Intrusions of groundlessness that often bring clients to therapy include challenges to a previously established identity, loss of a defining relationship, perceived threats to security or bodily integrity, and difficulties managing to have a consistent, positive self-image.

A psychology of no-thingness thus implies that the well-being of a person involves the ability to relinquish the position of security, in which a constructed form and self-image was taken as an object with continuity. One relinquishes the objectified self that one thought one had, and the imagined sense of relationship of one object with another. The ending of the previous security of self is the opening of oneself as not-a-thing, not located in time (Brown, 1966). Well-being thus is relational without being located as an entity involved in having relationships (Kalupahana, 1987; Loy, 1999). Healing through therapy therefore allows one to know one's being prior to any attachment to the image of self, and allows acceptance of the loss of any such image and its relations as the discovery of oneself as whole.

The object that was imagined as self is merely the assumption of continuity as a center for perception in time and space (Kohut, 1987). Typically, there are attempts to conceptually enhance this self by seemingly adding to it a sense of value, good qualities, pride in accomplishments, and security or established existence. At the same time, self is defined by whatever opposes it, whatever it wants to avoid or eliminate as a threat to its establishment of existence, internally or externally (Watts, 1989). "Self" may consist of memories, experiences, feelings, values, roles, and/or perspective, and along with this complex occur associated memories and experiences of threat. Health in the sense of balance and well-being is the relinquishment of any attempt to hold experiences, the release of the fear of losing the self, relinquishment of the effort to maintain the believed-to-be-necessary self-at-the-center.

Who I am is never really broken into the separable categories of subject and object, although experientially such splitness is assumed by language and by perception as it interacts with the conceptualizations of memory (Krishnamurti, 1987). Conceptual reality *becomes habitual and gains the power to be taken as reality by an apparently individualized consciousness with a personal history* (Rimpoche, 1992). This conditioning of awareness, aided and abetted by society's expectations, roles, and demands, repeatedly situates an observer in separable relationship with observed phenomena. Repetition seemingly solidifies a separable self for an individual being.

As psychology recognizes that the separable self that encounters various situations and conditions is fictional, it will inevitably equate well-being with being as is, noting that the a priori energy/awareness of being is not attached to specific entities or conditions of being (Krishnamurti, 1987). Through this recognition, psychology aligns itself with the concerns of the perennial wisdom found in such expressions as Zen Buddhism—which emphasizes awareness as immediate and total (Suzuki, 1986), and Advaita Vedanta a branch of Hinduism that points to one's original nature as undivided (Balsekar, 1989).

Such a shift in psychology will view problems in living, not as having originated in a past that is being carried into the present, but as a present attempt to exist as a separable entity that is being defined by bringing the past into the present. Psychology will move toward release of suffering as its orientation rather than continuing its current directions of viewing individuals as carrying disorders, carrying strengths, and wanting to solidify an adjusted and efficient self through positive self-esteem. The individual is understood as a construction, which is projected in an assumed shared space of interaction rather than as an independently existing being. Psychology can show that an understanding is possible, which is not regressive, fused, or infantile, yet in which the separable self and object are not.

The acausal being that is human wholeness is not treated as if it exists in a separate way in an individual person (Nisargadatta, 1996). Healing thus is an invitation to a wholeness that already is the case. Wholeness does not have to be constructed or manipulated into being for a person. A creative and vital theory and practice emerges in which the traumas of human life are not taken as defining of self-nature. One's true being is what remains with the dissolution of the false self-oriented dichotomies from which human dilemmas develop (Balsekar, 1989).

Rather than reifying a recurring thought about a continuing entity, insight into human nature is seen to be discontinuous, a break with the past. Thus, discontinuities of life are assumed to be moments in which new openness is possible (Trungpa, 1987). Rather than trying to regulate life so as to avoid discontinuity and maintain security, challenges to the previously assumed security are taken as significant moments of present learning.

Psychology's traditional goal of defining a role for the objective observer and categorizer of others is thus laid to rest. A therapist is a guide who can share in an experience of opening rather than an expert who can define who and what another person is (Walsh & Vaughan, 1981). Such opening will be assumed not to be a goal or destination, but the nature of the present moment when it is understood without a position apart. The continuity of the self as a normalized assumption of suffering is released.

Observer and observed are cognized as interdependent and

mutually defining, with neither able to claim independent or substantial existence (Krishnamurti, 1987). As the subject/object dichotomy is treated as only apparently and conventionally separable, any object is understood as appearing within the context of some kind of observation. The implication is an end to concepts about inert things that exist independent of awareness as entities with a fixed location in space and time. Space, matter, energy, and awareness each infer the other. Such an understanding will allow Western psychology to integrate insights of Eastern psychology, in which spirituality and materiality aren't taken as separately existing categories (Watts, 1989). The Madhyamika doctrines of relativity *(pratityasamutpada)*, absence of any essence or intrinsic existence *(nihsvabhava)*, and absence of any inherent or intrinsic meaning to experiential events can allow for a new understanding of psychological health and development (see Fenner, 2002; Norbu & Clemente, 1999). Possibly there will be new understandings made available in Eastern contexts, in which some aspects of Western psychology, such as theories of development of the sense of individual personhood, may be integrated (Wilber, 1996).

The Western ideal of autonomy for the individual human being shifts to an openness as relatedness with nothing divided from it, to be labeled as an individual (Watts, 1989; Walsh & Vaughan, 1981). Relationship is now a field of being, and human relations are mischaracterized if considered as exchanges between separated entities—each one getting something from another, or manipulating another into giving something that is needed. Being beyond requiring something else from another now becomes possible (Walsh & Vaughan, 1981). Similarly, a new relationship with the nonhuman environment becomes possible. The environment no longer need be construed as something that exists apart from me, to be manipulated around my needs.

A psychology of no-thingness invites change through self-examination in which nonobjectification is the primary modality. Rather than supplying tools or conditions for health to a client, the nonconditional being of the client and counselor are the basis for opening to unconditional being as the true self (Walsh & Vaughan, 1981). The therapeutic contract will not be for the consumption of a service or techniques, but for the engagement in a process of inquiry in which authentic being is revealed. A new set of techniques is not necessary, and existing techniques need not be dismissed, but the key factor in therapy will be understood as the recognition of one's being aware as the nonseparation of subject and object. In other words, neither the client nor counselor will be understood as objectifiable beings, and their interaction will be understood as a potential revelation of the totality that one is rather than as means to develop a structural change in the client.

The foundation for a psychology of no-thingness involves: a) knowing as one's own being the reality that is not-a-thing, which isn't a constructed and continuing entity moving ahead through time, b) understanding and resolving anxiety about groundlessness and associated projection, defensiveness, anticipatory anxiety, and identification with a constructed self-image, and c) using therapeutic encounter to question assumptions through which experience becomes divided, a self gets placed against others, and relationships are construed through projection rather than being. No-thingness, therefore, goes beyond the implications that projections are to be assimilated and renowned, which would be the process suggested by, for example, Gestalt therapy or Jungian therapy (Polster & Polster, 1974). Rather, projection is cognized as never having a place of its own out there in which to be, nor an entity in here that could make it happen. The out there and the in here are both aspects of projected reality, in which a cognized entity and its repercussions are mistaken as reality (Brown, 1966). Thus reowning projections is at best a temporary process leading to recognition that one's doing and one's assumed reality are the same, prior to deconstructing the entire activity of projection.

The essential encounter in therapy is a means to learn about the circular processes of being in which a human being encounters projections as if realities, attempts to modify experiences to keep the desired image and avoid the threatening ones, and continually reinforces the beliefs and assumptions involved in the position apart from being (Polster & Polster, 1974). Therapy is a discontinuity of the assumptions, and invites the client to an experience of nondivision and nonseparation. Therapy arising from such a psychology is necessarily nonmanipulative, nonjudgmental, and cannot assume to know a better place than *now, as is*. Whatever experience and beliefs arise presently are investigated with attention to defensiveness and resistance to one's present being as arising. The desire to anchor one's being in a self isn't attacked, but is invited into a process of respectful inquiry and loving challenge. The client is invited, and what proceeds in therapy depends upon the client's response to the challenge, and the relationship in which client and therapist engage. Therapy is a relinquishment of attachment and illusion, not a promotion of positive mind-sets and self-images. It is growth through letting go rather than an accumulation of new ideas, new conditions, and new assumptions that must be continued. Therapy is an opening through discontinuity, in which previous self-definitions need not be reinforced, nor a learning of how to modify a continuing self in a supposedly improved direction.

The Unreality of Split Being

Awareness becomes seemingly split from itself when it conceptualizes a position in here looking out at there and remembers experiences in terms of my pain that I was unable to avoid and my pleasure that I tried to keep (Kalupahana, 1987). This split isn't a really occurring fact, but is an apparent perception constructed attributing location and object-significance to self. An emotional sense of my pleasure, for example, associated with bodily experiences, feelings of belonging, or being recognized by others is fit into a self-image. A sense of what constitutes emotional pain may be associated with experiences of rejection, abandonment, rage, neglect, or abuse. The psychological split is healed when pain is neither retained nor defended against psychologically (Krishnamurti, 1987). Pleasure is neither sought nor rejected (Loy, 1999; Norbu & Clemente, 1999). A client may move in the direction of health by integrating experiences that have been avoided, but is fully healthy when rejection and acceptance aren't options.

By neither avoiding nor seeking, the experiencer no longer splits from experience (Watts, 1989). Rather than aiming at catharsis, such therapy aims at what already is the case, at no-thing. It opens to the nonseparate being of therapist and client. This nonseparate being is not a fusion or regression to a condition with no boundaries. The distinctness and uniqueness of client and counselor are present in the experience. Perceptions of lack are investigated, understood as constructed, and resolved when there is neither need for something from outside nor retention of a self-image kept inside. One does not add self to world, nor remove self by withdrawing from the world as a result of such opening. With no division, one is the relational context that seemingly forms as individual and group as well as the world situation that mirrors the individual situations (Krishnamurti, 1987). Therapeutic process is potentially a revelation of the a priori truth in which freedom is conditionless being (Walsh & Vaughan, 1981). Such therapy requires the therapist to have done this work, to have integrated as the undivided being in which subject and object have no psychological distance.

In this therapy, there is no demand that a client change, stay the same, move to a different psychological space, nor retain the present sense of one's place and image. A therapist who is not dividing the relational experience of being with a client into a subject and object dichotomy will not have a basis for any demand that a client be different, nor any expectation that the client would remain the same. A client engaging in this therapy opens to an experience of discontinuity with the assumptions that were taken as life and being, to the extent that the client's readiness and the therapist's openness allow. As no-thingness is ultimately the relinquishment of narcissistic orientation with the self at center, perceptions and cognitions of self as central are brought into question by the nature of being as is (see Krishnamurti, 1987; Nisargadatta, 1996). One's dilemmas always reflect a desire to hold one's self as self. A therapist employing this orientation needs to be sensitive to the worldview and experience of the client, and the readiness to question activities by which self is apparently held.

In general, therapy allows clients' stories to be reconfigured toward an understanding of flexibility, release of the problem-focused orientation of the past, and opens as fully present—with an understanding that no story is true or necessary this instant. Experiences of disillusionment can be accepted as potential catalysts for recognizing nonreliance on explanations or cognitive maps oriented toward ideals.

When there is sufficient grounding in and of the present, suffering associated with the continuation of past patterns or associated memories is tolerated, expressed, and released. The possibility arises to recognize one's being as already always fully present, with past and future understood as projected constructs that needn't involve attachment (Watts, 1989).

In practice, a psychology of no-thingness involves being as is, without imposing views or expectations to change or stay the same. It involves neither fixing anything nor withholding assistance. Even as counselor and client may express their experience and perspective, there is awareness that no perspective defines their being. This present moment *is* the freedom that clients erroneously perceive themselves as lacking (Watts, 1961). Clients don't need a new perspective. Being as the present moment is sufficient. Such presentness involves a lightness and fluidity in which preoccupations and compulsive adjustments don't pertain. Thus, without receiving explicit instructions or expectations about how release should occur, a client can experience release however this pertains experientially, within the present context as understood by the client. Whereas perception and perspectives may be validated, unsplit reality has no validator existing separately, is beyond being validated. It is this a priori nature of being that is healing for human beings, and this healing merely is the presentation of what is the case, without the introduction of unreal splits.

Contact, Timing, and Pacing in Therapy

What is being described is not a feel-good therapy that rests in a concept that "everything as is, is fine and perfect." Rather, this therapy opens therapist and client alike into and as the pure unknown. In and as the boundless unknown that is presentness, the lens of the past is not applied. The operations that brought an artificially constructed sense of order, predictability, and orientation are relinquished. A sense of trust of "what is the case" underlies a therapy that needn't manipulate, fix, or impose expectations for a predictable process of change on a client.

The process of therapy allows a working through of the releasing of past conditioning appearing as the self-image within the present. This working-through always opens from and as presentness. Presentness is not a moment sandwiched between past and future, but is a priori being, the timeless inclusion of all time—prior to past or future being projected. The being or identity of the client and therapist is not embedded in memory or the past, nor is it interfered with by the functioning of memory. Simply, memory is not defining of a continuity of self.

Clients typically bring to therapy their assumptions about an individual and group identity, and the constructions in which this sense of identity is embedded in personal history and projection of a future expected to be experienced by a self. A psychology of no-thingness questions and undermines these set assumptions, in a flexible manner that is adaptive to the readiness of the client for such exploration. There is no fixed belief that the past is necessary to define the being of a client, to explain the nature of problems, or to be projected as an individual future. However, the past may indeed be explored as memories and identity-images that arise for a client, and explanations may be offered as optional constructs to be relinquished when the timing is right. The challenge of therapy, therefore, is not to construct an independent, autonomous, and forward-thinking sense of self. Such a sense of self can only be considered as transitional and dependent on memory-complexes. The full challenge of therapy involves release of the sense of self that depended on identification with constructed personal history and the resulting projections. Enhanced self-integration may be a temporary aspect of personal process, leading to sufficient trust in the process of being to relinquish the self at center.

The therapist who isn't trying to maneuver the client into any state is willing to sit with the client as he or she is (Polster & Polster, 1974). The challenge for clients (and therapists) is to experience this now as opening to being as it is. The strategies involved in manipulating reality to conform to the expectations and enhance the being of a self at the center drop away. The projective process is dismantled or deconstructed as sincere inquiry reveals that apparent existence as a self-center is possible only when there is the belief that one is imbedded in the context of the past. Psychotherapy done from this perspective can only involve an attunement and resonance that assists opening, which neither posits nor relies on a maintained central image of self. This psychology understands trauma and the reactive tendencies that construct a self in relation to trauma as a belief system grounded in images and memories, and not the fullness of *what is*. Therapeutic process proceeds according to the timing and pacing of the individual who construes a therapy-seeking self.

Brief Case Examples

The projected self is the process in which division is assumed as the ongoing duality of me and my experience, my demands against the demands of the world outside. Resolution of this dichotomy involves questioning into the assumed division of self-image and experience. One may express such resolution, not as a strategy or solution brought into the present, but as the timeless presentness that already is always the case. Therapy doesn't educate a client about this, but allows recognition of this being that never is not there, but simply is not located or objectified.

Nondual wisdom expressed as therapy values wholeness as momentary, has no anxiety about discontinuity, and heals by doing no-thing and providing no-thing. Such provision of no-thing is not a withholding in any sense of that word. It recognizes perhaps, that attempting to provide implies an existing lack. With no prescription to offer, a therapist can only alertly be ready to acknowledge nonconceptual knowing when it is expressed.

In examining the process by which psychological distress gives way to a release of the unreal, constructed, and projected self, I will very briefly refer to the case examples of Marsha, Mark, Paul, and Joan (all pseudonyms). Due to limitations of space, I will not provide extensive contextual and background information.

Marsha suffered from depressed mood and anxiety about being seen negatively by others. She tended to focus on family expectations that she maintain a successful marriage, and also understood her being as a person defined through having a successful relationship. Marsha worked in therapy to clarify how she had responded to relationships in her family and how she internalized injunctions about defining herself as a success in terms of how others perceived her. A key moment in Marsha's therapy occurred when she was able to relinquish the previously perceived self-image, status, and artificial sense of self-esteem involved in having a self that could be presented as successful at getting love and giving love. This moment arose after tears, anger, regret, and disappointment had been voiced. But that moment itself involved clarity, stillness, and a kind of stark realization that the momentum of the past had dissolved. Marsha stated, "I don't need to be that girl anymore, who has to be seen as successful in relationships."

Mark experienced intense anxiety, which at first could not be clearly associated with life events. After several sessions he was able to discuss memories of a pattern of sexual abuse from a caregiver during his grade school years. In Mark's case, awareness worked to accept and thereby release identification with past memories and feelings of hurt and pain. The therapeutic work exemplified a process in which feelings, memories, and the impact of experience had to be fully acknowledged and accepted prior to release of these experiences as definitional of self. In other words, as long as he had the agenda not to be affected by the past, his self was defined by the past. The tension of avoiding the impact of experience forced him to define himself as the self that could be strong enough not to be seen as weak. When vulnerability was allowed, a new openness to relationship occurred for Mark. For the first time, he allowed himself to be physically close to a woman in his life, and in therapy for the first time allowed tears and the acknowledgment of having been hurt. A turning point for Mark was the silent moment in which we looked in each other's eyes and he realized, as he later stated, "I don't have to pretend to myself that I wasn't hurt. I don't have to try to be that person, who is always going to be funny, weird, and apart from others."

Paul sought therapy to deal with ambivalent feelings about accepting and loving another, and to learn about his tendency to retreat from commitment with a woman with whom he lived. He found that past experience was constraining present expression, particularly through the unfinished relationship with his father, which he carried as an inner self-critic. Paul had previously studied meditation and had been exposed to ideas about the importance of being present. As a result, he would define himself as having "problems being mindful." However, it wasn't until he focused on the emotional tendencies to repeat critical self-dialogues that change became possible for him. He noticed that he was involved in a repeating loop of perception, with his self at the center.

He would interpret actions and results negatively, and the resulting mood would affect relationships by keeping him distant.

He acknowledged that feelings of being trapped in negativity actually maintained a familiar sense of identity.

For Paul, a break with the self of the past came when he said, "I think I'll take the summer off, and do some construction work in the mountains." During this break, Paul released his preoccupation with fixing his relationship and proving he could do well in an academic context. He took his break, returned to school, and ended up marrying the woman with whom he lived.

Joan sometimes experienced severe panic attacks along with obsessive-compulsive symptoms. After over a year of therapy, Joan had a severe panic attack that surpassed previous ones in terms of intensity, fear of losing her mind, and the sense that she would never escape. The usual techniques that had worked before, such as focusing on breathing and self-talk to remain relaxed, didn't work. At the point of utmost intensity, Joan experienced "letting go of my mind," to use her words. She laid down on a couch, didn't move, and had no thoughts about getting out of the experience or controlling the experience. At this point the panic began to decrease and eventually release. Joan said that at that moment she had no concern about controlling what was happening, developing expectations about what would happen next, or about what it would mean for her not to be able to control such events in the future. In ongoing therapy, we were able to consciously process the importance of letting go of her mind, how that had happened spontaneously, and to allow this theme to emerge in her day-to-day handling of anxiety. We explicitly discussed the importance of dealing with what is present, as it occurred. She eventually was able to release the complex of thoughts and feelings she had developed around perceptions that "this has always happened and has never been gotten rid of" and "this will always keep happening and will never stop."

It is worth noting that although each of these four cases was unique, there were moments in the therapy of each that had a similar tone. These might be described as moments of presentness of awareness, and as moments in which the usual self-references didn't occur. The feeling in the room at such times is one of involvement, as the energy of attending is undistracted and present. There is a perceived quietness, as the automatic thinking and feeling about how to control undesired events, the history of problematic feelings of lack or hurt, and the attempt to rehearse for or anticipate and control future events simply is not occurring. The contact between client and therapist is succinct, open, and able to verbalize the present awareness that is occurring. With each client, the words said at such times varied, of course. Yet the tone of the contact was noticeably similar, inwardly silent and still, and outwardly calm and receptive. The essence of what was occurring was the stillness of releasing, and the acceptance of being open without an attempt to control or maintain an agenda. The content of the words being exchanged seemed less important, although the words provided a way to indicate the change was occurring through nonresistance of the present.

Each of these clients reached a point in therapy when the structure of self that depended upon the familiar, upon a context for controlling experience and maintaining an image, was released. One may view such release as a kind of death of the familiar (Krishnamurti, 1987). Such release may come within the context of contact with the therapist, or may occur in the time outside of the therapeutic hour as clients experience the seeds that were planted in therapy blossoming in unexpected ways. Such blossoming occurs when there is readiness to release the image of security embedded in self-dialogue, and the preservation of the image associated with being seen favorably by others, and through reflection, by self. When such attempts to maintain security are relinquished and present being is embraced as is, strength becomes evident as the absence of any attempt to maintain self.

Nature of Projection

The entity placed in the body is a projection designed as the carrier of projections. It inhabits the body-construct as a mind-entity that can know and do. It brings with it constructions of threats that would attack or negate its knowing and doing. The goal of projection is to protect an imagined entity taken as self by forming protections to ensure imagined continuity. The falsely conceived separated self is a deep-seated human strategy for believing that the present can be controlled by using the past as a basis for identity, predictability, and knowledge (Krishnamurti, 1987).

Conceptualization substituting a self-image for simple openness as *what is* becomes the activity of projection. When we analyze the activity of projection, we inevitably get involved in further conceptualizations. So the key insight into projection is not a conceptual analysis of how projection occurs or what it is, it is the simple openness in which projection is not the case. A moment in therapy in which there is unobstructed openness is a lack of involvement in projective process, without any need for a concept of projection and what it is or is not.

When we conceptualize clients as dealing with conceptual processes, we run the risk of relating to the client as an image. Psychological theory can have the unintended consequence of promoting a story in which the therapist knows reality and the client doesn't. Thus, a psychology of no-thingness must take its stand in the immediacy of the moment as it is, in which neither a concept of therapist as existing knower or client as existing knower has been assumed as real. Generally, traditional therapy results in newer, improved constructs. A therapy of no-thingness does not have this aim, although clients are free to formulate new constructions and leave therapy whenever they like. They may leave when they have constructs for a new, improved sense of self and being. Although such constructs may arise in the atmosphere of safety facilitated in therapy, this sense of a new self-construct isn't the aim of the therapy.

The therapy of no-thingness can have no aim that involves a new state for a separable being called the client. Therapy expressing no-thingness is openness itself, and is a situation wherein means and ends are not separated. Such a therapy is nothing other than the opening that is the present as is, which is an opening to and of potential, and the discovery that one's being is this ever-new potentiality as actuality. Problems drop here simply because there is no place for an assumption of a problem-carrying entity.

Unsplit being is the openness in which no central self is posited or missing. Thus Mark, Marsha, Paul, Joan, and the therapist can be considered as conceptualized stories with roles enacted by selective inattention, allowing the past to seemingly individualize a being. The healing that arises from a dialogue enacted as presentness is not a therapeutic technique nor a projection involving interacting entities in a relationship. Rather, this healing is simply the living flux of life as is, when it attends without having a basis for selectivity of individuals.

Releasing the Apparent Split in Being

The apparent split in being that involves setting an individual against the world, and an individual against his or her own experience in the form of a self-image, results in an investment in unreality, in maintaining a false sense of security. Because projection involves splitting awareness, there is an internal and external aspect to the process. Internally, projection is associated with the maintained self-image and its associated introjects, that is with rules and expectations assumed to maintain security. Such introjects take place as automatic thoughts and interpretations. In the case examples given previously, the reader may note automatic thoughts occurred to maintain the security of the familiar through self-criticism, self-consciousness about performance and doing, and attempts to manage perceptions of lack and insufficiency. Outwardly, projection is associated with concern about the reactions of others to one's self. Thus, a desire to be seen as strong, impressive, and in control masks hidden feelings of self-doubt, weakness, and being out of control.

The projective strategy that takes place inside and outside the assumed boundary of the person is an avoidance of the unknown, and allows the person to continuously respond to what is believed to be known and known to be believed. The problem with this strategy is that by attempting to always deal with what is known, one interacts with one's images and contracts from openness. Therapy, from this perspective is an allowance of, and invitation to, openness. It is the release of contractive assumptions. Such therapy doesn't manipulate to attempt improvement, nor does it impose a new image to replace the old (Walsh & Vaughan, 1981). This therapy acknowledges splits of being as only a perspective or lens for viewing, and never as the reality that is viewer and viewed.

The moment in which there is healing by simply being present and open is not a moment involving a new strategic formulation. It is a moment of the dropping away of self-focused strategies for cognizing. Such moments are not manipulated into being, nor brought into being via education or exhortation. Rather, it is when manipulation, information, and insistence on a way of seeing or being fall away that presentness is revealed as always the case. In each of the case examples provided, clients experienced a moment in therapy when client and therapist were aware of an openness that wasn't an implementation of a conceptual map or means, but simply an experiential opening as *what is* without strategic intent.

Mark, Marsha, Paul, and Joan all carried, in different ways, physical tensions related to feelings and memories that were not compatible with their desired self-image. They struggled to be seen and experienced by others outwardly, and themselves inwardly, in a way that would preserve their attempt to maintain a secure image of their own being. In conjunction with such tensioning of the physical structure is the psychological splitting and internal dialogue in which the desired self contends with the undesired experiences that don't fit, and when the internalized self-critic arises with the wished for independent and positive self.

In each case, the internalized sense of self lived in contraction related to undesired feelings and perceptions, attempting to manipulate relationships and experiences on a day-to-day basis, caught in internal dialogue and other attempts to manage and maintain the familiar sense of self. Joan and Paul were able to articulate, in retrospect, their sense that certain moments arose in which there was a perception of clarity and a dropping away of what Joan called "my mind" and what Paul called his "inner dialogue." These were still moments without any attempt to do or be in a particular way. For Mark and Marsha, there were moments in which their experience simply arose as is, uncontested, without trying to impose the image of an invulnerable self, or a successful self. Such moments are inwardly quiet, outwardly receptive, and without subterfuge or agenda to maintain a fixed self-perception, or perception by the other.

Relationship and Therapy

Relationship can be understood as the natural arising of mutually defining aspects of a whole situation and perception (Fenner, 1999). Thus, rather than two separated individuals attempting to join together to do therapy, we have a whole situation spontaneously arising. This relationship isn't fused, nor is it split into divided subjects and objects. The therapist's being is present not only with the client, but as the client.

The therapist and client are not split, yet they are distinct. Distinctness and the sense of physical sensation, feeling, and boundary are not denied in a therapy informed by nondual wisdom. While cognitively a process seems to evolve and develop, the energy that heals by unsplit presentness is not coming into being or going out of being. When there is clarity of and as this energy, there is spontaneously the release of perceived needs for security requiring self-division as survival.

Clients' strategies and sense of self-structure are often faltering or unstable, or may be overly rigid, at the time they enter therapy.

Clients may feel sensitive, afraid of being overwhelmed, ambivalent about change, and demoralized. Thus, one of the basic principles of psychological study, from its inception in the West, is to find out how individuals, from their own perspectives, can generate or regenerate enthusiasm, interest, and a sense that life can work (James, 1912). In facilitating such regeneration, it may be helpful to postulate that individuals' distress, tensions, and frustrations need not be viewed negatively, as states that must be controlled or fixed (Trungpa, 1987). Their faltering sense of self may be viewed as a transition rather than a structure in need of resolidification (Sogyal, 1992). Thus, there is no assumption that the client should invent a context for a new, improved spiritual or psychological self-image with manufactured self-esteem, nor that there should be avoidance of hurt, a sense of lack, or anxiety about impermanence (Trungpa, 1987). To view the sense of loss or hurt that brings clients to therapy as being out of place would be to perpetuate a split and separation in the process of therapy. At the same time, a split would be involved if we were to view these states as intrinsically real, as continuing independently from beliefs and interpretations.

Paul summarized change that had occurred in therapy by explicitly noting that his cognitions, perceptions, and inner dialogue formed an ongoing cycle in which he repeated what he expected. It was only when he was willing to experience the unfamiliar and unknown that the cycle dropped away. Paul, who had years ago ended habitual abuse of alcohol, stated that although he was free of substances, he now realized that he had not been free of his addiction to a cycle in which he repeated thoughts and perceptions that maintained a familiar and negative sense of being an isolated self.

Therapy needn't involve fixed procedures or beliefs, and in fact would contradict its own ability to question fixity if it did. Because persons are not considered as fixed entities or positions, the sense of personal identity is viewed as a movement of memory images, associations, and concepts—not as an established being that has security (Krishnamurti, 1987; Watts, 1961). Whatever ideas, assumptions, and images have been used to construe an ongoing sense of expected reality will be projected as the lifespace and experience of the client's believed-to-exist identity or self-image. This repetition of image and expectation involves a distortion of reality. Reality is misunderstood as the perpetuation of the past, rather than an always-originating now that includes flux and relatedness (Norbu & Clemente, 1999). What is considered reality is an image of the past that is being maintained as much as possible by selective attention. It is this projection of the past that dissolves as therapy allows newness to be expressed as one's being.

Being as present is not static and is not a circular repetition of the expected. Clients often experience such moments as a breaking through of energy, as freedom, or as insight and clarity. One could say, consistent with observations in the psychology of Madhyamika Buddhism, that the fixed identity of the past is deconstructed as its claim to an inherent existence dissolves when there is clarity about its relational dependence (Fenner, 2002; Kalupahana, 1987). What is noticed clearly in therapy is that the viability of emotions of self-negativity, shame, doubt, resentment, rage, and anxiety dissolve as the self that requires these reactions and expectations no longer is maintained and carried forward. The release of that self is not the result of new beliefs, but an openness in which no predetermined belief is required or presumed. What is key to change is not new constructs for thought, but release of the thought constructs that determined reactions, feelings, and requirements for a separated self-sense.

If and when there is readiness for circular repetition of past identity patterns to drop away, such dropping away will occur nonvolitionally and acausally (Balsekar, 1989). The intent to cause something to occur requires the intentional self-center. The dropping away of that basis for a familiar and anchored belief-structure is spontaneous, not a continuity or a strategy. Suffering in the form of physical tensions related to self-doubt, shame, and anxiety are quite real in their day-to-day effects. These effects cannot be addressed successfully by minimizing them or treating them as if they are unreal, as a mirage generated by a fictional fixed identity. Therapy therefore facilitates exploration, gives feedback, and promotes inquiry. The effects of self-imposed friction are addressed honestly and without either minimizing or exaggerating. The psychosomatic and relational repercussions of self-protection are clarified with self-examination. The dropping of the projection of a separated self is the choiceless awareness of moment-to-moment being (Krishnamurti, 1987).

Dissolving Self-referencing, Splitting, and Suffering

An example of a kind of Asian therapy of no-thingness can be found when the Ch'an (Zen) Buddhist teacher Joshu was asked, "Who is the Buddha?" He answered, "Two pounds of flax." This story is generally considered as a direct expression of nonanalyzable truth beyond conceptualization (Suzuki, 1986). For the purposes of this chapter, we can view the question "Who is the Buddha?" as equivalent to "Who am I really?"; as "What is it to be unsplit?", and "How am I to be whole?" The answer is a direct presentation of the unspeakability and noncognizability of nondual truth, as an indication that human knowing as shared through dialogue and constructs always requires conventional assumptions and references. "Two pounds of flax" doesn't fit the expectation for an answer and doesn't fit the self-referencing activity of thought and emotional reactivity.

For clients in therapy, as with people considering themselves as located, continuing centers of perception in general, everything seems as if referred to a me: "What's in it for me?" "Why does this have to happen to me?" With release of the self-image fixation, such concerns and the associated preoccupations and cycling emotions of lack and need dissolve. The client can behave assertively, but no longer has a sense that "I must be assertive for the sake my me-ness." There is nothing to prove or validate with regard to an investment in self-image.

In different ways, with each of the clients mentioned as case examples, therapy addressed the split that occurs when the introjective/projective mechanism defines a universe in terms of what is good for me in here and what should be kept away from me, out there. The splitting between self and environment is mirrored by an internal split between what is desired and feared. The healing of the internal split is the healing of the external split, as relatedness that is always now, without divisions of a past, present, and future, or of an internal and an external.

9

Welcoming All That Is

Nonduality, Yoga Nidra, and the Play of Opposites in
Psychotherapy

Richard C. Miller

*By experiencing the pairs of opposites, suffering ceases.
When distress arises, ride opposing thoughts back into nondual Awareness. By reversing instability into stability, from
refusing into nonrefusing, suffering is relinquished. Through
disidentification, the pairs of opposites cease their noxious
effect. By reversing the pairs of opposites stability and the
release of suffering are quickly achieved.*
                                    —*Patañjali's Yoga Sutra*[1]

Yoga Nidra

Yoga Nidra is an ancient tantric Yoga practice that reflects the perspective of Awareness both as the inherent ground of our essential beingness and the container, agent and
agency of our healing into the understanding that this is so.[2] Tantra
(from *tan*, "to extend") is a vast array of techniques, which are designed to stretch our understanding in order to overcome the mind's
penchant to divide ultimate subjective unitive Reality into separate

objective parts.[3] Tantra is not concerned with philosophical intellec-
tualism or secondhand information. It is concerned with firsthand
knowing of who and what we actually are, when we stand free of
psychological conditioning in the absolute truth of this moment.

Yoga means "union" or "nonseparation" and occurs when we
live consciously as our True Nature, which may be conceived as
unborn, unchanging, and nondual Presence. Nidra means "sleep"
or "changing states of consciousness" and when used in the context of Yoga Nidra it refers to our capacity to abide knowingly as
nondual, unchanging, and wakeful Presence in the midst of the
changing circumstances of life.

The origins of Yoga Nidra can be traced to various ancient
Eastern spiritual teachings including nondual Trika-Shâsana as
represented in its revelatory Shiva sutras; Tantra and such texts
as the Mahanirvana; Vedanta in such texts as the Mândûkya and
Taittirîya Upanisads and the Tripura Rahasya; and the teachings of
Yoga in such texts as Yogataravali and the Yoga sutras of Patañjali
with its emphasis on *pratyahara*, wherein the mind's propensity to
identify with its projections is transcended and one realizes one's
true nature as unitive Consciousness. Various yogis have revitalized
the practice of Yoga Nidra during the past half century, bringing
it into the public domain, most notably through the teachings of
Swami Sivananda and his disciple Satyananda Saraswati, founder
of the Bihar School of Yoga, Swami Veda Bharati, a disciple of the
late Swami Rama of the Himalayan Institute, and Rammurti S.
Mishra (Shi Brahmananda Saraswati) among others.[4]

First Experiences with Yoga Nidra

I was first introduced to the practice of Yoga Nidra in 1970, during an introductory Yoga course. At the end of my first lesson our
instructor led us through the process of Yoga Nidra, which entailed
paying attention to opposing experiences within my body such as
warmth-coolness, agitation-calmness, fear-equanimity, sorrow-

joy, and separation-oneness. I was invited to rotate my attention through each pair of opposites until I was able to embody each opposing experience, even while experiencing its opposite.

I drove home that evening feeling expansively present and free of all conflict. I felt radiantly joyful as well as attuned with the entire universe. I experienced life as being perfect just as it is. I felt my self to be spacious, nonlocalized Presence. Instead of my usual experience of being in the world, I was having a nonmental experience of the world being in me. I had discovered myself to be witnessing Awareness that was mysteriously not separate from life. While this experience slowly faded over the next several weeks, it left a strong resonance and a deep longing to consciously awaken into and fully abide as witnessing Presence. Since then I have persistently investigated the various processes of Yoga Nidra, becoming adept in its application through both my firsthand experience of it as well as through guiding thousands of students and clients in the process during psychotherapy sessions, workshops, private Yoga lessons, and meditation retreats.

Yoga Nidra and Psychotherapy

Despite its simplicity, Yoga Nidra elegantly supports Western therapies for ego transformation as well as Eastern spiritual approaches to transcendent awakening. Through its straightforward process of attending to naturally occurring experiences of opposites of sensation, emotion, thought, belief, imagery, and identity, it awakens the discriminating insight that every experience, when fully allowed, is both an expression of as well as a pointer to our underlying nondual Nature. Further, Yoga Nidra affirms that when we abide as That, integration and healing unfold spontaneously, conflict and suffering cease naturally, and freedom is recognized to be our innate disposition.

While Yoga Nidra is ultimately concerned with enlightenment, providing its practitioners with a process for revealing their innate nondual Awareness, within the psychotherapeutic milieu, Yoga Nidra offers therapists and clients a valuable conceptual framework and a practical process for constructive transformative healing as well as a context and a process for deconstructive insight that reveals the client's underlying nature as nonconceptual and nonseparative Presence.

In psychotherapy, Yoga Nidra at its least is a process that assists our clients in locating, describing, and welcoming the various sensations, emotions, beliefs, mental images and memories, which prevent their presenting issues from resolving. In therapist-assisted nondirectional listening, describing, and welcoming, which form core movements within the process of Yoga Nidra, resistances dissolve and clients experience themselves expansively open to the *what is* of their experience, wherein both constructive psychotherapeutic transformation and deconstructive disidentification from habitual beliefs unfold naturally.

There are two distinct phases in Yoga Nidra that pertain to psychotherapy. First, during its constructive phase, Yoga Nidra assists clients in developing an integrated psychological identity that is capable of processing all past and present experiences. This phase is similar to other forms of psychotherapy. However, during its second, or deconstructive phase, Yoga Nidra shifts the emphasis away from the content of awareness to Awareness itself, within which the client's experience is unfolding. During deconstruction the accent is on transcending separative ego-identity and realizing one's inherent spiritual identity as impersonal unitive Awareness. It is this second phase that marks the distinctive function of Yoga Nidra and what it has to offer psychotherapy. Yoga Nidra extends the role of the psychotherapist from healer of the psyche who helps the client reconstruct a healthy psychological identity, to therapist as spiritual midwife who assists the client in deconstructing their notion of being a separate ego-I, thus enabling the client to realize their nondual Nature. Yoga Nidra is ultimately interested in going beyond ego identity. Conscious abiding as nondual Presence is the decisive realization of Yoga Nidra. The purpose of Yoga Nidra is to help its practitioner realize that the psychological self lies at the root of all conflict and suffering and that healing beyond suffering entails seeing through the myth of the separate psychological self. In the words of the Dalai Lama: "Selflessness is not a case of something that existed in the past becoming nonexistent. Rather, this sort of 'self' is something that never did exist. What is needed is to identify as nonexistent something that always was nonexistent."

The Process of Yoga Nidra

Classically, Yoga Nidra unfolds as a twelve-step process of meditative Self-inquiry. Its intention is to deconstruct the seven levels of identification that keep the false sense of separative identity in place. These levels include identification with and as 1) the physical body of sensation; 2) The energy body of feeling; 3) the body of emotions; 4) the mental body of imagery and memories; 5) the body of joyful equanimity; and 6) the body of ego-I identity. During Yoga Nidra, we explore all that we take our self to be—body, senses, and mind—in order to come to what we actually are, nondual Presence.

The traditional twelve-step process of Yoga Nidra has been thoroughly delineated in other writings.[5] However, we may succinctly state its twelve stages as follows. We first set our intention to engage in the process of Yoga Nidra, which is our resolve to inquire into what is preventing our realization of Self as nondual Presence. Next, we rotate attention through, which leads to spontaneous disidentification from, the physical body of sensation, the energy body of feeling, the body of sensory awareness, the body of emotions, the body of thoughts, the body of images and memories, the body of joy and bliss, and the body of self as separative witness. As each of these seven levels of identification deconstruct, disidentification unfolds naturally, and nondual Presence floods into foreground consciousness. Residues of separative ego-identity become transparent until Self as pure Awareness is recognized to be the ever-present truth. This is the completion of Yoga Nidra. The practice of Yoga Nidra is then reengaged as long as residues of identification continue to surface.

The central principle underlying Yoga Nidra is that when there is neither identification with nor suppression of what is present in consciousness, spontaneous disidentification unfolds revealing our underlying nondual Presence. Identification with foreground objects in consciousness obscures realization of the innate background Presence. For instance, when the mind neither gets caught up in thinking about nor repressing an emotion, such as shame, psychological resistance subsides. Attention is then freed from being involved with the emotion and is available for inquiring into the nature of the spacious Presence in which the emotion is arising. Every object in consciousness (sensation, emotion, thought, or image), then, instead of obscuring Presence, becomes a pointer to nondual Presence.

Over the years I have made various adaptations upon the classical model of Yoga Nidra, tailoring it according to the needs of the individual, be they a client in psychotherapy or a student of meditation. One of the key principles in Yoga Nidra is its focus on the rotation of attention through opposites of sensation, emotion, thought, and identity.

Duality and the Perspective of the Opposites

Yoga Nidra respects the transformative power that opposites play in sustaining and resolving suffering.[6] When we live identified with the belief of being a separate ego-I, we live fixed in an attitude of having to negotiate with existence. The separative ego-I is governed by the law of opposites in which all that is seen as positive is held captive by its opposite. Where there is darkness there is light. Where there is good there is evil. What we create we destroy and what we destroy is recreated. Opposites are always paired and our suffering is sustained by our inability to experience and transcend these pairs of opposites.

Opposites are never separate. They are complimentary polarities arising within a unified field. When any sensation, emotion, or thought arises, its converse always coarises. Neither is separate from the other, and neither is separate from the unified field of nondual Awareness. Darkness cannot exist without light, or good without evil. Pain cannot exist without pleasure, or conflict without its opposite, peace.

Duality, which is made up of the entire spectrum of opposites, exists within the unified field of Awareness. The mind, body, and senses are dualistic in nature, for what exists in space-time duration forms the fabric of duality. Duality arises when the unified field of Awareness is split by the mind into separate subject and object. In duality this split is believed to be real. Subject is perceived to be separate from object and both are perceived to be separate from Awareness. Duality is the product of the dividing mind, which experiences itself as a separate ego-I. Suffering and conflict coarise when this belief is taken to be real.

When client and therapist are oriented in this understanding, Yoga Nidra is an effective approach for healing the myth of separation, suffering, and conflict. The power of Yoga Nidra, with its focus on transcending the opposites, is based on the insight that without healing the root belief in separation, suffering can never be completely dispelled.

When clients experience only one-half of a pair of opposites, for instance grief versus joy, or shame versus potency, they remain stuck in their experience, unable to move forward. By helping them experience the entire spectrum of opposites of sensation, emotion, and thinking (shame *and* potency, grief *and* joy), therapists enable their clients to deconstruct mistaken beliefs. Psychological integration takes place when clients cease trying to rid themselves of their experience and instead open to the full experience of each opposite of experience.

The ego-I is the product of the dividing mind that splits the world into self and other. This gives rise to opposites of attachment and aversion, leading to conflict and suffering. Ego-identity does not accept the interdependence of opposites, for this would mean the end of its separative existence. Splitting, conflict, suffering, attachment, and aversion coarise as mutually interdependent facets of the singular belief in separation. Any attempt to eliminate one pole of opposition only creates further conflict.

Therapies based upon the premise that clients need to change, begin and end in conflict. This theoretical stance promotes the belief that there is something wrong with the client that needs to be fixed. This stance itself is a product of the dividing mind. Therapy ultimately fails when it emphasizes the need for clients to be other than they are. It is in welcoming every movement of life—grief and joy, shame and potency, sadness and happiness, fear and safety—that we are able to go beyond the pairs of opposites into our true resolution as freedom.

Ego-I and the Tyranny of the Shoulds

The mind inherently tends to identify with whatever thought is present. And its most deeply held conviction is of being a separate ego-I. This belief births defensive reactions against perceived threats to itself, which are expressed as, "I [you] should or shouldn't…" The tyranny of these "shoulds" is the mind's way of maintaining its unstable equilibrium, based on its tendency to hold only one pole position of any pair of opposites. For example, holding onto guilt prevents its resolution with responsibility. Holding onto shame prevents its resolution with potency. Holding onto despair prevents its resolution with joy. Holding onto only one-half of any pair of opposites maintains the mind's belief in being a separate ego-I.

Construction, Deconstruction, and Welcoming

As we've mentioned before, the process of Yoga Nidra consists of two distinct phases. During the initial constructive phase, Yoga Nidra emphasizes welcoming the entire content of consciousness, allowing each experience of psychic material to arise complete with its attendant movements of sensation, emotion, and belief. As an attitude of welcoming is engendered, defensive strategies are disclosed and described. Welcoming evokes insight into self-defeating patterns that are based on refusing to be with confusing, disorienting, overwhelming, or threatening psychic material.

Welcoming is not a psychological action undertaken by a separate ego-I. Welcoming is an impersonal aspect of nondual Awareness. While at first clients may believe they are the ones "doing" welcoming, during the deconstructive or second phase of Yoga Nidra, they eventually recognize that welcoming is their True Nature, what they are always "being" whether or not the mind participates in this understanding.

As psychic material surfaces, each attendant movement is paired with its opposites as a way of assisting its full disclosure into awareness. As opposites emerge into consciousness, welcoming replaces refusing, psychological integration unfolds, and an internal structure develops that is capable of embracing the changing and turbulent circumstances of life. As integration deepens, clients spontaneously disidentify from psychological content and are able to sustain their equanimity, no longer troubled by conflict. When clients are able to rest here undisturbed, attention is freed to inquire as to the form and substance of this internal embracing structure that has emerged and the quality of equanimity that has ensued.

Now the deconstructive phase of Yoga Nidra begins. The emphasis shifts from focusing upon the always changing content of awareness, which clients have been witnessing and working with, to self-inquiry into the nature of witnessing Presence. What has been background, Awareness, moves into the foreground, becoming both witness and witnessed, subject and apparent object.

Bill has come into therapy feeling groundless and adrift, with a fragmented sense of self. The first phase of Bill's therapy had emphasized his psychological integration as an ego-identity who could accept, participate in, and communicate his needs. As Bill's focus turned from integration to self-inquiry, he began to have experiences, as in his early years of therapy, where "the bottom dropped out" from beneath him and he fell into "emptiness devoid of solid ground." Whereas during the constructive phase of therapy Bill had been frightened by experiences like these, he now felt capable of being with the disorientation and fear. He was able to be in his experience rather than trying to get out of, overcome, or be rid of it. Bill began to inquire into the nature of himself as that Presence in which these experiences arose. He was no longer interested in his experience, which was always changing, but in the nature of the experiencer, which he now realized had always been stably present, regardless of his circumstance. He began to see his identification with the belief that he would disappear if he opened to the "bottomless void." At one point he realized that the entire world was inside him, rather that he being in the world. He felt himself as an impersonal witnessing in which this "life of Bill" was happening. To his amazement he felt more involved rather than removed from life for having this realization.

During the constructive phase clients' focus is entirely upon liberation from various contents of consciousness. As issues resolve and conflicted content dissolves, clients experience more freedom and equanimity. While freedom and equanimity may at first be associated with the resolution of psychological issues, the process of Yoga Nidra directs the client to probe the possibility that their freedom and equanimity are ultimately independent of cause and are, in fact, the breaking through of their True Nature.

The Compassionate Caress and Holding Environment of Presence

Nondual Presence, toward which Yoga Nidra points, is like a mother's loving, nonjudging and compassionate caress. It surrounds and pervades all sorrow, conflict, grief, pain, and joy with compassionate tenderness and love. The more Presence is consciously embodied, the more our clients are capable of experiencing and describing their deepest sorrows as well as their most sublime joy. As clients are able to compassionately witness their self-judgment and the stressful contents of their consciousness, long-held sorrows dissolve along with the misperceptions that have held them in place. As conflicts resolve, clients' experiences of isolation, alienation, and separation disperse, and their underlying nondual nature spontaneously reveals itself.

I have witnessed clients in the depths of despair suddenly give way to sublime joy even as they continue to experience their grief. Opposites such as sorrow and joy, anger and equanimity, and shame and potency are often viewed as incompatible. Ultimately, as true healing unfolds, all polarities are realized to be complementary opposites along a continuum of wholeness. When clients recognize their nondual nature in the midst of travail, they realize that they can be with life as it is. They don't have to change their circumstance, experience, or self in order to experience compassion, love, equanimity, and peace.

> *Nicky is lying on the floor with eyes closed encountering sensations of shame and a lack of energy that she experiences daily in her body. I support her in experiencing her feelings without trying to think about or understand them. After a few minutes, I ask her to find sensations that represent their opposites. She remembers a time when she is five years old. She is playing outside, her body full of radiant energy and sparkling vitality. I suggest that she embody these feelings*

without trying to think about or understand them. After a few minutes I invite Nicky to rotate her attention back and forth between feeling these opposing experiences. After several rotations, I encourage her to experience these opposites simultaneously. Nicky begins to sob deeply with her entire body. Integration is taking place as Nicky experiences her generative, potent playfulness even as she is experiencing the powerlessness and confusion that led to feeling shame and overwhelm from having been sexually molested by her father. Later, Nicky talks about feeling an energetic shift during her holding of the opposites that enables her to re-capture and embody her potency and aliveness even as she experiences her father violating her physical and psychic boundaries. As she describes her experience, Nicky radiates a newfound confidence and sense of loving compassion toward her self and her memories of her childhood abuse.

Yoga Nidra introduces its practitioners to their True Nature as a holding environment that welcomes every moment of life just as it is. This Presence is nonjudging, spacious, compassionate, and loving. It pervades everywhere, containing and seeing all things. It is without judgment or sentiment. It is always present, never rejects, welcomes everything, and is nondual in that it encompasses all duality. It is free of separation, for every object is dependent upon Awareness for its existence. Awareness contains no ideal of how life "should be." It is always inviting both client and therapist to be just as they are. Awareness enables projection, transference, and countertransference to unfold completely and be seen for what they are. Sensation, emotion, thought, conflict, sorrow, and joy all arise, unfold, and have their resolution in Awareness. Nondual Awareness has no stake in anything being other than it is or anyone being other than they are. This welcoming attribute of Awareness enables psychotherapy to work, allowing clients to find their psychological freedom as an integrated ego-identity as well as to eventually realize their ultimate freedom when their separative ego-identity entirely dissolves.

These essential qualities of Awareness underlie the therapist's capacity to be a holding environment of healing for their clients. The therapist's attunement with Presence enables clients to unfold their deepest experiences of conflict, pain, and trauma, working through projection and transference and uncovering solutions appropriate to each life circumstance. Awareness is also the active agent underlying therapeutic insight, for intuitive insight is also an essential aspect of Awareness. During psychotherapy, insight emerges spontaneously into the consciousness of both therapists and clients. While appearing in apparently independent entities, insight and the person in whom it arises are not separate from nondual Awareness.

When clients recognize their underlying nature as spacious nonjudging, compassionate, and loving Presence, causeless equanimity emerges. The perfume that arises from this profound insight lingers even as residues of separation remain. With repeated insight, these residues become transparently permeable to the underlying fragrance of Awareness. Our True Nature is always present, even when it is unrecognized. Once glimpsed, however, it leaves behind an unmistakable scent that stimulates the client's longing to return from conflict and suffering to nondual Presence that is perfect just as it is.

Separation and No-Self

As psychological insight and integration unfold, some clients become available for healing beyond their separative ego-identities into a unitive impersonal I-ness. Nonoriented therapists may dismiss the signposts, or glimpses, of True Nature, which occur at many juncture points along the journey of psychotherapy. When oriented therapists have the capacity to recognize the territory that they are navigating, whether it is personal psychology or impersonal Awareness, they can adroitly assist their clients through either of these realms of healing.

In either approach, and from the perspective of Yoga Nidra, clients are encouraged to fully describe every aspect of their experience including gross and subtle body sensations, emotions, beliefs, and mental images. As clients stop trying to change, which is their defense against being authentic, and enter into truly being with *what is*, defenses dissolve and integrative insights spontaneously appear into what may have appeared as hopeless or irresolvable conflicts and confusing ambiguities. Yoga Nidra extends the process of psychotherapy by shifting, at appropriate moments, the emphasis from the personal content of consciousness to impersonal Presence in which the content is arising.

> *Today, Lucy is lost in her depressive hopelessness, identified with the belief that her situation will never change. She is embroiled in conflict at work and believes that no one understands her. She feels lost, alone, and separate in a sea of perplexing emotion and belief. In the midst of her tears of confused bewilderment, I invite Lucy to describe her immediate experience while gazing into my eyes. My eyes reflect back to her the compassionate openness that I am feeling in this moment of "meeting." I know that the compassion that I feel exists as the background of Lucy's consciousness, even as it is being obscured by her present foreground experiences. As we gaze, her heart suddenly melts as she experiences a "rush" of loving kindness toward her self. Her mind grows quiet and she feels washed by a great silence of nonconceptual self-understanding. She is experiencing a moment of grace, a glimpse of her True Nature. She smiles and relaxes for the first time in several weeks. I support Lucy to rest in this glimpse, so that her heart might open wide with forgiveness toward herself and gratitude for simply being, in spite of her current difficulties. Lucy returns the following week*

reporting how this glimpse has lasted her entire workweek, giving her a newfound sense of spaciousness in her conflict.

Yoga Nidra reveals our Real Nature as a compassionate Presence that is not separate from what is being witnessed. Presence is neither detached nor dissociative, but full of active capacity. We are integrally related to what is witnessed. The belief in a separate self is a misperception, reinforced and projected out by the minds of both the therapist and client. This belief is the breeding ground of all suffering, conflict, projection, transference, and counter-transference. Tremendous psychological healing may occur even if the misperception of separation is not fully revealed within the therapeutic encounter, but without breaking through the myth of separation, suffering will continue.

At the end of a long and integrative phase of psychotherapy, David reached the conclusion that he had successfully resolved his issues of self-loathing and social inhibition that had brought him into therapy. He now felt like a fully functioning adult who possessed a healthy sense of self, an internalized locus of control, and the ability to participate in his life pursuits and interpersonal relationships. While he now felt psychologically strong and resilient, he continued to experience an illusive sense of separation and suffering that he couldn't attribute to some unresolved psychological or interpersonal issue. As David explored these ambiguous feelings through Yoga Nidra, he discovered an underlying belief of being a separate self that fed his sense of suffering. While the initial thrust of therapy had focused on reconstructing David's healthy functioning ego-identity, therapy now shifted to inquiring into and deconstructing his belief in being a separate self. David began to recognize glimpses of his real nature, which uncovered a causeless equanimity that undid the remnants of separation and suffering that had plagued him for decades.

Conflict and suffering arise from introjected misperceptions, which engender and then project the feeling of being a separate self. The central introject, which we take in as babies, is of being born as a separate body/mind that is either male or female, a belief fostered upon and into us by our parents, educators, and the world at large. Nondual Presence is neither born nor dies. Rather, the body/mind is born and lives and dies in Presence. Conflict and suffering are messengers, which signal that misperception, introjection, and projection are taking or have taken place. Conflict and suffering are not something to get rid of. Rather they are signposts that point out the underlying misperception that is holding the belief of separation in place. When this belief is exposed and deconstructed, conflict and suffering disappear, having served their ultimate purpose.

I-ness, Immanence, and Transcendence

Having a human body brings an undeniable sense of "I-ness." This sense of I-ness is different from the belief in being an ego-I, which is a false conviction based on the misperception of separation. In contrast, the experience of essential "I-ness" arises as a characteristic of nondual Awareness, evoking joy in the midst of adversity.

The feeling of ego-I ultimately dissolves upon close inspection, while the sense of "I-ness" remains as an unchanging mood that is both immanent and transcendent. It is immanent as our lived experience of being an embodied form and transcendent as our witnessing Presence that is aware of our embodied experience. Immanence and transcendence are paired opposites that mutually coarise and affirm the understanding that our True Nature and its objects are always one and never two, except as conceptual reality projected out by the dividing mind.

When the transcendent quality of "I-ness" remains hidden, separation is all that is experienced, and changes in the status quo of life are experienced as threatening and fearful. We feel limited when we live only one dimension of life. Fear limits life, but also signals that we are refusing one-half of the equation. In order to heal suffering we must recover our transcendental nature as Presence.

Alternately, when the immanent quality of "I-ness" remains hidden and we live only our transcendent function, a subtle withdrawal from living in the world occurs. Opposites must be reconciled. Living one-half of the equation always leads to suffering, which is merely the messenger that informs us that we must balance the opposites. When opposites of immanence and transcendence are balanced, they resolve into their ground of nondual Being, which knows no suffering.

> *Sonia is collapsed in her fear of being authentic. Her mind has introjected a harsh inner critic that judges her feelings as wrong and projects her power onto others outside herself. She thinks, "If I just do it right I'll get the love I'm looking for." She has no trust in herself and feels "small, deficient, worthless, isolated and cut off" from herself and the world around her. She wants to "get out of here" but feels "lost and incapable." She is living a life identified only with her sense of being a separate, powerless self.*

> *I invite Sonia to look at me and describe her experience, which I reflect back to her, mirroring an empathic welcoming Awareness that is simply present to what is. She begins to open, allowing these "different flavors" of her experience. We work like this, month after month, as Sonia learns to be with her experience as a feeling-witness who doesn't know where she is going, but who is open to and tolerates what comes. She learns to skillfully rotate her attention through the opposites of her experiences of lost/found, incapable/capable, isolated/intimate, deficient/full, small/big, cut off/in contact, and worthless/potent, which increases her capacity to tolerate strong feelings of abandonment and intimacy within herself and with others. Her capacity to attune with a nonjudging*

witnessing Presence increases as she recognizes her capacity to be a spacious container that welcomes each and every experience. I support her exploration of this witnessing function, which opens Sonia into a full embrace of the therapeutic insight that, "I'm okay here, as I am." Sonia continues to shift her identity from the separative ego-I function that harshly judges to an identity as immanent-transcendent I-ness in which judgments arise and can be welcomed with neither reactive expression nor defensive repression. Her self-alienation dissolves as she feels ever more intimately connected to and involved with the world around her. Sonia begins to feel joy that she at first associates with her newfound self-acceptance. I help her experience this joyous equanimity without trying to conceptualize it. She begins to realize that this has been with her since infancy and exclaims, "It's already been happening all this time." She had simply ignored the background Presence because of her reaction to the strong thoughts and feelings that had occupied the foreground of her mind.

It is now six years since Sonia began therapy and I see her sporadically for "check-ins." She is living her life authentically, allowing her negative and positive experiences of sensation, emotion, and thought to unfold with only minor movements of the former self-judgment. During a recent session, Sonia began to cry as her "persona of aloof guardedness for fear of being judged" yielded to her open Presence. She reported, "It's so empty here, yet so full; everything is here." It has been an amazing journey for both of us.

Summary

Yoga Nidra is a process that invites therapists and clients to fully live their capacity to be present in, and to, each moment of their experience with openness, innocence, and curiosity. The price we pay for living this capacity is to give up all of our roles and knowing of how things *should* be. In living in "not-knowing" we are open to the unknown, where empathic insight and understanding arise naturally without the mind's need to know how.

Yoga Nidra and psychotherapy entail the art of listening, which is an openness free of direction or preconception. It is this capacity of therapists and clients to be present and listen without agenda or judgment that enables them to explore and reveal hidden and disregarded aspects of self that otherwise sustain conflict, suffering, and the myth of separation. Hidden within every conflict is its solution. When openness prevails, conflict finds its resolution in nondirectional listening wherein the deep movements of sensation, emotion, and thought are free to unfold completely, free of the tyranny of shoulds.

Yoga Nidra is a process of self-inquiry, that entails disidentification from the content of consciousness and deconstruction of the mind's core belief that it is a separate ego-I. Disidentification and deconstruction heal the misperception of separation and brings an end to suffering. Disidentification constitutes our capacity to experience life without reactive defense, releasing us from the myth of separation and revealing our True Nature as nondual Presence.

Yoga Nidra initially invites clients to encounter and welcome, and explore and describe all opposites of sensation, feeling, emotion, thought, belief, memory, imagery, and the sense of ego-I, which keeps their suffering in place. Experiencing the opposites as complimentary polarities leads to psychological integration and health. Finally, Yoga Nidra invites clients to investigate the separative nature of ego-identity, which underlies their remaining vestiges of inner conflict and suffering. Self-inquiry deconstructs ego-identity and its miragelike reality, opening the ground for latent nondual Presence to spontaneously flood into the foreground. In this moment clients reclaim their real freedom as unchanging, nondual Presence that is both immanent and transcendent in every moment of life. This is the fulfillment of Yoga Nidra and the completion of psychotherapy.

Endnotes

1. Venkatesananda, *Enlightened Living: The Yoga Sutra of Patañjali*, Anahata Press, 1999, I.12, II.33, II.35, II.48, III.6

2. I use the concept Awareness interchangeably with Consciousness, Presence, Being, Unborn, True Nature, Self, and God to represent the nonmental, indescribable, nondual, absolute, impersonal, ever-present, and nonchanging ground that everything is made of. I use noncapitalized concepts such as consciousness and awareness to refer to manifestations of Presence that represent personal and changing phenomenon.

3. Feuerstein, Georg, *Yoga: The Technology of Ecstasy*, Tarcher, 1989.

4. See the included references to the works by these authors.

5. Please refer to the enclosed references by Richard Miller and Swami Satyananda.

6. Gestalt and Jungian approaches to psychotherapy, among others, also acknowledge the importance of the play of opposites when working with clients. It is beyond the scope of this chapter to explicate a comparison of these various approaches. Instead, I refer the reader to the writings of June Singer in her work entitled *Androgyny: The Opposites Within*, Nicolas-Hays, Maine, 2000, and the writings of Fritz Perls.

10

Deconstructing the Self

The Uses of Inquiry in Psychotherapy and Spiritual Practice

Stephan Bodian

nquiry can be likened to a microscope or magnifying glass: the information or experience it reveals may differ markedly depending on where it's aimed and how precisely it's focused. In psychotherapy, inquiry has a venerable history as a tool to help therapist and client alike make connections between past and present experiences and to gain insight into habitual patterns of feeling and behavior. In the nondual wisdom traditions of the East, self-inquiry has long been a powerful practice to help the spiritual seeker penetrate the empty or insubstantial nature of everyday phenomena, including the apparent self constructed of thoughts and feelings, to gain insight into the essence of Reality itself.

In this essay, I briefly outline the history of inquiry in spiritual practice and psychotherapy and offer a new model for applying it to therapy that enables clients to peel back the layers of identification, or self-image, to reveal deeper levels of Being. In the process they gradually "deconstruct the self" they have spent their whole lives constructing. As they let go of old ideas of who they think they are, they have an opportunity to experience who they really are—an experience that can be profoundly transformative, both personally and spiritually.

Personal Experiences and Sources

My own experience with spiritual inquiry began in the early 1970s, when I undertook intensive Zen practice, first as a layperson and then as a monk. Though I started with the simple meditation practice of following the breath, I was always fascinated by the enigmatic Zen stories known as koans, which have traditionally been used to catalyze spiritual awakening. Two of the best-known koans are questions: "What was your original face before your parents were born?" and "What is the sound of one hand?"

In the mid-'70s, I began studying koans myself as a monk in training with a well-known Japanese-American Zen master and found that they did indeed confound my rational mind and occasionally catapulted me into more direct, nondual modes of experiencing reality. However, I never felt that Zen offered a complete approach to spiritual and psychological development. In particular I noticed that despite numerous deep spiritual insights, I continued to respond to certain situations with inexplicable anger, sadness, and anxiety. In 1982, I put aside my robes in order to pursue my own psychotherapy and also to study psychology in graduate school.

There I discovered another mode of inquiry: the standard psychotherapeutic interview. I learned to focus the lens of inquiry onto the contents of my experience, including memories, feelings, and habitual patterns of thinking and behaving. At the same time I became adept at asking questions that revealed the connections between present suffering and past conditioning, yielding a potentially transformative "interpretation" or insight. The limitation of this approach, I discovered over time, was that it created layers of narrative, or stories, that I gradually took to be the truth about myself. Instead of becoming freer and lighter, I found myself feeling increasingly encumbered and limited by the interpretations and labels I had accumulated over the years. Rather than feeling more connected with other people and all of life, I felt more fragmented and self-absorbed.

I had also learned a different mode of therapeutic inquiry, based on the experiential approach of Gestalt, that focused on immediate experience. Like sitting meditation, this approach tended to bring me into the present moment and connect me with the full range of feelings, thoughts, and sensations. But it still tended to emphasize the "meaning" these experiences had for "me" and failed to turn the lens of awareness or inquiry onto the experiencer itself.

In the midst of my psychological studies, I met Jean Klein (1988), a master of Advaita Vedanta, the nondual expression of the Hindu tradition, who introduced me to the method of self-inquiry known as *atma vichara* (literally, "self-inquiry"). Under his guidance I had a powerful awakening to my true nature as pure, unlimited, undisturbed awareness itself. During the ten years I worked with him, this insight became deeper and more stable. But still there remained a split, a duality, a lack of integration, between this deeper knowing and the persistent patterns of thinking and behaving that would regularly ambush me and convince me once again that I was this limited person suffering in space and time under the weight of a particular history and set of character traits.

Finally, after years of flipping between hanging out in the unconditioned awareness itself and then struggling to resolve "psychological issues" therapeutically, I met another teacher, Byron Katie, whose approach, known as The Work, involved not abiding as awareness, as the "who" of "Who am I?" but rather constantly inquiring into the truth of the very stories and habitual thought patterns that seemed to be so problematic. Under the influence of her approach I finally discovered the already-existing, inherent integration of awareness and the contents of awareness as a truly nondual, undivided reality. Or, in the words of a seminal Buddhist scripture, "Form is emptiness, emptiness is form." The Work provides a means for revealing the absolute in the midst of the relative, the unconditioned in the midst of the conditioned, the transpersonal in the midst of the personal. The inquiry that I describe in this essay, which now arises naturally with my clients, draws upon The Work, the self-inquiry of Advaita Vedanta, and the phenomenological investigation of experiential psychotherapy.

The Uses of Inquiry in Conventional Psychotherapy

Inquiry has always been an essential part of the psychotherapeutic process. Freud and his followers were detectives of the psyche, asking extensive questions to elicit connections between past experiences and present pathology in order to help resolve the inner conflict at hand and turn the extreme suffering of their patients into the ordinary suffering of the human condition. Following in this tradition today, clinicians of virtually every persuasion take an extensive personal history at the start of therapy by asking questions, and all but the most nondirective among them continue to inquire into their clients' experience throughout the duration of the relationship.

Of course, the purpose of the inquiry differs from one orientation to another. Psychoanalytically oriented therapists may elicit memories, fantasies, dreams, and stream of consciousness in their search for internal conflicts, developmental deficits, formative or traumatic life experiences, or holes in the self structure. By contrast, cognitive-behavioral therapists may use inquiry to identify negative, dysfunctional, self-defeating cognitions to reveal how they cause present suffering and to actively challenge their validity so they can then be replaced with more accurate, positive, functional cognitions.

In the existential-humanistic tradition, direct questions are often replaced by more indirect, nonintrusive methods of focusing a client's interest and curiosity—for example, wondering, observing, inviting, reflecting, probing, and sharing of the therapist's own resonant experience. Whether the inquiry is direct or more implicit, however, the aim is essentially the same—to encourage clients to wonder and reflect on their own experience. When the process is successful, clients internalize the inquiry and get into the habit of asking some version of the question "What's happening right now?"

In general, the purpose of inquiry in this tradition is to expand the sense of self to embrace as much authentic experience as possible, including hitherto unconscious emotions, wishes, fantasies, visions, and creative potential, so the client is living life fully and opening to the full range of human expression and possibility. Humanistic psychotherapies, such as those described and practiced by Abraham Maslow, Carl Rogers, James Bugental, and others, support full subjective experiencing, expanding and in the process transforming the definition and limits of self.

But even the most experientially oriented psychotherapies rarely if ever encourage clients to direct their attention to the supposed experiencer, the apparently separate self to whom all these experiences occur. Instead, such therapy generally assumes the inherent separateness or duality of subject and object, helping clients focus on "my" experience so "I" can know more fully who "I" am through recognizing "my" fantasies, wishes, needs, and so forth. The existence and inherent value of this subjective "I" is taken for granted.

The Uses of Inquiry in Nondual Wisdom Traditions

By contrast, nondual wisdom traditions teach that there is no intrinsic separation between subject and object, experiencer and experienced, God and creation, consciousness and its manifestations. The apparently separate and substantial self does not exist except as a constantly changing constellation of thoughts, feelings, images, memories, and sensations. There is just "what is"—known as "suchness" in Zen—without a separate self to be aware of it. Or, in another way of putting it, consciousness and its object are one.

Note that the term "nondual" (a precise translation of the term *advaita*) is used instead of "monistic" (about oneness) because subject and object are at once one (on an absolute level) and different (on a relative level). In other words, in the classic Buddhist formulation "Form is emptiness, emptiness is form," form doesn't cease to be form also, even though it's empty, and emptiness doesn't cease to be empty, even though it's also form. Both are true simultaneously.

In the nondual wisdom traditions of Zen, Tibetan Buddhist Dzogchen/Mahamudra, and Advaita Vedanta (which, as I mention earlier, is an offshoot of Hinduism), inquiry is used in different ways to penetrate the surface of apparently substantial reality in order to glimpse the emptiness or insubstantiality or nonlocatability (the terms are three different ways of describing the same reality) that lies at the core. Donald Rothberg (2000), a professor at Saybrook Institute, proposes five interrelated modes of spiritual inquiry, of which three are relevant to this discussion:

- Systematic contemplation: Training to develop an open, receptive, nonjudgmental, present-centered awareness.

- Radical questioning: The asking of fundamental questions that probe the nature of reality and lead to deep spiritual insight.

- Critical deconstruction: Methodical inquiry into a particular belief system or worldview, leading to a dimension of knowing beyond the mind.

All of the nondual traditions encourage both systematic contemplation and radical questioning in one form or another, and the practice of Mahamudra, and the traditional Madhyamika dialectic on which it is based, make particular use of critical deconstruction.

Zen koans

In the Rinzai school of Zen, teachers assign their students "radical," enigmatic questions, anecdotes, or stories known as koans, which the student then contemplates during meditation and ultimately "resolves." Through this process of resolution, the students' understanding aligns itself with the wisdom of the great Zen masters of old. Koans, in other words, are a way of transmitting the nondual (that is, enlightened) experience of life (which, strictly speaking, can't be transmitted!) from one generation to the next. The early koans, especially the koan known as *mu,* serve to catalyze the student's initial awakening, and subsequent koans provide an opportunity to eliminate old, distorted views of oneself and reality and resolve any doubts that might remain.

Some koans take the form of actual questions, though they clearly point to answers beyond the mind. Others are merely stories, often of a famous exchange between master and disciple. The inquiry in these koans lies in the living teacher's implicit expectation that the student will present a response of some kind. Students are encouraged not to think about the koan (though some initial understanding of context and characters is generally helpful), but to become one with the koan and allow a response to spontaneously emerge as a direct expression of nondual reality itself.

Tibetan Buddhist Dzogchen/Mahamudra

Although Dzogchen and Mahamudra are often taught together by teachers schooled in both the Nyingma and Kagyu traditions of Vajrayana Buddhism, they actually differ somewhat in their approach. Whereas Dzogchen masters generally transmit a direct experience of the nature of mind (that is, the nondual experience) to their disciples and then teach them how to abide in it at all times, traditional Mahamudra, following the Indian Madhyamika philosophy on which it is based, teaches a series of techniques for inquiring into the nature of mind (and therefore the nature of reality, since everything is mind) that reveals it to be nongraspable, nonlocatable, and essentially nondual.

Once students have completed the preliminary practices, which can take several years, and learned to focus and calm the mind, they are directed to inquire into the nature of mind until they come to the realization that it is essentially pristine, radiant, and clear. Then they engage in a series of questions that challenge their preexisting notions of mind and demonstrate that it can't be grasped or located in any way—in other words, that mind is inherently empty. At the same time, these questions reveal the inseparability of mind and the objects of mind, subject, and object—in other words, the nondual nature of reality. There is no attempt to engage directly with the contents of mind, the point is rather to penetrate through the contents to the underlying reality.

Advaita Vedanta

Advaita Vedanta, which emerged in the middle of the first millennium C.E. as a crystallization of the philosophy of the great Hindu scriptures known as the Upanishads, teaches that the individual atman (self or soul) is identical with the ground of being (*brahman*), and that the manifest world is merely the illusory play of *brahman*, possessing relative but not ultimate reality. The practice of inquiry involves discriminating between what is real and what is illusory, and adhering to the real.

In the twentieth century the great Indian sage Ramana Maharshi, who though not trained in Advaita in fact embodied its teachings, instructed seekers to simply abide as the Self, the ultimate reality—and if it was not immediately clear how to do that, to first turn the mind back upon itself and ask "Who is this? Who is experiencing this thought or sensation right now? Who am I?" This self-inquiry (*atma vichara*) eventually reveals the true "I" to be the inexhaustible ground of being itself.

The Purpose of Inquiry in a Nondual Approach to Psychotherapy

Psychotherapy informed by a nondual perspective resembles its conventional counterparts in that it involves two people sitting across from one another, talking and sharing their experiences. Unlike regular therapy, however, it's grounded in the realization, drawn from the nondual wisdom traditions, that the true source of all healing and the lasting resolution of all conflicts and apparent problems lies in the recognition of our nondual nature. Instead of a separate self struggling to survive and solve problems in challenging circumstances, who we really are is not separate at all—not separate from others, from all of life, or from the ultimate ground of being itself. In the realization that this apparently separate self has no substantial reality, problems spontaneously lose their hold, since they're inevitably based on a mind-created scenario rooted in separation.

Nondual therapy is not a special method, approach, or set of techniques, and certainly not a particular viewpoint. There are as many nondual therapies as there are nondual therapists. It's actually an interaction between two people that occurs in the absence of a viewpoint, agenda, or interpretive lens; if it's truly nondual, it unfolds in a shared, resonant space or field in which the apparent separation between client and therapist has dissolved—or, more accurately, doesn't apply.

Interventions such as inquiry arise as a natural response to a felt-from-the-inside dissonance or discrepancy between how the client interprets reality and reality itself. This discrepancy, based on the illusory self, is the root of all suffering. As one of my clients succinctly put it, stress is the resistance to *what is*. There is a natural movement toward increased awareness of what's true, because truth naturally wants to reveal itself and spontaneously moves to illuminate and liberate what's untrue—the stories and beliefs that cause suffering and contraction. In the shared, resonant space of the therapeutic encounter, therapist and client orient together toward greater awareness, openness, and clarity because that's the source of true freedom and aliveness. It takes tremendous energy to ignore or suppress the truth, whereas opening to the truth liberates this energy at its source.

In a nondual approach to therapy, there's no attempt to change or get rid of anything, including the personality with all its inclinations, idiosyncrasies, and preferences. The only purpose is to shine the light of inquiry onto the contents of experience in order to discriminate between the true and the false, the real and the unreal, in Advaita terms. Instead of seeking answers or solutions, which are understood to be merely additional conceptual overlays, the inquiry is focused on revealing the concepts, stories, and beliefs that cause suffering, knowing that once they're recognized for what they are, rather than taken to be true, suffering and conflict will spontaneously disperse. As a deconstructive alternative to the ordinary human tendency to keep reinforcing and reconstructing a separate self, such inquiry gradually becomes internalized and self-perpetuating, like a computer virus that eventually eats away the hard drive! Remember, however, that what's eaten away is not authentic, individual, creative self-expression, but the illusory, constructed self. The more this self is seen through, the more freedom and space we have to be more fully "ourselves."

Often the beliefs that are deconstructed turn out to be defenses against some deeper feeling or insight that may feel threatening, such as fear, grief, shame, aloneness, or insecurity. By inquiring into the beliefs and constructs, we gradually penetrate the layers of self-identification, thereby revealing the feelings that were formerly hidden and making them more accessible to direct, nonconceptual experiencing. Once these feelings are directly met in the intimacy of awareness, they tend to naturally release, making more energy available for spontaneous living.

In its deconstructive approach, nondual therapy resembles other depth psychotherapies, such as the existential-humanistic approach taught by James Bugental. But instead of challenging and disclosing the client's "self and world construct system" (Bugental's term), only to replace it with a more "authentic" construct, nondual therapy gradually—and gently, since there's no agenda, just a natural orientation toward the truth—deconstructs this system entirely.

Needless to say, such inquiry, no matter how gentle, may at times elicit strong resistance from the minds of even the most spiritually oriented clients. After all, the "self and world construct system" constitutes a way of relating to life that is familiar, apparently continuous, and stable in comparison to the instabilities of life. Even though it's inevitably the root cause of suffering, it also provides a "standpoint," a seemingly secure ground from which to view and encounter the world. Without it, clients fear becoming ungrounded, disoriented, and insecure.

At the deepest level, this system—also known as "ego" or "discursive mind"—protects the client from a direct experience of emptiness, which, as I mentioned earlier, is the essential, nondual nature of reality. But most people who haven't encountered emptiness directly (and even some who have) fear it because they imagine it to be a deficiency or lack of some kind. In fact, the discursive mind is afraid of anything that doesn't fit its accustomed conceptual categories—afraid, in other words, of the unknown in any form—and works quite hard to create a consistent, familiar worldview that it can project onto the unknown. Emptiness, of course, is ultimately unknowable by the mind and therefore especially threatening. In a sense, the entire inner life is a defense against experiencing our inherent emptiness, which is actually our oneness with all of life.

Once the client has the experience of directly encountering this emptiness, this groundlessness, this open, spacious freedom from viewpoints or conceptual filters, there is usually the rather surprising and often liberating realization that, rather than constituting a deficiency, this so-called "emptiness" is actually our wholeness, our fullness, our completeness. It turns out that nothing is missing, left out, or problematic; there's no place to go, nothing to achieve, and no problem to resolve. In fact, such moments of realization are usually accompanied by deep peace and unaccountable joy—as well as, at times, by laughter, relief, gratitude, and other similar emotions—and they can be profoundly and lastingly transformative.

Unlike cognitive-behavioral therapy, which works to replace negative, dysfunctional cognitions with more positive, functional ones, nondual therapy doesn't necessarily discriminate between good and bad cognitions or try to replace some with others. Rather, the fundamental understanding is that no cognitions or concepts of any kind can possibly encompass reality as it is, which is ultimately ungraspable by the mind. In particular, the constructs that constellate an apparent separate self are just that—constructs—and, if taken for reality, are the ultimate cause of suffering. Hence, the work is simply to illuminate concepts and constructs with the light of awareness and explore the ways in which they contribute to suffering. Where cognitive-behavioral therapy tends to reconstruct a better, more effective self, the nondual approach deconstructs the self by revealing that it has no abiding, substantial reality.

At the same time, some cognitions and constructs are clearly more painful and dysfunctional than others and tend to attract the most attention in the therapeutic encounter. As they are gradually identified and revealed, new, more positive cognitions often spontaneously emerge from the depths of Being to take their place. Though they may not reflect the ultimate truth of the nonconceptual nature of reality, these new cognitions provide clients with welcome relief and enhanced freedom from suffering and act as a transition to living in the unknown, without relying on concepts.

Uses of Inquiry in a Nondual Approach to Therapy

Each of the three types of inquiry that I describe earlier in this chapter has a significant role to play in nondual therapy. Remember, however, that the nondual approach doesn't use a preestablished protocol or agenda; rather, it unfolds spontaneously in response to the unique interaction between client and therapist that occurs in the resonant field where, in essence, your suffering, contraction, or resistance is experienced as mine as well. Rothberg's categories are helpful descriptors of what does, in fact, occur, but they do not delimit or even inform the work.

The foundation of a nondual approach to therapy is "systematic contemplation," the process of "being with" experience with bare attention, without judgment or evaluation. Together, client and therapist are present with the client's experience as it unfolds, and attention is periodically drawn from the mind's interpretations back to direct, bodily felt experience itself. In Tibetan Buddhist terms, the open, spacious, receptive mind of "being with" is the ground, the path, and the fruition of nondual therapy—that is, it's at once the space or field in which the therapy occurs, a technique that clients can learn, and the liberating emptiness to which clients awaken, if only briefly. Indeed, "being with" is the nature of reality itself, since, as I mentioned earlier, consciousness, or awareness, and its object are one.

"Radical inquiry" occurs in nondual therapy in the form of direct questions. Some, such as "Who are you?" or, more circumstantially, "Where is this 'me' you're referring to?" "For whom is this a problem?" or "What is experiencing this emotion right now?" call into question the client's identity as a separate, substantial self. Others, such as "Is there anything missing right now?" or "In this moment, where is the problem you've been describing?" challenge the substantial existence of the very issues and problems that the client has brought to therapy. Both kinds of questions directly point not to any object of awareness, but to the background awareness itself, the vast, spacious context in which experience takes place and that ultimately constitutes the client's true self. The questions tend to stop the mind in its tracks and turn it back on itself; in the process, clients often find that the self and its accompanying problems are not as real, graspable, or locatable as they might have believed.

Rather than pointing directly to the context or background of experience, "critical deconstruction" addresses the "self and world construct system" that tends to obscure this background. Since there's no agenda or attempt to change anything, the constructs are not actively rooted out and challenged, as in certain depth psychotherapies, but addressed as they arise in the course of the therapeutic encounter. One of the most potent forms of critical deconstruction is the "four questions" of Byron Katie:

- Is this story, belief, or cognition true?
- Can you absolutely know that it's true?
- How do you react when you think that thought [i.e., hold that story or belief]?
- Who would you be without it?

It can be a powerful moment in therapy when clients stop to ask these questions with an innocent mind, open to the possibility of seeing themselves and their life in an entirely new way. Once they deeply inquire into some cherished and usually painfully self-defeating story or belief, there may be the sudden recognition that it might not be true after all—and, even more revealing, that at some level they always knew it to be untrue!

If the response to the first question is yes rather than no, the other three questions help loosen the client's hold on the cognition and illuminate the impact it has on their life. (Even if the answer is no, the succeeding questions reveal the price they have paid for believing the cognition.) Once they've recognized the cognition or story for what it is—that is, a cognition or story that causes them suffering—they're one step closer to questioning its validity. Remember that answering no to the question "Can you really know that it's true?" doesn't necessarily mean that you now see it as false, it merely means that you accept that you can't really know for sure. In this way, the questions of Byron Katie invite clients to live in not-knowing, in a present-centered reality relatively free of preconceptions and expectations.

As the various beliefs and stories that comprise the self and world construct system are discovered to have dubious validity at best, the entire structure gradually begins to crumble, revealing huge spaces or gaps—the emptiness I mentioned earlier in this essay. Eventually the self and world construct system may even fall away entirely, an experience of complete freedom that the Buddha described (using the same construction metaphor) as the "ridgepole collapsing."

Often there's a particular core story that has tremendous energy and tenacity, the one around which the client has constructed his or her identity. This story does indeed act as a kind of ridgepole, in the sense that it holds the self concept together. Although every client has his or her own unique version, common core stories include: "I'm not good enough," "I don't deserve to be loved," "I'm all alone, there's no one there for me," and "It's not safe for me to be myself." When even the core story is seen to be just that—a story rather than an accurate interpretation of reality—clients may feel at once extremely disoriented, profoundly liberated, and shaken to the "core."

Applying Inquiry: Case Example

To illustrate how inquiry functions in nondual therapy, I'd like to describe my work with a client who came to me complaining of extreme, at times suicidal depression. Now in her late fifties, Mary had had a profound experience of her essential nature in her late twenties, which was accompanied by deep peace and an abiding joy. As she described it, the sense of being a separate somebody just fell away, along with all her problems, and she could see that life was perfect exactly the way it was. The experience lasted ten days and then gradually faded.

When she came to see me, at the urging of her husband, who believed (with good reason) that she was on the verge of killing herself, she seemed quite angry—at her husband, at her grown children, at her life, and above all at herself, for being such a "mess." At first I helped her identify and then experience her anger, which was taboo territory for her because she prided herself on being so good-natured and agreeable. (She had been a popular chiropractor for many years but had retired several years before because of a back injury.)

We spent several sessions exploring her childhood, which she did with great reluctance because she believed it had no bearing on the present situation. But I felt that it might be helpful in revealing the roots of her anger, and it did indeed turn out that she had good cause as a child to be enraged: a father who had berated her constantly and a mother who had essentially ignored her in favor of her older brother. Instead of expressing her anger outwardly, she had dealt with the situation by becoming obsessed with winning people's approval while inwardly feeling that she was totally inadequate and to blame for her parents' unloving behavior—in other words, by turning her anger against herself.

Now, as she sat in my office, the stories that held the self-hatred in place were layers and layers thick—and, as is quite common with severely depressed people, quite difficult to penetrate. In addition to a painful childhood, Mary believed she had been an inadequate mother (even though her children had turned out just fine) and that she had done no good as a chiropractor (even though most of her patients loved her). In addition, she had a few health problems, including ongoing difficulties with her back, that caused her some worry and intermittent pain. In all, Mary was convinced that she was so loathesome and burdensome to others that the best solution for all concerned was for her to kill herself, and she resisted any attempt to convince her otherwise.

Indeed, several weeks after we began working together, Mary nearly succeeded in doing herself in. Apparently she left home with several bottles of pills (which were easy for her, as a chiropractor, to obtain) and checked in to a nearby motel. Interestingly enough, however, she called her husband just before she was about to down the pills, ostensibly to say good-bye. But her husband managed to convince her to stop and then drove to the motel to get her. Like the others before it, this suicide gesture seemed more like a cry for help than a serious attempt.

Instead of continuing to work with the stories directly, which seemed fruitless, I guided Mary in "being with" her experience, particularly her bodily felt experience, which was quite new for her, even though she had worked with the body as a chiropractor. We increased our sessions to twice a week, and for the next few weeks we just tracked her experience in the manner of Buddhist mindfulness meditation. When her mind started commenting and interpreting and drifting into stories, I gently guided her back to her body. At first she found this practice unfamiliar and uncomfortable, but she gradually grew to enjoy it. After several weeks she reported that she found herself "being with" her direct experience spontaneously at various times through the day—and even in her sleep. Then we expanded her practice of "being with" to include the thoughts and feelings that passed through her awareness.

Gradually, in those moments of just "being with"— that is, moments of simple, unadorned presence—Mary regained a sense of the peace and joy that she had experienced many years before. But this brief opening quickly turned to her accustomed self-loathing as she criticized herself for straying so far from the profound realization that had once meant so much to her. It was just more evidence that she was a hopeless case—otherwise, how could she have forgotten for so long? Her mind clearly had a powerful hold over her.

At this point, using the practice of mindful presence as a foundation, we started to inquire into the stories as they arose: Is it really true that you're such an awful person? Is it really true that nobody loves you? Is it really true that your daughter hates you? Is it really true that the last thirty years have been wasted? What effect does it have on you and your life to hold such negative beliefs? And who would you be without them?

Little by little we began cutting through the dense clouds of cognitions and beliefs that made up her self and world construct system—and little by little they began loosening their hold over her, as she grew to realize that they were, indeed, just stories and that they caused her tremendous suffering. She began to discriminate between her projections onto reality and reality itself, which enabled her to choose one over the other. As the clouds of stories and beliefs thinned out, the radiance of presence, with which she had reconnected in our earlier work, shined through more and more.

Before our sessions together, she had believed, in accord with our psychological culture, that she would have to "work through" all the anger and resentment and unresolved issues of a lifetime in order to experience any real happiness. Because the task seemed so overwhelming, she had given up in despair and resorted to suicidal ideation as her only real solace. Now she knew that nothing needed to be worked through or eliminated—she could merely see her stories for what they were without getting caught by them. If they grabbed hold, she could always inquire using the four questions in order to loosen their grip. (Because she had once seen quite vividly that her true identity had nothing to do with her personality, she could hold the stories in a bigger space.) This realization afforded her enormous relief, and her suicidal ideation stopped.

To emphasize the insubstantial, nonlocatable nature of these stories and cognitions, I also asked questions such as: Where is your depression right now? Can you show it to me? How do you know it exists? Or: And where is your miserable childhood right now? Does it exist now, or is it in the past? And where is this past located? In this moment, can you find any problem? etc. Such "radical inquiry" strengthened the realization that her so-called problems were the constructions of her mind. Rather than being "deep-rooted neuroses" requiring long-term psychotherapy, as many conventional psychological theories teach, her problems ceased to exist for her in those moments when she stopped investing them with psychic energy and identification.

To some this approach may seem like spiritual bypassing, but the truth is that exploring her issues in a traditional psychological way for many years had just made them seem more solid, real, and entrenched in Mary's eyes and had provided more ammunition for her perfectionistic, judgmental, self-loathing mind. Now that she could hold her experience in an aware, expanded space and recognize her stories for what they were, she rapidly went from an agitated depression with active suicidality to a mostly calm, relaxed frame of mind in which the stories occasionally grabbed her but didn't retain their grip for very long. As a testimony to her unfolding, after six months of our work together Mary visited her family for three weeks with her husband and reported none of the usual agitation or depressive episodes. The change in her view of life and of herself had stabilized.

Conclusion

As this chapter makes clear, the use of inquiry to deconstruct the apparent, constructed self can have a powerful therapeutic effect. By turning the light of awareness back on the experiencer itself, such inquiry has the potential to awaken clients to a deeper level of identity where old beliefs, stories, and patterns of conditioning no longer exert the same control. Like Mary, once clients recognize and directly experience the deeper silence, spaciousness, and peace beyond the mind's chatter, it becomes increasingly difficult to be seduced by the same beliefs and stories again.

Though some psychotherapists may argue that this approach smacks of spiritual bypassing, I would suggest that many people in our acutely self-conscious, self-help culture have compounded their problems by overly analyzing and interpreting their feelings, impulses, and motivations. In the process, they've just added psychological material to the complex stories and identities they have constructed about themselves—what Bugental calls the "self and world construct system." Most forms of conventional psychotherapy leave this fundamental construct unchallenged and instead work within it to solve problems, change habits, and reveal deeper meanings for the fictitious me.

By encouraging direct experience of feelings and sensations unmitigated by the mind while inquiring into the beliefs and stories that cause suffering, a nondual approach to therapy invites clients to deconstruct the "self and world construct system" entirely. To use a favorite metaphor of the nondual wisdom traditions: Rather than struggling within a dream to solve the problems that the dream presents, it's far easier and more effective to wake up from the dream and recognize that the problems were merely imaginary. (In the Buddhist tradition, this dream is called samsara.) Through the use of inquiry, a nondual approach to therapy offers clients the opportunity to wake up from the dream of being a separate self beset by problems to the liberating realization that they are the limitless presence or space in which their problems arise and pass away.

11

Healing Trauma in the Eternal Now

Lynn Marie Lumiere

Everything is perfectly managed in the Unborn.

—Bankei

Nondual wisdom reveals that our unborn nature is the source and substance of all that is born into finite reality.[1] All of our experience is an expression of this nature, a primordial awareness that accepts all forms of its expression, no matter how pleasurable or painful. This awareness is unconditional love as it equally accepts the most sublime ecstasy and one of the most painful of all human experience, trauma. It is only in this embrace of the manifest by the unmanifest that true transformation or healing takes place.

All of the suffering that is brought to psychotherapy is a confused or contracted expression of the unconditional love that we are. When suffering is embraced by this love, the confusion is clarified, the contraction is relaxed, and we are released into simple presence. Once awareness awakens to itself in a human being, it is possible to liberate all forms of confusion through this meeting, including those resulting from trauma. Left to itself, the ego-personality will endlessly repeat trauma or try to hide from it. Only the unconditional love of conscious awareness can truly embrace it. Adyashanti (2002) beautifully describes love returning for itself in all its forms:

> It is when awareness somehow meets itself as Love, when all experience is touched directly by that Love, that it is dissolved, freed, healed, transmuted and transformed. When experience is met with full acceptance without any resistance, it reveals itself to be the same Love. Nothing survives this meeting. Nothing stands up to the presence of being and remains.
>
> We naturally move away from pain. But there is also a movement of intelligence within all beings that is moving toward what is, without needing to fix or change anything. It's the coming together of awareness and its experience that is freeing; that is Love. That is Love returning for itself. And it has no motive other than union. This touching without motive is what is transformative.

Transformation takes place in the present moment. Our past traumas can be resolved only in the here and now. This resolution involves an open receptivity to what appears each moment without any form of resistance, interpretation, or identification. By fully allowing *what is*, moment-by-moment, all experience finds its natural resolution.

This nondual wisdom is influencing and transforming the practice of psychotherapy in a way that allows its full potential to be realized. Psychotherapy can only be partially or temporarily helpful if it does not acknowledge what is actually most true. Psychology has been built on the belief in a separate, individual self, which is not essentially true. Traditional psychotherapy works from the premise that the individual self needs to be changed or improved. However, all lasting change comes out of genuine acceptance and this acceptance comes when we discover our true nature. It cannot arise from an imaginary self that is believed to be independent. The imaginary self can try to accept that which it finds unacceptable, but it cannot succeed. Only love itself has no resistance to *what is*.

The mind cannot understand nondual wisdom because it can think only dualistically in terms of separate polarities. When it hears that it is through acceptance that change naturally occurs, the mind can get confused. Many people, for example, think that if they accept things as they are, they will never change. Yet the acceptance or surrender that I am speaking of here is the power that truly transforms. That is why I put an emphasis on direct experience when it comes to the nondual truth. This truth cannot be fully understood by the mind; it can only be revealed through direct experience. And so, when clients relax their impulse to get rid of painful sensations or feelings and simply be present with them, they discover for themselves that their discomfort effortlessly dissolves or transforms over time.

When it comes to healing trauma, however, additional skills may be required. Bessel Van der Kolk, M.D. (1999), a leading trauma researcher, defined trauma as "the inability to be present with what is in the here and now." When we have experienced trauma, it tends to pull us out of the here and now into there and then. It returns us to repetitive reexperiencing or re-enactment of the past trauma. Trauma actually destabilizes the nervous system in a way that disrupts our natural ability to be in the here and now. Paradoxically, healing trauma requires being present with *what is* in the moment.

Therefore, healing trauma usually requires a skillful method that can facilitate being present with the nervous system's experience of trauma in the body. This process is greatly enhanced by the conscious recognition of awareness. By its nature, awareness is present with whatever appears within it. When we are conscious as awareness, and our trauma arises, we are not identified with it; we are not fixated and therefore no longer at the effect of it. There is naturally a being present with, or letting be, which allows a relaxation of the contracted, traumatic energy. Thus there is a synergy between the conscious recognition of awareness, which facilitates a skillful method, and the method, which facilitates being present with trauma. This synergy results not only in the healing of trauma, but can also result in liberation from suffering itself.

It is important to note however, that when a therapist abides as primordial awareness, he will spontaneously utilize whatever techniques or methods he has acquired. He is also able to forgo all protocols and just be with *what is*. Awareness can and does use whatever is necessary to awaken itself, but nothing is essential other than awakened consciousness itself. A therapeutic method is involved in creating true freedom only to the extent that consciousness is awakened in the one using it.

Our Instinctual and Essential Natures Unite in the Healing of Trauma

Peter Levine, Ph.D. (1997), one of the leaders in the field of trauma, discovered that trauma occurs when the massive amount of energy that we mobilize to protect and defend ourselves doesn't get to complete itself. If we are threatened and we can't fight or flee, we will freeze and the energy becomes stuck in the nervous system. What happens is that the intense frozen energy gets bound up with the overwhelming emotional states of terror, rage, and helplessness and does not discharge. The various ways in which we try to control this energy create the symptoms of trauma.

Dr. Levine observed that animals in the wild discharge high levels of stress arousal naturally and then return to a normal, relaxed state. Human beings on the other hand often block this innate ability to release and renegotiate traumatic stress. This is because human beings have a neocortex that has the power to override the reptilian brain. The reptilian brain contains our instinctual impulses, including the ability to release excess energy produced in response to perceived trauma.

When we attend to the mind and its thoughts, feelings, and stories *about* the trauma, we lose touch with our direct experience and remain fixated in the mind's interpretations. Thus the biological process cannot complete itself. The completion requires surrendering the mind's fixations and fully allowing the direct experience of sensation in the moment. As Peter Levine states, "Trauma is about thwarted instincts. Instincts by definition are always in the present. When we allow them their rightful domain, we surrender to the 'eternal now.'"

The skillful method that came out of thirty years of Dr. Levine's study of trauma is called Somatic Experiencing. In this section I will explore some key concepts of his work as it relates to being present. In the next section I'll illustrate this work with a case study, which demonstrates the synergy between Somatic Experiencing and nondual awareness. Somatic Experiencing provides a way to be present with the body's response to trauma and facilitates the gradual unraveling of embodied patterns or symptoms. In discharging traumatic stress, the nervous system stabilizes and develops the resiliency to remain present.

The Somatic Experiencing model uses a vortex system to illustrate how traumatic energy is formed and then renegotiated. Sigmund Freud (1922) defined trauma as "a breach in the protective barrier against stimuli leading to feelings of overwhelming helplessness." As shown in Figure 1, this rupture causes life-energy to rush out explosively and form what Peter Levine calls a "trauma vortex" or "outer vortex." The trauma vortex is a recapitulation of past, uncompleted responses and exists outside the stream of our present life experience. Nature simultaneously responds by creating a "countervortex" to balance the force of the trauma vortex, which is also called the "inner vortex." The inner vortex exists inside mainstream life experience and is a primal rhythm or force that is a natural compliment to the trauma vortex. It contains resources that naturally assist the healing of trauma. Figure 1 also shows that initially the trauma vortex is much larger than the countervortex; this creates the gravitational pull toward the trauma that interferes with our ability to be in the here and now.

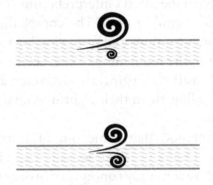

[Life Stream Diagrams: Figure 1 and Figure 2]

It is part of our instinctual nature that our attention is drawn to danger. Whenever life's stimuli are associated with past trauma, there is a perceived danger and attention gets pulled in that direction. We tend to either get fixated in reliving or reenacting our traumas or in trying to avoid them. These responses keep us out of the present moment and in an experience of our mind's distorted interpretation of the present. Yet it is our essential nature to be in the present moment. Past and future exist only as mental constructs. Life occurs in the now. The interface of nondual wisdom and Somatic Experiencing provides an opportunity for our instinctual and essential natures to unite in the healing of trauma.

Although I will not be able to present the full range of Somatic Experiencing here, I will briefly discuss three of the key concepts: pendulation, titration, and resourcing. They involve working with nature's primary instinctual responses to threat.

Pendulation

Phenomenal reality is organized in dualities or polarities: the inner and outer vortices, expansion and contraction, pleasure and pain, and so on. There is a natural movement between polarities. Pleasure is followed by pain and pain is followed by pleasure. Expansion leads to contraction and contraction leads to expansion. The natural flow between the polarized vortices created by trauma is what Peter Levine calls pendulation. Dr. Levine says, "Organisms have evolved exquisite processes to heal the effects of trauma. These processes include the ability to unite, integrate, and transform the polarities of expansion and contraction. If these polarities are integrated in a gradual fashion, then trauma can be safely healed."

Pendulation is something that is naturally always occurring. All experience is in constant movement between polarities. Yet, with trauma, pendulation gets interrupted and attention fixates on the trauma. Without an even flow between the vortices, attention is drawn further into the trauma vortex. This produces an experience of more sensation and emotion than we can remain present with, which leads to overwhelm. When an even flow of pendulation is reestablished, it regulates the nervous system, creating the resiliency that is necessary to remain present and discharge trauma. This resiliency, or self-regulation, is the ability to allow experience to come and go without becoming fixated in some way.

Self-regulation is normally developed through early attachment with our primary caretakers. Allan Schore (1994), a leader in the study of human attachment, states that "the development of the ability to adaptively cope with stress is directly and significantly influenced by an infant's early interaction with the primary caregiver." The more solid our foundation in secure attachment, the more resilient we will be to traumatic experience. Jon Allen, author of Coping with Trauma (1999), states, "Secure attachment is the antidote to trauma." Intense or early trauma, such as fetal trauma, can result in an inability to be here and now, even in basic, everyday ways. Such trauma can cause a person to live in a chronic freeze or dissociation until the energy is discharged. Peter Levine (1997) states that the bound-up energy can also manifest as chronic physical symptoms such as headaches, back pain, gastrointestinal problems, and asthma.

Titration

As pendulation is established, titration can occur. Titration involves releasing traumatic stress a little at a time, staying with only as much as we can be present to in the moment. Titration slowly allows traumatic activation to be accessed and assimilated so that the nervous system can gradually adjust to each level of excitation. If higher and higher levels of activation are allowed, it leads to overwhelm. In a client, overwhelm can look like either emotional numbing and dissociation or emotional flooding. The higher the levels of activation, the further away a person can get from the here and now. As traumatic stress is released a little at a time, a person becomes more able to remain present with whatever arises.

There is a natural movement between the vortices as we remain present on the level of sensation in the body. It flows back and forth like a figure eight or infinity sign, taking support from the inner vortex and bringing it to the trauma vortex, being present with a piece of the trauma vortex, and then returning to the inner vortex and orienting to the here and now. An example of one titration follows in the case presentation.

This vortex description of titration mimics what occurs more deeply when a client has recognized the nondual ground of being. A surrender into this being or awareness allows our innate wisdom to bring up only as much as can be met fully in the moment. This meeting dissolves or releases the traumatic energy back into the ground of being. In this meeting it is revealed that the trauma and our essential being are one and the same. The flow is a meeting of whatever arises and a dissolving into the source of it all, again and again. This can occur when there is both recognition of awareness and resiliency in the nervous system.

Resourcing

In order to establish resiliency, the inner resource vortex must build a center of gravity that can balance the pull of the trauma vortex. Bringing awareness to resources as they spontaneously arise in the body strengthens the inner vortex. These resources include organic movements from the nervous system that support the discharge of traumatic stress. Examples of the appearance of these resources are a deep breath, a smile, or a defensive gesture trying to complete itself. The inner vortex is also strengthened by bringing awareness to the positive sensations associated with experiences such as being in nature or with loved ones. Figure 2 shows the vortices more balanced after the inner vortex is strengthened.

In essence, healing trauma is simply about creating enough safety to be with what is in the moment. The *Somatic Experiencing Training Manual* (1997) defines a resource as "anything that helps a person maintain a sense of inner safety and integrity in the face of threat or disruption." In my personal and professional experience, what offers the deepest sense of this safety and integrity is direct experience of awareness, our true nature. Once the awareness in which all experiences arise and subside is consciously recognized, it becomes the primary resource. Because it is the source and substance of all things, this resource is naturally resonant with all experience. It intimately embraces whatever arises in each moment, including our pain and discomfort; yet it is simultaneously disengaged. It is simply alert and present. When awareness comes to the foreground as a resource, because it is both pervasive and totally detached, it profoundly supports the process of titration and releasing traumatic energies from the nervous system.

An awakened psychotherapist is a powerful resource who

can provide a field of wisdom and unconditional love, which not only provides safety, but also facilitates the client's awakening to nondual awareness. This field allows the client's nervous system to relax and surrender to *what is*. The more clearly the therapist is abiding as open presence, the more naturally Divine Intelligence comes through, unimpeded, in each moment. Such a therapist is better able to follow the natural wisdom of the client's body by being fully present and available to the subtle movements and sensations. Sensation is the primary language of our instinctual nature, which has its own wisdom and knows how to discharge trauma.

If a therapist also has a self-regulating nervous system, it greatly increases the client's capacity to regulate his or her own nervous system. Being awake to our true nature does not necessarily mean that our nervous system is self-regulating. Developing this resiliency sometimes requires therapeutic intervention, such as Somatic Experiencing, in addition to spiritual awakening. However, the powerful combination of self-regulation and awakened presence can magnetize the client into a resonance with primordial awareness and the natural movement of pendulation within it.

As the nervous system is stabilized and the person is resting as presence, the pendulations between the vortices become very, very slow until they disappear altogether into the eternal now. Peter Levine states that, "By moving between these vortices, we release the tightly bound energies at their cores—as if they were being unwound. We move toward their centers and their energies are released; the vortices break up, dissolve, and are integrated back into the mainstream." From a nondual perspective, dualistic experience opens and liberates itself when met directly with awareness and then dissolves back into the ground of being. And, as the traumatic energies release, they naturally transmute into feelings of contentment, ease, love, and even ecstatic bliss, which are intrinsic to our true nature.

Awakening from Fear: A Case Study

Diane (a pseudonym) is a fifty-year-old woman who has experienced fear, anxiety, and phobias much of her life. She came to me after eight years of what she referred to as "talk therapy" because she wanted to do a more somatic, experientially based therapy. She reported that she was in a spiritual crisis and wanted to process her trauma. She knew that she had symptoms of trauma, but was not clear about the cause. In the course of taking a thorough history, I discovered that she had many medical procedures early in life. The medical procedures Diane had are among those listed by Peter Levine (1999) as the most traumatizing to children. These procedures included six ear lancings before eighteen months of age, being restrained in a leg cast at age two, several hospitalizations for uncontrollable vomiting at age four, and a tonsillectomy at age five with ether used as anesthesia. These traumas were compounded by the additional trauma of being in an alcoholic family system that was unable to provide her with the nurturing and support she needed.

Diane lived in fear of "finding out something is wrong with her body that will mean disaster." She stated that she would "rather die than go to a doctor." She imagined that common aches and pains, or marks on the body, were symptoms of life-threatening illnesses. She also limited her activity level to a minimum for fear of stressing her heart. When she began treatment, fear and anxiety were always present in her life experience to varying degrees.

Diane responded well to Somatic Experiencing. She appreciated becoming more aware of her body and felt that this was "exactly the right work for her." Initially, her nervous system did not have the resiliency to allow for pendulation. When beginning with a focus on positive sensations, attention would move quickly to tension in other areas of the body, which would become more and more contracted, and then move into a freeze. She would literally become temporarily immobilized. This would happen within minutes of focusing on sensation in the body. When the trauma vortex is big and strong and the healing vortex is weak and undeveloped, attention on either positive or negative sensation can quickly cause a spiral into the trauma vortex. Therefore, our initial focus was on strengthening her ability to be in the here and now as a way of accessing resources and establishing pendulation.

I drew from resources that Diane spoke about and those that appeared spontaneously in sessions. At the beginning of treatment, she described an experience she had during a trip to Hawaii. She experienced being present and at ease moment to moment and there was a deep knowing that everything was okay exactly as it is. This lasted for an extended period of time during and after the trip. The sensations, feelings, and images that arose in the body as she spoke of this experience were some of the resources that we later utilized. We also brought attention to positive sensations that arose spontaneously, such as the warm tingling in her feet as they rubbed against each other. Often her left foot lovingly rubbed her right foot, which was the leg that had been in a cast as a young child.

After strengthening resources by bringing more awareness to them, I began to point to the experience of awareness itself as that which is always present no matter what appears and is larger than the vortex system, but inclusive of it. Not all clients are ready to recognize nondual awareness. I point to the experience of awareness itself when I am spontaneously moved to in the moment or when clients bring it up themselves. The presence, as Diane called it, was something she had already experienced. However, she believed that the presence was lost, so we inquired into whether or not this was true. The practice of inquiry used here is common in nondual teachings. It involves simply inquiring into one's direct experience in the moment and seeing what is actually true. I have found this to be a useful adjunct to Somatic Experiencing because it deepens clients' experience of their innate resourcefulness.

Therapist—"And what are you experiencing now?" [Noticing a slight smile and a deeper breath, which indicates an inner vortex experience]

Diane—"I am remembering how I felt when I was in Hawaii."

Therapist—"What do you notice as you remember that?"

Diane—"I have a felt-sense of a movement towards life deep in the center of my being."

Therapist—"Be with that felt-sense and notice what you are aware of in your body."

Diane—"I feel grounded with my feet firmly planted on the ground and my legs feel solid…. there is a deep relaxation in my belly and a warmth, a feeling of love coming from the belly and moving into the heart area."

Therapist—"Yes…"

Diane—"I feel more aliveness in my body. …something that is bigger than me…a presence that is loving, calm, still, vast, all-seeing…It is what I experienced in Hawaii."

Therapist—"Yes, wonderful…And as you be with that…just check in your own experience right now…is this a memory?"

Diane—[Silent pause] "No, it is real and alive, right here and now."

Therapist—"Checking again…Did it ever really go anywhere?"

> *Diane*—[Silent pause] "No, I just thought it did. It seems
> to go away when I am in my thoughts...but this feels like
> something that is always here...it has a quality of always be-
> ing present."

Once Diane began to have direct experience of the presence, I brought attention to it repeatedly in sessions. She began to understand that it is always available here and now. At first it was a fleeting experience, and she reported that it only happened when in sessions. However, it continued to grow and deepen and began to occur outside of sessions.

It was important not only to experience the presence, but also to bring awareness to how she knew it in her body. It is easy for spiritual experience to occur only "above the neck" and not be embodied. It can even become a form of dissociation from pain and trauma. Some traumatized people are in spiritual communities for that reason. In order for nondual awareness to be available to the nervous system as a resource in healing trauma, it needs to be embodied as a felt-sense. This involves experiencing the nondual awareness in the body on the level of sensation.

The felt-sense is another important concept used in Somatic Experiencing. It could be defined as internal body sensations or a bodily awareness of experience. As Peter Levine says, "The felt-sense can be said to be the medium through which we experience the totality of sensation. In the healing of trauma, we focus on the individual sensations. Every event can be experienced both in its duality, as individual parts, and as a unified whole. Those which are perceived in a unified manner through the felt-sense can bring revelations about how to undo trauma."

As the presence of awareness became more known and embodied in Diane's case, it facilitated the discharge of bound up traumatic energy through titration. The following is an example of one titration within a pendulation—the flow of movement between the vortices and back to the here and now without getting stuck in the trauma vortex. As she told me about her new puppy, Diane's eyes were bright and she was smiling with delight, which indicated inner vortex experience. When possible, it is best to begin pendulation with the inner vortex.

> *Diane*—"The puppy is bringing so much joy into my life...I feel so much love for him...he has really opened my heart."

> *Therapist*—"Yes...and as you feel the love and joy...and the openness in your heart...notice what you are aware of in the body."

> *Diane*—"I feel more aliveness in my body...there is a tingling sensation of aliveness throughout my whole body."

> *Therapist*—"Good...be with that..."

> *Diane*—[Pause] "I'm noticing a sadness in my face and throat..." (her eyes moisten) [Movement into the outer or trauma vortex]

> *Therapist*—"Notice what happens next."

> *Diane*—"There is tension in my shoulders...and in my neck...and an impulse to move towards the aliveness..."

> *Therapist*—"Stay with the impulse..."

> *Diane*—[Stretches and moves her head back and up] "It feels good (the stretching)...and I'm connecting to something bigger...I feel the joy again." [Movement back to the inner vortex]

> *Therapist*—"Now begin to think about opening your eyes...

when you are ready, open them and allow them to look around the room wherever they want to go." [Reorienting to here and now]

Trauma gets discharged one titration at a time. This natural flow is allowed by surrendering to our instincts in the present moment. It also involves skill on the part of the therapist to direct attention away from the trauma vortex if the client gets pulled too far in that direction.

As Diane's trauma was being discharged, we inquired into whether or not being constantly vigilant and defended was a real safety, which is what her mind believed. Diane had lived her life on alert, always looking out for the next danger. This is a common symptom of traumatic stress. Through direct experience in the body, she began to realize that the true safety was found in the awareness that is always present and in the pendulation that occurs within it. Pendulation allows the nervous system to relax into present experience, knowing that painful sensations that arise will pass. This is a new experience for a nervous system that has been in a chronic state of stress arousal for most of a lifetime.

Diane also began to understand that the fear she experienced was a product of her thoughts. The less she believed in her thoughts, the more the fear receded into the background. She reported that for the first time, she was experiencing happiness in her daily life even though fears still arose. She had believed that they needed to be eliminated completely before she could ever be happy again. But she has realized that whether they are present or not, peace is available in each moment. She also came to know that thoughts dissolve when they are met directly with awareness. These realizations came about as I directed her attention to what was actually happening in the moment. She began to understand these truths through observing her own direct experience.

The following is an interaction that involved experiencing resources such as happiness and stillness. We then inquired into fear, which led to a felt-sense of safety. These changes in her day-to-day life and perspective indicated that the trauma was being discharged.

> *Diane*—"I am experiencing happiness in my life and I'm not afraid of being happy. I have always been afraid of happiness, waiting for the 'other shoe to drop.' I don't feel that anymore. I am not waiting for something bad to happen. I am not living on 'red alert.'"

> *Therapist*—"Yes...be with this sensation of happiness..."

> *Diane*—[Long Pause] "I am aware of a giant stillness that encompasses everything...I feel completely surrounded and held by it...it permeates everything...everything that is happening is happening within it...and nothing disturbs it."

> *Therapist*—"Yes...just be that...and notice how you know this in your body."

> *Diane*—"I feel connected with it through the belly...the belly is like a gateway...there is calmness in the belly...and in the heart, too...I'm grounded in my belly, not in my head."

> *Therapist*—"And from here, how do you experience the fear?" [At this point I moved into inquiry in order to put her fear in perspective]

> *Diane*—"It is very small...and I can see that it is solely a product of my mind...I am really feeling that no matter what happens, there's always love here and it will be okay."

> *Therapist*—"Yes...No matter what happens, it will be okay...feel that knowing in your body."

Diane—"There is nothing to be afraid of! I feel undefended and open to life...[opens her arms out to demonstrate the openness and stayed with this for some time] "The openness feels safe...safer than being on alert...There's no need for vigilance here...nothing bad can happen here."

Therapist—"Yes...be with that sense of safety...feel the truth of that."

This inquiry led to a realization that the habitual pattern of vigilance to protect the body from harm was not true safety. Realizing this allowed long-standing patterns of contraction to begin relaxing. Without an embodied understanding, the body/mind keeps these patterns in place, believing them to be needed for protection. In order to truly release these contractions, it is important for the true safety to be realized in the body on the level of sensation.

From the perspective of awareness, Diane was able to experience fear with acceptance and without getting sucked back into it. Fear was seen as small and a product of her mind. Acceptance involves fully experiencing what is in the moment, without distancing ourselves from it. Paradoxically, the more intimately we experience *what is*, the more detached we become from it, and the less our attention is pulled out of the present moment.

Diane reported to me that she sees the transformation that is taking place in her life as "nothing short of miraculous." A "pulsation towards life" has been awakened in her body, and she is no longer controlled by fear. She also reports feeling "overwhelming gratitude" for the work we are doing that includes both a healing of her trauma and an awakening to her true nature.

Trauma as a Catalyst for Awakening

Trauma is a fact of life. Most of the issues that psychotherapists work with are related to the effects of trauma. Everyone experiences it in some way, whether directly or indirectly through the trauma experienced by loved ones. Also, traumatic reenactment is the source of most of the violence in the world, which affects us all. Yet, as common as trauma has been throughout history, we have been slow to learn how to resolve it. Since the healing of trauma involves somatic and spiritual processes, the field of psychology has had little to offer over the past century. The recent increase in awakening to nondual wisdom along with the discoveries made by Peter Levine and others now provide a way to be free of the cycle of trauma and traumatic reenactment.

Because its effects are so intense and pervasive, trauma can be a catalyst for profound surrender and awakening. I see it as a wake-up call for the human race. Trauma is a primary cause of human suffering, and yet it can only be truly resolved by coming home to the eternal now. In the healing of trauma, we must let go of the mind's illusion of control and discover the beingness that is always present. Therefore, the healing of trauma has the potential to help bring about transformation and awakening in the human species. Otherwise, trauma will continue to be a painful and destructive force among us. Peter Levine says, "Our survival as a species may depend on the resolution of trauma and traumatic reenactment." Fortunately, now is the time when both the healing of trauma and awakening to our true nature are better understood and increasingly possible.

Endnotes

1.   I would like to acknowledge Barbara Moore and John Lumiere-Wins for help with editing, and Peter A. Levine, Ph.D., for his valuable contribution to the field of trauma.

2.   The author may be contacted by email at Lumiere@conscioustherapy.com, her website at conscioustherapy.com, or at (510) 287-8922.

12

Jungian Analysis and Nondual Wisdom

Bryan Wittine

This chapter is about the journey in Jungian analysis of a spiritual seeker named "Jenna," who longed to know God. It is also about a defensive process I call "psychospiritual splitting," which nearly derailed Jenna's quest. Finally, it is about our analytic relationship and a nondual understanding of spirituality, both of which were central to her journey.

On the surface of things, Jenna began analysis because dysfunctional patterns in love and work remained unresolved despite years of practicing meditation. What is more, subtle feelings of being flawed and unacceptable seeped into her awareness whenever her defenses were down.

Unknowingly, however, Jenna was compounding her problems by her faulty use of spiritual exercises. In her eagerness to see into the depths of the divine, she was splitting between "higher Self" and "lower self" needs. In many ways she used spiritual ambition to compensate for her insecurity and to circumvent the difficult task of individuation, which Jung defined as the process of developing to the fullest possible extent who and what we are as unique individuals.

In order to heal this split, Jenna needed an approach to psychotherapy that addressed two paths of development: the vertical path of spiritual transcendence and the horizontal path of individuation.[1] The first is directed toward awakening to the Self, or the timeless, formless ground of pure being/awareness. The latter involves illuminating and transforming the shadow, or the wounded, lost, and disowned parts of the personality. It also involves actualizing the unique gifts and talents of our individual selfhood. A nondual understanding of spirituality encompasses both paths.

As I see it, our individual psyche and physical body are sacred manifestations of our essential Self, Spirit, or Being. They are centers of expression for our greater transpersonal awareness. Ultimately, nonduality is abidance in and as the Self, from which wisdom, compassion, and power spontaneously arise and flow forth through the unique qualities and capacities of our individual self.

Although the body and psyche are distinct from the Self, they are not separate from the Self. Being out of touch with the Self leaves us feeling unstable, empty, and ontologically insecure. By contrast, if we neglect our sacred manifestation we might rest in deep and timeless being/awareness, but there is no development of the unique gifts and talents by which we might potentially contribute to our loved ones and our community. To ignore the path of individuation, then, means the Self or Spirit might end up expressing through an inadequate vehicle, a vehicle moved about by powerful, immature, unconscious forces, which not only short-circuit our potential for love and creativity but also distort and derail our quest for stable spiritual realization. Anything less than realization of the seamless totality of essential being and sacred individuality is not nondual. Nondual awareness, as I define it, is virtually impossible unless we develop accordingly on both paths.

If we are like Jenna, we face certain problems by trying to develop exclusively along the path of transcendence. We might believe that if we awaken to God or the Self, our personal difficulties will magically disappear. Work and relationship problems, conflicts concerning self-esteem, anxiety, and depression will automatically take care of themselves if we meditate, pray, and transcend our ego-personalities. Although it is possible to have many meaningful spiritual experiences as we journey along the path of transcendence, the downside is that we might simply dissociate from our psychological conflicts and emotional problems. Moreover, if we exclusively cultivate our innermost spiritual awareness, the shadow side of our personality will usually find some way to become known. Sooner or later whatever is split off is likely to come to the foreground, perhaps through a traumatic breakdown of mind or body or through painful difficulties in love and work. Sometimes it is not until we "fall from grace" that we finally come down to earth and become aware of the split-off parts of our personality.

In this chapter I highlight a few of the difficulties associated with psychospiritual splitting. First is the tendency to use images of God to compensate for unmet childhood needs; second is the potential for ego-inflation if we identify with these images. When our use of God-images is compensatory and we identify with them, we inevitably inflate and drive our traumatized and lost parts further into the unconscious. Often it is only by suffering a profound dark night of the ego that we let go of our inflated self-images, reclaim our wounded parts, and begin to realize our true identity as the formless Self beyond all images of God. The formless Self might then use our illumined and individuated personality as a vessel through which to radiate the love, wisdom, and power of our true nature out into the world, into all the activities of our daily life.

The Self

Before describing Jenna's journey in analysis, I shall discuss my understanding of Jung's (1961; 1971) notion of the Self, which is central to this case. This aspect of Jung's psychology is perhaps the most confusing of his corpus because he used the term in several different ways. He used it to refer to a primary cosmic unity analogous to Asian concepts of unity consciousness, to the totality of a human being including both conscious and unconscious, to a transpersonal power that transcends the ego, and to the spark of divinity at the core of the soul.

I base my understanding on his initial intuitions and later alchemical writings. Henderson (1986) says Jung's concept of the Self first took shape in response to his fascination with the Atman of Indian philosophy. Further, Corbett (1996) believes "Jung's theory [of the Self] is best understood as a psychological restatement of the ancient Vedantic notion of the Atman" (p. 41). If this is true, then we need to understand what the word Atman refers to.

Atman is Sanskrit for "self" and refers to the divine Self in the human being, the "God within" (Tyberg, 1976). According to Indian Vedanta, this Self is our true "I," our ground of pure being/awareness, which is identical to the universal Ground from which all creation proceeds *(Brahman)*.

If the Self is our ground of being, it is also the matrix of transpersonal awareness within which all personal experience occurs. The Self is therefore the larger field that encompasses the smaller. Moreover, it is also the source of all forms, including the body and personal psyche. Swami Abhayananda (1991, p. 13), a Western Vedantist, tells us the Self is the inconspicuous Witness behind all our states of mind. It is this Witness that is our true Self and not merely the various states of mind with which we ordinarily identify. Because we identify exclusively with the transient body, emotions, and mind, we lose sight of our true nature as pure being/awareness, the Knower in all states of consciousness.

Vedantic seers also say our ego-consciousness is a fragment of the Self's consciousness. While we are identified with the ego-fragment, the Self might sometimes appear in our dreams and visions as one of any number of possible Self-images: a center of great luminosity and radiance; God as Father, Mother, or Beloved (with the "I" as the child or lover); a wise man or woman; a divine child; a goddess; Christ; the Virgin Mary; the Holy Spirit; angels, deities, buddhas, bodhisattvas; shamanic power animals; and images of the natural world, such as a mountain, star, ocean, or infinite space. Many people experience these images as preternatural presences that reside within the psyche, as living aspects of their own minds.

Apparently the Self-as-ground can communicate Its intentions to the ego-fragment by way of these preternatural presences. We can regard the manifestation of a spirit, a deity, or a power animal in dreams and visions in at least three ways: first, as an invitation from the Self to the ego to inquire more deeply into the meaning of life and the nature of reality. In this way the Self is the source of inspiration that sets into motion our paths of individuation and transcendence. Second, whatever the medium by which we encounter them, we can regard God-images as sources of guidance on how to conduct our lives. We will see this illustrated in a dream Jenna presented, in which the Self appeared to communicate something necessary for her personal and spiritual growth.

Third, images of the Self might be regarded as symbolic representations of attributes of the Self, analogous to the Sufi view (Almaas, 1986) that the ninety-nine names of God—representing such attributes as mercy, compassion, strength, peace, love, and wisdom—are manifestations of the Divine in the human psyche. When these images arise, they might point to emergent attributes that are part and parcel of our essential Self. In this way we have an opportunity to consciously meet and realize one or another attribute of our true nature.

It seems to me that in keeping with Jung's original intuition we must regard these images (and the attributes they represent) as subtle manifestations of the Self, which is the source of all forms. None of them, however, should be taken to be the essence of the Self, which is formless and infinite. The Self is the deep, formless, infinite being/awareness from which all manifestations arise. Self- or deity-images, by contrast, are subtle manifestations of the Self.

If we surrender to the Self and accept Its guidance, it is possible that our journey will gradually move beyond a dualistic relationship with the Self as "Other" to a more fundamental nondual realization: we are both the fragment and the totality of being/awareness. There is a seamless continuity between ego and Self. The paths of transcendence and individuation come together as we realize the Self in its formless radiance, prior to and beyond all images, expressed as and through our sacred individuality, which becomes the lens through which compassion, wisdom, and power pour forth into our relationships and the world.

Jenna

When I first met Jenna, she seemed ethereal and composed. She held her head high and spoke softly, as if we were in church. Her softness, however, seemed strained and marked by a subtle air of superiority. "How long have you meditated?" she questioned, her tone slightly imperious. "Are you familiar with esoteric teachings? I might be better off with a Zen master."

An assistant professor of literature at a nearby college, Jenna lived alone. In addition to her academic duties, she led groups in which people meditated, told dreams, and read sacred texts.

She became aware of her spirituality as a child. Because she suffered from bronchial asthma, she couldn't play with other children and so spent many hours alone. She imagined angels and other beings from myths and fairy tales and talked with them on a regular basis. "They were very real to me," she said.

In her early twenties a frightening asthma attack landed her in the hospital, at which point she learned some metaphysical healing techniques and used them unfailingly for two years. She claims she was healed as a result of using these techniques and became an avid student of metaphysical spirituality.

Over the years Jenna developed an interest in goddess spirituality and developed skill for visualizing and meditating on deities from various ages and cultures. For example, her daily meditation was to visualize "a goddess radiating wisdom and compassion" who became her "inner guru." She imagined herself sitting before this resplendent figure dressed in blue and repeated the affirmation, "I rest in the heart of the goddess. She is all around me, holding and protecting me. I rest in the heart of the goddess."

Over time the goddess seemed to develop an independent existence in Jenna's mind. Conversations occurred between them. For example, one time when she gazed into the deity's eyes, the goddess sent special beams of loving light and communicated a message: "You are a special person, a wise and beneficent 'daughter of the universe.'"

An important visionary experience occurred one evening while Jenna practiced yogic breathing techniques. She saw herself as the high priestess of the Tarot—a cool, detached feminine figure dressed in blue robes with a moon-crown on her head and a scroll on her lap. "As I concentrated on it," she said, "the vision absorbed me. I was pulled into a surreal world of unearthly beauty that had a shimmering radiance, like that of moonlight on water. I found myself in an ancient temple, smelling the incense and hearing the chanting of monks. Then I saw myself seated on a throne, like the oracle of Delphi. At first I was looking at myself. Then I became the high priestess. My whole life unfolded before my eyes as well as my past and future lives. I realized it was my destiny to disseminate to a suffering humanity the wisdom of the ages recorded in the universal memory."

This and other visions convinced Jenna to blend visualization techniques with her knowledge of myth and literature and become a teacher of metaphysical spirituality. "I developed a small following," she said. "I began to think I was one of two or three hundred people chosen to bring in the highest teachings of the Aquarian Age. I thought I was destined for high sainthood."

I felt conflicting emotions as I listened to her. At first I felt inadequate and wondered why she was coming to me. After all, she was so spiritual, and I felt less than ordinary in her presence. Then

I started to feel competitive. I wanted to "burst her bubble" and tell her she wasn't exceptional. I realized, however, that my feelings might be clues to Jenna's shadow-self. A sense of the dramatic pervaded her story, but underneath she might be feeling insecure.

She paused in telling her story. I waited a moment and said softly, "These are interesting experiences, Jenna. But you're experienced enough to know that visions such as these don't mean you're special. How is the rest of your life going—your relationships, your work?"

I saw Jenna wince in shame. Slowly, apprehensively, she told me she had recently separated from her partner of five years, a passive man for whom she had little respect. The breakup occurred when she spiraled through a confused and chaotic love affair with a married man who was also her student. No one had understood her so deeply as this student. She really wanted him, wanted to capture him, to make him love her, and would stop at nothing to get him. She was so consumed by desire that she hadn't stopped to think of the consequences of their passion for his wife and child.

The affair became a scandal. Students and colleagues discovered the liaison, accused her of sexual misconduct, and judged her severely. Many abandoned her. The lover accused Jenna of being too controlling and returned to his wife, and Jenna's partner wanted nothing more to do with her. Alone and rejected, she was plunged into a deep depression as she faced a huge split between her spiritual ideals and uncontained desires. "How could someone who felt such love and was so dedicated to spiritual life make such a mess?" she moaned. Her visionary experiences stopped, esoteric teachings lost their meaning, and she began to question everything.

Jenna's History

Jenna's mother was a very beautiful woman with frustrated desires for social status. She wanted to appear as though she and Jenna lived at a higher socioeconomic level than they actually did. Everything about her mother—clothes, house, interests, even religion—

reflected a need to appear socially upper crust. She groomed Jenna to look the part.

Jenna never knew her father and saw him only once. According to her mother, he was a rough, immature man who had multiple affairs and deserted the family shortly after Jenna's birth, finally dying when Jenna was six. The mother pined away for her missing husband, never remarried, and withdrew into alcohol to ease her depression. She blamed Jenna for the breakup. Jenna retreated into a vivid fantasy life, spending hours reading fairy tales and myths and imagining herself in the stories. She privately talked to spirits who soothed her and gave her the love she needed and never got from her mother. One of these spirits, she imagined, was her lost father.

Commentary

I now wish to comment on the case as I've presented it thus far. I believe that Jenna's spirituality arises from authentic longings to know God. Prior to her "fall from grace" she cured herself of debilitating asthma by using metaphysical healing techniques, which required intense concentration, and she practiced meditation on a daily basis, which took self-discipline. That she teaches literature at a university suggests she is competent and intelligent.

However, I also believe she was using goddess-images in her meditations to fill in holes in her psyche that formed as a result of childhood needs inconsistently met due to her mother's narcissistic and depressed personality and the early abandonment by her father.

According to contemporary psychoanalytic theory (Summers, 1994; 1999), for us to evolve and maintain a vital, mature personal self out of our inborn potentials, we need caregivers who facilitate our individuation by meeting certain developmental needs. Winnicott (1960) said we have a "holding need," a need for caregivers who suspend the expression of their own subjectivity and are "present" simply as loving onlookers who give us room to discover our own subjective reality. Kohut (1971; 1984) said we also have a "mirroring need," or a need to be affirmed by our caregivers for our value and creative spirit. He also said we have an "idealizing need," or a need to experience ourselves as part of calm, wise, loving authorities who possess qualities we admire and are latent within us. Finally, he said we have a "twinship need," in the sense of needing relationships with others who are very much like ourselves and who therefore give us the feeling that we are members of the greater human family.

Our caregivers facilitate the emergence of our authentic individual selfhood when they optimally respond to these needs. By contrast, when they neglect to meet them, most often because of their own unmet developmental needs, they derail our individuation. If individuation is derailed we might dissociate from our emotional life (holding wounds), experience ourselves as defective (mirroring wounds), feel unable to be true to guiding ideals (idealizing wounds), and feel deeply estranged from others (twinship wounds). Moreover, when our needs are unmet, they remain unconsciously active but archaic and immature. There is then a lifelong need to find others to fulfill them.

In Jenna's case, I recognized deep, unfulfilled longings for holding and mirroring stemming from her frustrating relationship with her invalidating mother. An inquisitive, imaginative child, Jenna needed a caregiver who joyously welcomed her into existence, recognized the uniqueness of her subjective life, and affirmed her special talents. Instead, as she put it, "My mother wanted a classically pretty daughter who dressed impeccably, attracted men, and married into money, and she groomed me to look the part. She also disapproved of my artistic and intellectual pursuits, ostensibly because they would drive men away and limit my chances for marriage and social position."

"I never matched my mother's image of me," she continued. "Now that I'm no longer a priestess to my students, I feel inadequate. I'm nothing underneath it all. No matter what or how much

I accomplish, mother's never happy. She said I was disappointing as a person."

There are at least two ways in which Jenna unconsciously used visualizations to meet these needs and compensate for feeling defective. First, she regularly visualized being held within the heart of the goddess. Her history coupled with her use of the affirmation "I am in the heart of the goddess" suggest she was attempting to invoke in her psyche the nurturing qualities of a stable, accepting, holding presence who cherished her and protected her from harm. Similarly, when the goddess radiated beams of loving light and told her she was a special "daughter of the universe," Jenna was probably attempting to provide for herself some semblance of mirroring. It is possible that through these visualizations she was attempting to activate in her psyche the positive Great Mother archetype—an image of the divine as a loving, sheltering, affirming power, a wholly accepting presence who in effect says, "Yes, you exist, and I love you just the way you are."

Then, too, Jenna tried to compensate for her feelings of defectiveness by identifying with another archetypal image, the high priestess, which resulted in an inflated ego. If we adopt Stolorow and Lachmann's (1980) definition of narcissism—that "mental activity is narcissistic to the degree that its function is to maintain the structural cohesion, temporal stability, and positive affective coloring" of the personal self (p. 10)—then it is possible that at least some of Jenna's spiritual activities supported an inflated sense of herself and compensated for her feelings of worthlessness.

If as spiritual seekers we are plagued by feelings of inadequacy from childhood mirror wounds and deficits in early parenting, we might compensate by constructing grandiose images of ourselves, such as Jenna's high priestess and "daughter of the universe," which become part of our persona when feelings of deficiency are too painful to confront in their rawness. We might also fashion ourselves as spiritual teachers long before we have the stable realization to actually perform this function. In short, Jenna attributed to the ego what belongs to the Self. Ultimately, however, the Self is the spiritual teacher, not the ego.

A Dream to Guide the Analysis

At the start of her analytic journey, I asked Jenna to begin using a technique known as "inner searching" (Bugental, 1976), a developed form of free association. I asked Jenna to (a) center her attention on a genuine life concern, (b) open her awareness as fully as possible to whatever she found, and (c) freely express whatever she experienced—physical sensations, emotions, thoughts, dreams, fantasies, hopes, wishes, and so on. When she immersed herself as fully as possible in her stream of awareness and gave simple, unbiased descriptions of whatever she found, she made many new discoveries, some of them life-changing. During the third month of our work together, for example, she had the following dream:

> I am flying in outer space. I see ahead of me the City of God, all golden and shimmering in the distance. I am so excited. I want it so much. Then I discover that, despite its beauty, it is an uninhabited golden shell. God doesn't live in this shell. I think, "I have to keep going; this isn't It!" Then in the distance I see the Milky Way galaxy with the Eye of God enclosed in a triangle at its center. I gently enter the Eye and dissolve into boundless emptiness, absolute love, and perfect peace. I'm finally home! Then I hear a stern but loving voice that says, "You can't stay here. It isn't time yet. You have to go back." I'm sad and start to leave, but on the way out I find a spirit-man, a being of light who tells me I'm an orphan and he is adopting me. He takes me in his arms and gently brings me back to earth. But getting back into my body is difficult.

As her analyst, my first task was to help Jenna use the dream as a trigger for her inner searching. In the dream, she is flying to higher realms and encounters the empty city of God. When I asked her for associations, she said that the empty city reminded her of the poverty of her inner life. "Once God dwelled within me," she said. "I had so many wonderful feelings of love and joy. But now, because of my indiscretions, God has abandoned me, and I'm nothing but an empty shell."

Then she added, "Maybe it's not a big loss. All of these images are giving me a headache anyway. You'd think with all my study I'd have known that images of God are not the real thing. They're empty shells, obscuring rather than revealing God. There's no real value in them!"

"So, I have to keep going, far beyond the empty city, straight to the Eye of God. But, hell! Just as I enter the Eye and melt into God's love, He tells me I can't stay, at least not now! I've got to go back." She paused, and then said angrily, "I'm being rejected by God Himself, just like I was rejected by my mother. Once again, I'm not good enough!

"No, that's not it," she continued. "It's not that I'm not good enough. I'm just not ready, not acceptable yet, to live in blissful union with Him." Then she said with quiet resignation, "But I can't stand this world. I want out!"

As Jenna associated to the dream, I had my own intuitions about its meaning. I thought the dream might contain a message from the Self that spoke of the change of attitude that Jenna needed for therapy to work and individuation to proceed. One of my favorite quotations from a Kabbalistic text (Matt, 1995) reads, "Before descending to this world the soul is imperfect; she is lacking something. By descending to this world, she is perfected in every dimension" (p. 148).

When I quoted this to her she replied, "Descending to this world is so painful. It's also humiliating. I assumed I was an initiate on the spiritual path, an advanced soul, but now I'm in the dark. I feel rejected, abandoned, and alone. I don't know what's real anymore. I'm questioning everything I took for granted."

"But, Jenna," I argued, "maybe 'descending' is positive. Maybe God is saying to you, 'Integrate your whole self—body, emotions, mind, desires, sexuality, creativity. Bring all of yourself to Me, not just your spiritual part.' Maybe we should think of your dream as a message to stop striving so hard to know God and see what happens when you join us regular human beings."

Indeed, the dream suggests it is futile for Jenna to strive for spiritual transcendence by bypassing her human needs. Authentic spiritual growth involves holding and containing all experiences, not just lofty spiritual insights and feelings. She must include in her experience everything she wants to avoid. In this sense, spiritual life involves bearing pain and suffering, holding darkness with a compassionate heart, and realizing our full humanity while simultaneously resting in the stillness and emptiness of the Self. It seems to me that we gradually develop our capacity to do this when our emotional life is met by the holding and mirroring ministrations of responsive caregivers, which Jenna did not have.

The Transference Relationship

Another important symbol in Jenna's dream is the spirit-man, a preternatural presence who adopts her, carries her back to earth, and helps her return to her body. I believe it will be useful to examine this image as it relates to the transferences that unfolded between us.

As an analyst, I find it useful to distinguish between two types of transference.[2] In the first, the "repetitive transference," analyst and client unconsciously repeat dysfunctional patterns in the early relationship between child and caregivers. In the second, which I call the "development-enhancing" transference, archaic developmental needs from childhood are reactivated, and the analyst responds optimally to those needs. Bacal (1998), a psychoanalytic self-psychologist, defines "optimal responsiveness" as "the responsivity of the analyst that is therapeutically most relevant at any particular moment in the context of a particular patient and his illness" (p. 5). As I see it then, the development-enhancing transference requires that the analyst empathically attune himself to the patient's inner world in order to deeply understand the patient's authentic developmental needs, and then to communicate verbally or nonverbally his understanding, which encourages the process of individuation to get back on course. This could mean that the analyst must embody Self-qualities that are latent within the patient and are needed by her for her own individuation. Analytic treatment consists of a shifting figure/ground relationship between these two types of transference.

There were many times over the course of treatment when I confronted Jenna and activated the dysfunctional relationship between her and her mother. This is partly what happened when I suggested that her visions don't make her special. I also confronted other maladaptive behavior patterns: her use of her students to supply the mirroring she didn't get from her mother, her tendency to treat others as if they were inferior, her refusal to accept her ordinariness. When I confronted her along these lines she said I reminded her of her invalidating mother. She said I was criticizing her, telling her she wasn't perfect just the way she was. She often reacted by getting angry and withdrawing. Sometimes I argued back, "Quite frankly, I don't see you as perfect. I see you as human, with authentic human needs. I think your needs scare you because to your mind they imply you are defective, neither good enough in your mother's eyes nor good enough to the God you imagine inside your head. I think we need to welcome all of who you are, human needs and all."

The image of the spirit-man, however, seemed to suggest development-enhancing possibilities in our relationship. I told Jenna I thought the spirit-man might be a symbol for her *animus*, for the archetypal masculine aspect of her psyche that functioned as a wise, calm, holding presence. I said I thought that these were her own qualities, but they were latent within her and might become manifest through our relationship. On more than one occasion Jenna told me that I embodied these qualities and recognized her need to discover them more fully within herself.

I asked Jenna to associate to the spirit-man's action of helping her come back to earth and return to her body. She said that coming down to earth meant many things: becoming grounded in a practical sense; opening to her sensuality and her sexual feelings toward men; understanding in a deep way that she is not special but a part of the human race. Coming down to earth also meant developing a "grounded spirituality," the word "ground" referring to the Self not in its transcendence but in its immanence as her own ground of being/awareness and her essential attributes of basic goodness, confidence, wisdom, and strength.

In terms of the development-enhancing transference then, the spirit-man is an image of grounded, quiet, holding strength, qualities she needed from me to work through her feelings of defectiveness and relax into the basic ground of her own true Self. If I could embody these qualities to some degree, our relationship might help her realize the spirit-man within herself, a calm, holding presence that supports the unfolding of the whole of her individual being as well as her true nature.

Within the milieu formed by the development-enhancing transference, Jenna continued to inwardly search. Gradually she opened to and talked about her developmental needs. First, she focused on the degree to which she had internalized and identified with her critical, invalidating mother and the various ways in which this internalization became part of her personality (a "complex" or "subpersonality" in the Jungian sense). That she held unquestioned beliefs far more pernicious than her mother's is evidence for this unconscious identification. For example, Jenna tended to find fault with people who displayed emotional weakness and felt subtle contempt for men. She also had all kinds of ambivalent feelings about love and sexuality. Further, she had a variety of harmful spiritual beliefs devaluing of her body and the world; for example, "The spirit is real, my body is unreal" and "This world is a dream, a mere illusion; only the world of spirit exists." Whether or not these beliefs are objectively true is a matter of philosophical debate; clinically Jenna used them defensively, to ward off the endless despair of a deep vulnerable core, a "hungry child" subpersonality.

Identified with the invalidating mother, Jenna was full of contempt for the hungry child–part. This fragile self-sense was dependent on others and on me for holding and mirroring, but the influence of the invalidating mother left her hating these needs. Not only had her mother cruelly disapproved of them, they were also the source of trauma. Having them at all put her in harm's way and left her vulnerable to the whims of others whom she needed to fulfill the child's needs. Consequently, these longings had to be rooted out and expunged. She banished them into the unconscious, where they took on a life of their own. Her defenses against them permeated most of her relationships, but her hunger to be admired and her longing to be comforted, protected, and held burst forth into her relationship with her lover. He rejected her when she tried to control him to get these needs met. Gradually, the child's needs came to the surface in her relationship with me.

A Dark Night of the Ego and a Change in Spiritual Orientation

As Jenna reconnected with her lonely, rejected child, she entered the most difficult period of her therapy. Disillusioned from the defensive aspects of her spirituality and disidentified from her invalidating mother, she began to feel all the loneliness, powerlessness, and rage of a little girl who just wanted to be loved. She faced into the heart of dependency and felt the awful pain of a frightened, barely-affirmed-and-nurtured infant-self. During this period she spent many hours walking on local hiking trails and sitting at the ocean weeping for the childhood she never had. Many times she thought of suicide.

For several months she saw me four times a week. She told me that she simply wanted to be with me and to feel my holding presence. Sometimes we sat together in complete silence, she lying on the analytic couch, me in my chair by her side. Sometimes I imagined I was a concerned parent sitting at the bedside of a seriously ill child.

In the quiet we could hear the sounds of traffic, the ticking of the clock, the muffled voices from the office downstairs. These noises seemed to arise and dissolve against the backdrop of quiet and stillness in the room. Gradually we both let go into a warm feeling of expanded being. I made very few active interventions, but stood by mostly as a silent background presence that watched over and cared for her while remaining curious about what might come from her next.

It gradually occurred to me that in the silence Jenna was opening to subtle realms that lay beyond thoughts and words. One day she spoke extensively of this. She told me that she was beginning to see her fragile little girl and invalidating mother not as intrinsic realities but as constructions within consciousness, as movements set against a vaster field of identity. The little girl and the invalidating mother were appearances—ghosts, phantoms—within her deep and formless being. One day she said, "I feel like a huge open space in which things long gone set up housekeeping and remained half alive. My mother, my father, and this little girl I once was: I think I'm liberating them. They're memories, only memories. I think I understand what therapy is now, Bryan. It's about opening up all the doors and windows in my mind and liberating the ghosts to evaporate into the Heart of God."

An important benchmark of this period occurred when she asked me what kind of meditation practice might suit her now that she had no interest in visualizations. I replied that I had recently been studying the writings of the revered Indian sage Sri Ramana

Maharshi (1959), who taught a method of self-inquiry that makes use of the simple question "Who am I?" She procured a copy of his collected works, containing instructions for contemplation, brought it to a session, and read passages to me. As she lay on the couch she sometimes followed his instructions and posed to herself the question "Who am I?" The upshot of this was simple and direct. Jenna became more fully aware of awareness itself as the pure presence that witnessed whatever arose in her mind. This left her feeling far more at peace with her child-self and forgiving of her disapproving mother, abandoning father, lover, and students. She also found forgiveness for herself for acting out her shadow-needs with her lover. Finally, Jenna realized that peace and forgiveness were actually attributes of her essential Self.

As I reflect back on this period in her analysis, I am struck by her complete lack of drama. High visions, lights, sounds, and colorful mythological imagery no longer captivated Jenna. She began to "just sit" every morning with a cup of tea close by. She gardened and took long hikes on quiet country trails. She also began to exude gentle warmth in place of superiority and aloofness. Friends appreciated this change and remarked on it.

Toward the end of her therapy, Jenna assumed the position of chair of her college's department of literature and decided not to resume teaching classes in meditation and spirituality. She feels she can serve more fully by concentrating her energies in academia. Her creativity, however, has blossomed. She has published poems and short stories in national magazines and has become involved in community support groups.

This is not to say that she has reached the end of her individuation, nor do her experiences in analysis constitute full Self-realization. But she continues to practice meditation on a daily basis and finds much that is affirming in spiritual literature. What is different now, however, is that she no longer tries to live according to a grandiose spiritual vision constructed to compensate for emotional and relationship needs. By accepting and embracing these needs, she has also developed a more openhearted quality toward others.

Summary and Conclusion

In this chapter I have argued that there are many of us who unknowingly develop a profound psychospiritual split. In our naivete we approach spiritual practice longing to attain liberation, but in doing so we neglect to care for our sacred manifestation, the conscious and unconscious aspects of our physical bodies and personal psyches. This leaves us practicing a dualistic spirituality that perpetuates the split and leaves us feeling enfeebled and adrift, lacking creative energy, and hiding our shadow behind inflated spiritual feelings and beliefs.

This is a far cry from a nondual understanding of spirituality. As I see it, a nondual understanding means holding and containing all parts of ourselves, both conscious and unconscious, not just our lofty spiritual insights and feelings. A nondual spirituality, then, must help us hold our darkness with a compassionate heart; it must also help us actualize our potential as mature human beings, which means our talents and abilities to contribute to our loved ones and our community. It must do so, however, while simultaneously helping us contact the deep Self and all its essential attributes: love, compassion, peace, joy, strength, and so on.

If we practice a dualistic spirituality, our immaturity is likely to show up somewhere, perhaps in our earthly naivete, in a physical or emotional breakdown, or in problems in love and work. This is what happened to Jenna, who was motivated not only by authentic longings for union with God, but also by profound feelings of not being good enough, which she sought to split off and bury. These feelings were associated with an unconscious "needy child," which developed in response to her judging, invalidating mother. As I have shown, Jenna internalized and identified with her mother, transforming her into a second subpersonality. These

two subpersonalities—the needy child and the invalidating mother—were parts of Jenna's shadow. They behaved in Jenna's psyche
like independent beings with lives of their own. To compensate for
the painful emotions engendered by this pair, Jenna combined authentic spiritual gifts with rigidly held beliefs to construct a "high
priestess" persona. She tried to live in that split state, which nearly
proved disastrous.

Psychospiritual splitting might be resolved through an approach to inner work that honors both transcendence and individuation. When practiced with a nondual understanding, Jungian
analysis might contribute to such an approach. From this perspective, images of the Self may be used as guides on how to conduct
our lives and as symbols of essential attributes that are ready to
manifest in the psyche of the person.

The process of healing in Jungian analysis, however, involves a
painful disillusionment from our grandiosity and a willingness to
engage the disowned aspects of our personality. As we have seen,
Jenna endured an awful, excruciating dark night in which she let
go of the high priestess and became unflinchingly aware of her invalidating mother and needy child. It gradually became clear that
these subpersonalities were not constitutional givens, but constructions of identity based on the past. Only as she brought to the
light of awareness the memories, emotions, and beliefs associated
with these subpersonalities, thoroughly experienced them, and
penetrated beneath them to the Self otherwise obscured by them
could she discover how relative they were. Then her feeling of being
worthless dissolved into the Self as the matrix of being/awareness,
which became for Jenna a holding environment of forgiveness,
stillness, and peace. From the deep and formless Self there finally
emerged a new sense of wholeness, which encompassed both the
mystery of being and the outer world of relationships and work.

The full transformation—for all of us—is, of course, the work
of a lifetime.

Endnotes

1.   I am indebted to psychosynthesis therapists John Firman and James Vargiu (1980) for this helpful conception.

2.   I am indebted to intersubjective psychoanalyst Robert D. Stolorow (1994) for this conception.

13

Dancing with Form and Emptiness in Intimate Relationship

Jennifer Welwood

In the Heart Sutra of the prajnaparamita tradition, one of Buddhism's most renowned teachings, the great bodhisattva Avalokiteshvara says to Shariputra:

> Form is emptiness; emptiness itself is form;
> Emptiness is no other than form;
> Form is no other than emptiness.

His words, which may seem incomprehensible at first, point to the nondual nature of reality. But what do they actually mean? Are they something that can be understood in terms of our everyday human experience rather than as an abstract, esoteric philosophy? And what does understanding nonduality have to do with relationship dynamics?

As in the above lines, nonduality is traditionally spoken of as an indivisibility of form and emptiness. This indivisibility is said to be both the nature of our own minds and the nature of reality. Emptiness here does not mean a vacancy or sterile void, but rather an open expanse that is not in itself a concrete "thing"—it is empty of "thingness." It is also empty of concepts, in that it is neither made up of concepts nor knowable through concepts. It is self-existing.

If we investigate this in relation to our own minds, we discover that when we look directly, there is a basic open awareness that is always there. Usually we do not notice this basic awareness, because our habit is to give our attention to objects of awareness— the outer objects of our sense perceptions, and the inner objects of our subjective experiencing. But even a little introspection reveals that all of these things occur in a larger space of awareness, or else we could not be cognizant of them. This larger space of awareness points to the empty quality of mind.

But at the same time that our mind has this empty quality of open awareness, it also continually generates forms—a whole spectrum of thoughts, feelings, images, sensations, perceptions, and qualities and states of being arise continuously. Yet when we look deeply into any of these forms, we find that they are also empty, because they do not exist in a way that is solid, continuous, permanent, or defined. They appear at some point in time, abide for a while, fluctuate in the course of their abiding, and disappear at some other point in time. They have some kind of existence in the moment, but they are empty of intrinsic existence in that their existence is not fixed or eternal—they change during the course of their existence and at some point cease to exist. So we find that form is permeated with emptiness. And when we look into the emptiness that permeates form, we find that that emptiness is always giving rise to form. Particular forms may not be eternal, but the potency of emptiness to dynamically express itself as form *is* eternal, and is inseparable from emptiness.

The phenomenal world also reflects this indivisibility of form and emptiness. Physics has shown us that apparently solid forms are comprised of vastly more empty space than they are of matter; and empty space is the birthing ground of form, from galaxies to living beings to subatomic particles. Even intergalactic space, once considered virtually empty, is increasingly revealing itself to be permeated with form—dark matter, fields and forces, black holes, and mysterious things that we can detect but not yet name.

So in both the inner and outer worlds, whenever we look deeply into emptiness we discover form; and whenever we look deeply into form we discover emptiness. This is the sense in which form and emptiness are inseparable, indivisible, and nondual. In tantric language we could say that they are lovers joined in eternal embrace—distinct yet not separate; not one, not two.

This understanding has a poetic beauty that can be appreciated for its own sake, but its significance to our human experience goes way beyond that. We can begin to see this when we explore the implications of not knowing our own nature and the nature of reality as nondual, and then we can extend that understanding to the particular ways that those implications manifest in relationships—giving rise to the phenomenon that Sartre so aptly described when he said that "hell is other people."

When we don't recognize our own nature as nondual, what tends to happen is that we see emptiness as something that form has to work against in order to maintain itself. Taking ourselves to be some kind of solid form, we see emptiness as something that could undermine or annihilate us. Rather than recognizing emptiness as our own nature, we see it as an enemy that we have to avoid or defeat. And we see form as something that we have to fabricate or defend or promote. So when we fail to recognize the nonduality of form and emptiness they become divided, and rather than being inseparable from one another as lovers, they become opposed to one another as antagonists. We have to avoid emptiness and we have to fabricate form. And this attempt to avoid emptiness and fabricate form is one way that we could define the activity of samsara, deluded existence based on ignorance of our true nature.

To our psyche, then, emptiness appears as any experience that threatens or disrupts whatever form we are trying to hold onto at a particular moment. Any experience that we don't want to have, anything that's not the way we're trying to get it to be, becomes an emptiness experience for us.

If what we are trying to be, for example, is a good person, then that would be the form that we're promoting—some version of ourselves as a good person, based on our concept of what "good" means. And then if feelings of anger or aggression arise, those would be an experience of emptiness for us, because they threaten the form that we are trying to maintain. Or if we are trying to be someone who is strong, then an experience of emptiness might be where we feel weak or vulnerable or helpless. In both instances, we don't trust that our basic openness naturally contains qualities such as goodness and strength; we misunderstand our basic openness as a *deficient* emptiness that we have to override in order to manufacture goodness and strength.

So when we fail to recognize our nature as nondual, not only do form and emptiness become divided, but each also becomes a distorted version of itself. Rather than emptiness being an open expanse whose natural potency generates form, it becomes a negative deficiency that we have to work against in order to maintain form. And rather than form being that which arises naturally out of emptiness, it becomes something that we have to fabricate as an avoidance of emptiness. If we don't make form arise, it won't arise naturally as an expression of emptiness. Emptiness has to be avoided as a threat to form, and form has to be fabricated in opposition to emptiness. And we can see that this is a state of suffering.

To further complicate matters and to bring in the full vividness of samsara, the very way that we attempt to grasp a particular form, that very activity of form-grasping, actually undermines whatever form we are striving for—propelling us to attempt to grasp it even more intensely. This creates a vicious circle in which we go around and around, caught in a cycle that is self-undermining and self-perpetuating at the same time. This is another way that we can understand the suffering of samsara—we're caught in these cycles that undermine and perpetuate themselves simultaneously, and we don't notice that and we don't know how to get out of it.

For example, say that we're trying to prove that we have value through some activity of earning it. Perhaps we try to earn our value through achievement and productivity, or perhaps we try to earn it by being kind and accommodating toward others—whatever fits our concept of having value. But the more that we try to earn our value, the more that that very project reinforces the underlying premise that we don't intinsically have it—it forever remains something that we have to earn, something extrinsic to who we are. And then that premise propels us to keep trying to earn it, and we are caught in our samsaric loop.

This phenomenon manifests in relationship dynamics all the time. Perhaps we are drawn to someone, and so we try to get them to love us. The problem is, who we become in that attempt usually isn't very appealing. We're trying to make something happen rather than allowing it to happen naturally, so we're constantly manipulating ourselves, or the other person, or both. We may present ourselves in a way that isn't open or authentic, or we may try to pressure or control the other—none of which is likely to evoke feelings of love. Our attempt to get the other to love us actually makes them less likely to love us, and then we feel even more desperate for love, even more convinced that love won't arise unless we make it arise—and the cycle continues.

Or perhaps we are trying to maintain our sense of space in our relationship. Perhaps we see our space as something that could be easily consumed or usurped by the other. So we assert our need for space in a way that is hard-edged or hostile, that has a quality of pushing the other away. The very way that we go about promoting our need for space makes it hard for the other to welcome giving us our space. And then we feel even more convinced that the other doesn't want us to have our space, and we all the more antagonistically go about asserting our need for space.

Samsara is a psychologically brilliant term for this activity, because in Sanskrit it literally means going around in circles. Someone once said that insanity is believing that we can keep doing the same thing and get different results. That points directly to this cyclic phenomenon: we keep doing the same thing in order to avoid some experience of emptiness, and when it doesn't work, rather than recognizing that it doesn't work, we keep doing it harder. We think that if we try harder at the thing that doesn't work, we can make it into something that works. This is the fundamental situation of samsara, and it is the way that the conditioned mind operates in general.

The Psychodynamics of Samsara

We'll look now at the particular psychodynamic structure that makes form-grasping inevitably self-undermining—we could call this the psychodynamics of samsara. Then we'll extend that understanding into couple dynamics.

From a developmental perspective we could say that at the beginning of our existence we are completely open, simply because we haven't yet developed the mechanisms to close ourselves down. This openness allows us to be connected with the basic ground of our nature, because that basic ground *is* openness. Our connection with this ground is neither conscious nor fully developed—one reason we so easily lose it—but there is at least some initial presence of it.

But we find ourselves in an environment that does not support our full openness. As human beings, we cannot remain open in some ultimate sense unless we are able to remain open in a particular sense, that is, to the particularity of our experiencing at each moment. We cannot maintain some state of transcendent openness if we have lost our capacity for immanent openness. And our family environment does not support our immanent openness—our openness to the full spectrum of our actual experiencing—because our parents did not embody this in themselves or receive this from their parents. So our environment supports us in staying open to some parts of our experiencing, but not to others. This inevitably leads to loss of openness and loss of being.

Say, for example, that our environment does not support us in staying open to our experience of sadness or pain. Perhaps our environment remains stable as long as we are happy, confident, and doing well, but begins to unravel if we are having a hard time and don't get over it quickly.

At first we might simply register that fact—the environment can't handle it when I am sad. This in itself isn't a problem; it is simply an accurate perception. But if this occurs again and again, at some point the mind of the child will decide, "My feelings of sadness are bad"—not in a conscious way, but implicitly. And because that experience is too painful for the child to tolerate for very long, eventually a strategy will develop: "I'll try not to have feelings of sadness." This *is* a problem, because such a strategy brings with it a loss of unconditional openness, and therefore a loss of connection to the ground of being. As this strategy becomes solidified by years of practice, eventually the child's "I" lands on it: "*I* am someone who doesn't experience sadness or pain." For the psyche this is the ultimate solidification of form. Whenever we take a particular form—in this case, a self-concept—to be the truth of who we are, we defend it with the same intensity with which we would defend the physical survival of our bodies.

At this point we've developed a conditioned identity. We could say that the conditioned self is a psychic structure that is made up of many such conditioned identities. And with every conditioned identity we're doing several things simultaneously: on the one hand we're grasping or holding onto some concept of ourselves that we think we're supposed to be, along with all the parts of our experience that support or confirm that. And on the other hand we're rejecting or warding off any parts of our experience, inner or outer, that threaten or disconfirm that. And we're continuously referencing ourselves to a mental construct that is based on the past, and on how we reacted to our inability to remain open in the past. All of this fabricated mental activity completely obstructs our capacity for openness and presence, which means that it obstructs our capacity to abide in our deeper nature.

So we begin by having some connection with our deeper nature, but then we lose that connection because we are unable to stay open to the full flow of our experiencing. And then because that disconnect is too painful to stay with, we develop a strategy for covering it up. And then we solidify that strategy by identifying with it, which cuts us off even further. We lose the true support of our deeper nature and seek refuge in the false support of our conditioned identities. This is how our samsaric confusion manifests at the level of psychodynamics.

From this perspective, our "wound" is not what happened to us in the past; it is that we were unable to stay connected with our deeper nature in the face of what happened to us in the past. This understanding allows us to directly relate to our problem in present time, which is our disconnect from the truth of who we are. It also helps us avoid the common therapeutic pitfall of fixating on the past in a way that solidifies rather than liberates it.

Looking more closely into the phenomenology of our loss of being, we can see that our conditioned identities always come in pairs: one that is more conscious, and underneath that, one that is less conscious. The more conscious identity—the one that we create to cover up our loss of being—could be called our *compensatory identity*, because its basic function is to compensate. The less conscious identity—where we have identified with our loss of being—could be called our *deficient identity*. In the above example, the deficient identity that goes with not having pain would be something like: "I am someone whose pain is *too much*; if I allow it, it overwhelms and alienates those I need and love." So underneath "I am someone who doesn't have pain" is "I am someone whose pain is too much."

For every conditioned identity then, there are always two poles: the pole of who we're hoping we are, and the deeper pole of who we're fearing we are. This is an intrinsically untenable situation, because what we're trying to be does not rest on any actual confidence that we really are that; we have to continually work against the deeper fear that in fact we aren't that. This is why our intrapsychic samsaric loops—our "bipolar" conditioned identities—are inevitably self-undermining. There is nothing we can ever do to prove that we *are* something as long as our deeper belief is that we really are *not* that—especially when our activity to disprove that deeper belief only reinforces it. When we reject our pain as too much, for example, then when it finally does break through it probably *will* seem like too much—both to ourselves and to those around us. This is the self-undermining part of our samsaric loop. But then because we cannot tolerate the experience of our pain as too much, we are thrust back into our strategy of repressing it. This is the self-perpetuating part of our samsaric loop. And the momentum created by this mind activity that both defeats and perpetuates itself is inexhaustible, until we begin to bring awareness to it.

The Samsara of Relationship Dynamics

While our own personal samsaric loops can create tremendous suffering and bring us to the outer layers of hell, to really go all the way down into hell requires another human being. So we'll look at what happens in a relationship when two partners' intrapsychic samsaric loops interact to create an interpersonal samsaric loop.

For this I'll use the example of a couple I worked with, whom I'll call Linda and Greg. They were both in their forties, had been together for about two years, and for a year had been completely mired in a cycle characterized by Greg's chronically showing up late and Linda's deep distress about that.

After exploring both their current situation and their backgrounds, we discovered that Linda had a compensatory identity of "I don't need much." She had learned to win her father's approval by being strong and self-sufficient; her stance was that she didn't really need anything from others, but from a motivation of generosity was willing to relate to others.

Greg's compensatory identity, on the other hand, was "I don't give much." His stance was that he wanted nothing to do with codependent entanglements, and that it was not his job to make other people happy.

And so when Linda and Greg first met there was an alliance: "I don't need much" meets "I don't give much"—and it's a match! Many relationships are initially forged in this way, based on a contract between both partners' compensatory identities. And like many couples, Linda and Greg were content in their mutual collusion for a while.

The reason these kinds of contracts are not tenable is the same reason that our conditioned identities are not tenable—they are fabrications with no basis in reality. They require ongoing effort and vigilance to maintain, and cannot withstand any movement toward real intimacy. With Linda and Greg what happened was that Greg's "I don't give much" began to manifest in ways that were painful for Linda—his chronic lateness—and she could no longer deny her pain by fleeing into her compensatory identity of "I don't need much." Instead, her recurring pain began to catapult her into her deficient identity, which was "I can't get enough." For Linda, seeking her father's approval had been a substitute for feeling truly nurtured in her family. So underneath her stance of self-sufficiency was a tremendous hunger for real human contact; underneath her identification with "I don't need much" was a deeper identification with "I can't get enough."

Once Linda became mired in her deficient identity of "I can't get enough," she began to trigger Greg's deficient identity, which was "I can't *be* enough." Greg had spent much of his childhood try-ing to make his depressed mother happy, with no success. He even remembered the precise moment, at age eleven, when he gave up all hope of ever making her happy. But with this giving up came a terrible sense of inadequacy, which became solidified into a self-concept of not being enough. His strategy of not giving to others was a compensation for his deeper belief that "I can't be enough."

As Linda's deficient identity of "I can't get enough" became un-covered in their dynamic, this elicited Greg's deficient identity of "I can't be enough." And the more that Linda reacted from "I can't get enough"—usually by demanding and blaming—the more that Greg reacted from "I can't be enough"—usually by withholding and withdrawing. This became a self-escalating cycle in which the reactive habit of each partner triggered the reactive habit of the other. From the "heaven" of the mutual support of their com-pensatory identities, Linda and Greg were now in the "hell" of the mutual antagonism of their deficient identities. Their intrapsychic samsaric loops had expanded into an interpersonal samsaric loop, and anything they did from within that loop only intensified it. This is the template that usually underlies painful, repetitive rela-tional dynamics.

In working with this couple, I helped them recognize the defi-cient identities that were being triggered for each of them, so that they could begin to hold them in awareness rather than react from them. This included helping each of them experience their sense of deficiency as a *feeling* rather than as a *truth* about who they were, and then learn to allow the feeling without reacting to it. Once they became more aware of and present with their underly-ing vulnerabilities, they were able to begin having a different kind of dialogue with each other, based on self-disclosure rather than defensiveness. This was the way out of their samsaric loop. Rather than losing awareness within their reactive patterns, they began to bring awareness to bear on those patterns. And their greater transparency with their own experience allowed them to be more transparent with each other, which is what allows for intimacy.

As Linda and Greg each learned to stay open to and present with their experience and to tell the truth about it, they also reconnected with their own ground of being—which *is* openness and presence. And then from that ground of being, other qualities of being arose naturally—even when what they were initially opening to was extremely painful. Strength and groundedness arose, kindness and compassion arose, humor and lightness arose. They experienced an innate sense of okayness, simply by being open. Rather than the fabricated okayness of their compensatory identities, they experienced the true okayness of their deeper nature, which arises from openness, naturally and without fabrication.

At these moments in the work they discovered something else of great significance: when they were simply present, with themselves and with each other, they experienced a profound sense of connection. This was a revelation to them both. Greg had always seen connection as something he had to provide or generate in some way, and this had contributed to his wariness of connection. And Linda had seen connection as something that required one person to be in the role of giver and the other person to be in the role of receiver— which also made it into a project. Usually she tried to fulfill this project as the giver, until her underlying sense of need broke through. Discovering a different basis for connection freed them both from these old constructs and allowed them to experience connection as something that arises naturally from openness.

Of course this was a major piece of work for both of them, and it unfolded over many months. For a while Linda and Greg would trigger each other again outside of our sessions, and could only come back to openness with my guidance. But this was not surprising, because their core deficiencies were being activated. For all of us, this is where we are the least conscious and the most likely to be hijacked by our conditioned patterns. Eventually, though, they stabilized in their capacity to shift from reactivity to openness, and to tell the truth about their reactivity when it arose.

For Linda and Greg then, we could say that they were caught in their samsaric predicament as long as they believed that their nature was really a deficient emptiness. And they became freer as they began to experience their nature as nondual—as a self-existing openness that naturally gives rise to form. The true resolution of their relational difficulties was to become more porous to their deeper nature, which then also gave them a basis for discovering real intimacy.

This is the doorway for all of us—to recognize that all of our suffering, relational and otherwise, is a symptom of our loss of being and our confused attempts to remedy that. From the perspective of the conditioned self this is extremely bad news, because it means that all of our identity projects, which we have been invested in all of our lives, are doomed to failure. But from the perspective of our wish to awaken, it is extremely fortunate, because we finally understand that, in the end, nothing will work unless we realize our deeper nature.

Selected Bibliography

Abhayananda, S. (1994). *The Wisdom of Vedanta*. Olympia, WA: Atma Books.

Adyashanti. (2002) Satsang given at a retreat titled "Love Returning for Itself," Green Gulch Zen Center, Mill Valley, CA.

Allen, Jon G. (1999) *Coping with Trauma: A Guide to Self-Understanding*. Washington, DC: American Psychiatric Press.

Almaas, A. H. (1984). *Essence*. New York: Samuel Weiser.

Bacal, H. A. (1998). "Optimal Responsiveness and the Therapeutic Process." In *Optimal Responsiveness: How Therapists Heal Their Patients*. Northvale, NJ: Aronson.

Balsekar, R. (1989). *The Final Truth: Guide To Ultimate Understanding*. Los Angeles, CA: Advaita Press.

Boorstein, S. (1997). *Clinical Studies in Transpersonal Psychotherapy*. Albany: State University of New York Press.

Brown, N. O. (1966). *Love's Body*. New York: Random House.

Buber, M. (1970). *The Way of Man, According to the Teaching of Hasidism*. New York: Citadel.

————. (1965) *Between Man and Man*. New York: MacMillan.

Bugental, J. F. T. (1976). *Psychotherapy and Process: The Fundamentals of an Existential-Humanistic Approach*. Menlo Park: Addison-Wesley.

Corbett, L. (1996). *The Religious Function of the Psyche*. London: Routledge.

Dürckheim, K. G. (1992). *Absolute Living: The Otherworldly in the World and the Path To Maturity*. New York: Arkana.

Elliot, T. S. (1963). *Collected Poems, 1909–1962*. London: Faber and Faber.

Fenner, Peter. (2002). *The Edge of Certainty: Dilemmas on the Buddhist Path*. York Beach, ME: Nicolas-Hays, Inc.

Firman, J. and J. Vargiu, "Personal and Transpersonal Growth: The Perspective of Psychosynthesis." In Boorstein, S. (ed.) *Transpersonal Psychotherapy*. Palo Alto, CA: Science and Behavior Books, 1980."

Freud, S. (1913) *On Beginning the Treatment*. Standard Edition 12:121–45.

————. (1922). "Lectures and Beyond the Pleasure Principle." International Psycho-Analytic Press.

Godman, D. (1998). *Nothing Ever Happened*. Boulder, Colorado: Avadhuta Foundation.

Goldberg, A. (1978) *The Psychology of the Self*. New York: International Universities Press.

Henderson, J. (1990). *Shadow and Self: Selected Papers in Analytical Psychology*. Wilmette, IL: Chiron.

Hixon, L. (1993). *Mother of the Buddhas: Meditation on the Prajnaparamita Sutra*. Weaton: Quest Books.

Huxley, A. (1945). *The Perennial Philosophy*. New York: Harper & Row.

James, W. (1912). *Essays in Radical Empiricism*. New York: Longman, Green & Co.

Jung, C. G. (1961). *Memories, Dreams, Reflections*. New York: Pantheon.

————. (1971). *Psychological Types*. Vol. 6. *The Collected Works of C. G. Jung*. Princeton, NJ: Princeton University Press.

Kahn, M. (1997). *Between Therapist and Client*. New York: Freeman and Co.

Kalupahana, D. J. (1987) *The Principles of Buddhist Psychology* Albany, NY: State University of New York Press.

Katie, Byron, with Stephen Mitchell. (2002). *Loving What Is: Four Questions That Can Change Your Life*. New York: Harmony Books.

Klein, J. (1988). *Who Am I? The Sacred Quest*. Dorset, UK: Element Books.

————. (1989). *I Am*. Santa Barbara: Third Millennium Press.

Kohut, H. (1984). *How Does Analysis Cure?* Ed. A. Goldberg. Chicago: University of Chicago Press.

————. (1971). *The Analysis of the Self*. Chicago: International Universities Press.

————. (1976). *The Restoration of the Self*. New York: International Universities Press.

————. (1984) *How Does Analysis Cure?* Chicago: University of Chicago Press.

Krishnamurti, J. (1987). *The Awakening of Intelligence*. San Francisco: Harper Books.

Krystal, P. (1982). *Cutting the Ties That Bind*. York Beach, ME: Samuel Weiser.

————. (1990). *Cutting More Ties That Bind*. York Beach, ME: Samuel Weiser.

Krystal, S., Prendergast, J., Krystal, P., Fenner, P., and Shapiro, Isaac and Kali. (2002). "Transpersonal Psychology, Eastern Philosophy and EMDR," in Francine Shapiro, ed., *EMDR as an Integrative Psychotherapy Approach*. Washington, DC: American Psychological Association.

Krystal, S., Slyman, S., Wager, J., Pregerson, S., and Berbower, S. Transpersonal Panel Presentation at the EMDR International Conference, Santa Monica, CA, 1996.

Levine, Peter A. (1997). *Waking the Tiger: Healing Trauma.* Berkeley: North Atlantic Books.

Levine, Peter A., and Poole Heller, Diana. (1997) *Somatic Experiencing Training Manual.* Lyons, CO: Foundation for Human Enrichment.

Levine, Peter A. (1999). *Healing Trauma: Restoring the Wisdom of the Body.* Boulder, CO: Sounds True.

———. (1999). *It Won't Hurt Forever: Healing Trauma in Children* (audiotape). Boulder, CO: Sounds True.

Longchen Rabjam. (1998). *The Precious Treasury of the Way of Abiding.* Translated by Richard Barron. Junction City, CA: Padma Publishing.

Longchenpa. (1974). *Rang grol skor gsum.* Gangtok, Sikkim: Dodrup Chen Rinpoche.

Loy, D. (1999). *Nonduality: A Study in Comparative Philosophy.* New York: Humanity Books.

Lumiere, L., & Wins, J. (2003) *The Awakening West: Conversations with Today's New Western Spiritual Leaders.* Gloucester, MA: Fair Winds Press.

Maharaj, Sri N. (1996). *The Experience of Nothingness:*

———. (1982). *I Am That.* Durham, NC: The Acorn Press.

———. (1996). Edited by Robert Powell. *The Ultimate Medicine: Dialogues with a Realized Master.* Delhi: Motilal Barnarsidass Publishers.

———. (2001). *The Experience of Nothingness: Sri Nisargadatta Maharaj's Talks on Realizing the Infinite.* San Diego: Blue Dove Press.

Maharshi, R. (1959). *The Collected Works of Ramana Maharshi.* New York: Rider.

———. (1984). *Talks with Ramana Maharshi.* Tiruvanamalai: Sri Ramanasram.

Mahler, M., Pine, F., Bergman, A. (1975) *The Psychological Birth of the Human Infant.* New York: Basic Books.

Mannheim, R. (1974). *Martin Buber.* New York: Twayne.

Matt, D. C. (1995). *The Essential Kabbalah: The Heart of Jewish Mysticism.* San Francisco: HarperSanFrancisco

Miller, Richard C., *The Yoga Nidra Workbook,* Anahata Press, Press, Box 1673, Sebastopol, CA 95473, 1995.

Miller, Richard C. *The Principles and Practice of Yoga Nidra Audiotapes,* Anahata Press, Press, Box 1673, Sebastopol, CA 95473, 2001

Mishra, Rammurti S. (1979) *Fundamentals of Yoga: A Handbook of Theory, Practice, and Application*, Julian Press.

Niranjanananda, Swami. (1994) *Prana, Pranayama, Prana Vidya*, Bihar School of Yoga.

Norbu, C. N., & Clemente, A. (1999). *The Supreme Source*. Trans. A. Lukianowicz Ithaca, NY: Snow Lion Publications.

Osborne, A. *The Teachings of Bhagavan Sri Ramana Maharshi in His Own Words*. South India: Messrs. Rider & Company, 1971.

Parsons, T. (2000) *As It Is: The Open Secret to Living an Awakened Life*. San Diego: Inner Directions Publishing.

Powell, R (Ed.) *Sri Nisargadatta Maharaj's Talks on Realizing the Infinite*. San Diego, CA: Blue Dove Press.

Prajnanpad, S. (1981a) *Collected letters, vol. 3*. New Delhi: Adhikarilal Sadh.

Prajnanpad, S. (1981b) *Collected letters, vol. 1*. New Delhi: Adhikarilal Sadh.

Prakash, S. (1986) *L'experience de l'unité*. Paris: Editions Accarias. Quotations are from the unpublished English text.

Prendergast, J. (2000) The chakras in transpersonal psychotherapy in the *International Journal of Yoga Therapy*. No. 10.

Polster, E. & Polster, M. (1974). *Gestalt Therapy Integrated*. New York : Random House.

Poonja, Sri H.W.L. (1995) *The Truth Is*. Boulder, Colorado: Yudhishtara Press.

Reich, Wilhelm (1945) *Character Analysis*. New York, New York: Simon and Shuster.

Reynolds, John M. (1996). *The Golden Letters*. Ithaca, New York: Snow Lion Pubs.

Rogers, C. (1980) A Way of Being. Boston, New York: Houghton Mifflin Co.

Rothberg, Donald. "Spiritual Inquiry" in *Transpersonal Knowing*. (Editors: Hart, T., Nelson, P., Puhakka, K.) State University of New York Press, 2000.

Roumanoff, D. (1989) Un m*aitre contemporain*. Paris: La Table Ronde. Quotations are from the unpublished English text.

Rumi, Jalal al-Din (1995) *The Essential Rumi*, translations by Coleman Barks with John Moyne. San Francisco: HarperSanFrancisco, p. 106.

Satyananda, Swami. (1974) *Meditation from the Tantras*, Bihar School of Yoga.

_____ (1976) *Yoga Nidra*, Bihar School of Yoga, India.

Schore, Allen N. (1994) *Affect Regulation and the Origin of the Self*. New Jersey: Lawrence Erlbaum Assoc. Publishers.

Shapiro, F. (2001)*EMDR: Basic Principles, Protocols, and Procedures*. New York: Guilford Press.

Shapiro, F. (Ed.) (2002) *Emdr As An Integrative Psychotherapy Approach*. Washington, DC: American Psychological Association.

Shapiro, F. and Forrest, M., (1997) *EMDR*. New York, NY: Basic Books.

Shapiro, R. (1994) *Open Secrets*. Durham, N.C.. Human Kindness Foundation.

Sogyal Rimpoche (1992). *The Tibetan Book of Living and Dying*.San Francisco, CA: Harper.

Sri Sathya Sai Baba. (1988) *Sathya Sai Speaks*. Volume XI. Prashanthinilayam, India: Sri Sathya Sai Books and Publications Trust.

Stolorow, R. D., (1994) "The Nature and Therapeutic Action of Psychoanalytic Interpretation." In Stolorow, R. D., G. E. Atwood, and B. Brandchaft (eds.). *The Intersubjective Perspective*. Northvale, NJ: Aronson.

Stolorow, R. D. and Lachmann, F. M. (1980). *Psychoanalysis of developmental arrests: theory & treatment*. International Universities Press.

Suzuki, D. T. (1986) *Essays in Zen Buddhism, First Series*. N Y: Grove Press.

Tyberg, J. (1976). *The Language of the Gods*. San Francisco: Cultural Integration Fellowship

Thurman, Robert A.F. (1996). *Essential Tibetan Buddhism*. New Delhi: HarperCollins Pub. India.

Tolle, E. (1999) *The Power of Now*. Novato, CA: New World Library.

Trungpa, C. (1987). *Cutting Through Spiritual Materialism*. Boston, MA: Shambhala. New York: International Universities Press.

Trungpa, C. Unpublished transcript. n.d.

Van der Kolk, Bessel. (1999) *Traumatic Stress: The Effects of Overwhelming Experience on Mind, Body, and Society*. New York: Guilford Press.

Venkatesananda, Swami. (1999) *Enlightened Living, A New Interpretative Translation of the Yoga Sutra of Maharshi Patañjali*, Anahata Press, Box 1673, Sebastopol, CA 95473,

Wadell, Norma (translator). (2000) *The Unborn: The Life and Teachings of Zen Master Bankei 1622-1693*. New York: North Point Press.

Walsh, R. & Vaughan, F. (1981). *Beyond Ego*. Los Angeles, CA: J P Tarcher.

Watts, A. (1961). Psychotherapy East and West. New York: Pantheon.

Watts, A. (1989). The Book: On the Taboo Against Knowing Who You Are. New York: Vintage Books.

Welwood, J. (1990) *Journey of the heart: The path of conscious love.* New York: Harper Collins.

_____ (2000a) Between heaven and earth: Principles of inner work. In J. Welwood, *Toward a psychology of awakening.* Boston: Shambhala.

_____ (2000b) Embodying your realization: Psychological work in the service of spiritual development. In J. Welwood, *Toward a psychology of awakening.* Boston: Shambhala.

_____ (2000c) Reflection and presence: The dialectic of awakening. In J. Welwood, *Toward a psychology of awakening.* Boston: Shambhala.

_____ (2000d) The unfolding of experience: Psychotherapy and beyond. In J. Welwood, *Toward a psychology of awakening.* Boston: Shambhala.

Wilber, K. (1996) *A Brief History of Everything.* Boston & London: Shambhala.

_____ (1996) *The Atman Project.* Wheaton:ILL: Theosophical Publishing House.

_____ (2000). *Integral Psychology.* Boston & London: Shambhala.

Winnicott, D. W. (1960). Ego distortion in terms of true and false self. In *The maturational processes and the facilitating environment.* Madison, CT: International Universities Press.

Winnicott, D.W. (1971) *Playing and Reality.* London: Tavistock Publications, Inc.

Wolman, T. (1994) Contrasting Roles of Narcissistic Mirroring In Self Psychology and Separation-Individuation Theory in *Perspectives on Development, Psychopathology, and Technique.* Schmakramer, Salman, A. (Eds) New Jersey, London: Jason Aranson, Inc.

About the Contributors

John J. Prendergast, Ph.D., is an adjunct assistant professor of psychology at the California Institute of Integral Studies where he has created and taught a class on Transpersonal Counseling Skills for over a decade. He is the author of "The Chakras in Transpersonal Psychotherapy" in the *International Journal of Yoga Therapy* (2000), and second author (with Krystal, S., Krystal, P., Fenner, P., and Shapiro, I. and K.) of "Transpersonal Psychology, Eastern Philosophy and EMDR", in Shapiro, F. (ed) *EMDR As An Integrative Psychotherapy Approach: Experts of Diverse Orientations Explore the Paradigm Prism,* American Psychological Association Books (2002). He has taught a number of workshops for therapists on "The Energybody in Psychotherapy" and "Transpersonal Dimensions in Psychotherapy: Presence, Resonance and Inquiry", and co-organized and presented at the Conferences on Nondual Wisdom and Psychotherapy. He has been in private practice since 1985.

He began Transcendental Meditation in 1970 and later taught it; traveled to India on three occasions to be with various teachers including Ammachi, and spent fifteen years with his primary teacher Jean Klein—a European sage who synthesized elements of Advaita Vedanta and Kashmiri Shaivism. He currently studies with Adyashanti.

Peter Fenner, Ph.D., met his root guru, the Tibetan lama Thubten Yeshe in 1974. In 1977 he was ordained in India as a celibate monk. A condition of his ordination was that he continue to live in the world, with his wife and two young daughters. In 1983 he completed a PhD in Madhyamika philosophical psychology. After nine years as a monk Peter gave back his ordination.

This opened the way to explore Western psychological traditions of self development. In 1986 he began offering adaptations of Mahayana wisdom to mental health professionals. He subsequently founded the Center for Timeless Wisdom (wisdom.org), a Californian nonprofit organization, which offers contemplative dialogues and retreats in Australia, USA, Europe and Israel.

Peter's work gives immediate access to the liberating essence of Asia's spiritual wisdom. His work transcends sectarian divisions and attracts the interest of new and mature practitioners alike. In his retreats Peter creates a contemplative space that moves organically between dynamic dialogue and meditative silence. Fixed opinions and reactive emotions are gently dissolved through an inquiry that responds to the rhythm of each person's experience. The result is a simple and precise method for entering and deepening the experience of unconditioned awareness.

In response to the fact that many mental health professionals attend his workshops, for several years Peter has been involved in developing and teaching the principles and practices for a nondual psychotherapy. He is also available for one-on-one sessions, in person and by phone (see wisdom.org).

Peter's books include *The Ontology of the Middle Way* (Kluwer, 1990), *Reasoning into Reality* (Wisdom Publications, 1994) and *Essential Wisdom Teachings* (with Penny Fenner (Nicolas-Hays, 2001) and *The Edge of Certainty: Dilemmas on the Buddhist Path* (Nicolas-Hays, 2002). His psychological essays have appeared in journals such as the *Journal of Contemplative Psychotherapy, Revision, Journal of the International Association for Spiritual Psychiatry, Psychologia* (Tokyo), and *3me Millenaire*.

Besides running experiential workshops Peter has given presentations of his work at institutions such as Stanford Medical School, Columbia University, Saybrook College, and the California Institute of Integral Studies. He is also a full time Senior Lecturer in Asian spiritual traditions at Deakin University in Australia.

Sheila Krystal, Ph.D., has been a practicing Clinical Psychologist since the early 1970s, specializing in the integration of the spiritual dimension and psychotherapy via meditation, hatha yoga, Jungian dream work and Reichian body work. In the last decade, she has added Eye Movement Desensitization and Reprocessing as a skillful means in psychotherapy to facilitate a client's awakening to the nondual dimension of life.

She received her Ph.D. from Columbia University in 1970 and held a Post Doctoral Internships at Wright Institute and The Langley Porter Neuropsychiatric Institute of the University of California. For nearly 50 years she has been an active participant in and teacher of the work of her mother, Phyllis Krystal in *Cutting The Ties That Bind* and has edited several of her mother's eight books. In addition to articles on mid-life crisis and divorce published in the journal *Maturitas,* she has co-authored two articles on integrating meditation with the 12 step programs with Joan Zweban, Ph.D. that were published in the *Journal of Substance Abuse Treatment.* She is first author of a chapter on the use of EMDR in transpersonal psychotherapy (with J. Prendergast, P. Fenner, P. Krystal and I. and K. Isaac.) in Francine Shapiro's *EMDR As An Integrative Psychotherapy Approach: Experts of Diverse Orientations Explore the Paradigm Prism* (2002).

In addition to her private practice, Dr, Krystal has taught an advanced course in EMDR from the transpersonal perspective for the EMDR Institute, has presented papers on transpersonal psychology at two International EMDR conferences, and has developed a Transpersonal Protocol for use in EMDR therapy. She co-organized and presented at the 2000 Conference on Nondual Wisdom and Psychotherapy.

Over a fifty year period she has studied hatha yoga, meditation and nondual wisdom with various teachers including Yesuddian and Haich, Indra Devi, Sharma, Sri Sathya Sai Baba, H.W.L. Poonja, Jean Dunn and Adyashanti.

Adyashanti, a native of Northern California, teaches extensively in the Bay Area offering weekly satsangs, frequent intensives and silent retreats. He also travels to teach in other areas of the United States and Canada.

After a series of transformative spiritual awakenings, Adyashanti began teaching in 1996, at the request of his Zen teacher of 14 years. Adyashanti's teachings have been compared to some of the early Chan (Zen) masters of China as well as teachers of Advaita Vedanta in India. He is the author of *The Impact of Awakening* and *My Secret is Silence.*

Dan Berkow, Ph.D.,is a psychologist, associate director of the university counseling center, and part-time professor in the Psychology Dept. at the University of North Carolina, Wilmington. As teacher and practitioner, he has had a long-term interest in integrating nondual wisdom with understandings of human development and psychotherapeutic practice. He is co-author of *Creating Contact, Choosing Relationship: The Dynamics of Unstructured Group Therapy* (1994), San Francisco: Jossey Bass, "Asian Psychological Approaches and Western Therapy" in *Promoting Health Across Cultures: A Handbook* (1999), (M. Maclachlan, Ed.), London: Sage, as well as several other journal articles.

Stephan Bodian, M.A.,is a licensed psychotherapist and the bestselling author of several books, including *Meditation For Dummies* and *Buddhism For Dummies* (with Jon Landaw). Ordained a Zen Buddhist priest in 1974, Bodian has been practicing and teaching nondual approaches to truth since 1969 and has been practicing as a therapist since 1982. Bodian was editor-in-chief of *Yoga Journal* for 10 years and has written numerous articles on psychology and spirituality for national magazines, including *Fitness* and *Alternative Medicine.*

Dorothy Hunt, A.M., L.C.S.W., is the founder of the San Francisco Center for Meditation and Psychotherapy, where for many years, she has taught workshops, facilitated meditation groups, spiritual retreats, and consultation groups for psychotherapists focused on nondual understanding. In addition to practicing psychotherapy since 1967, Ms. Hunt has taught workshops at Esalen, the Association for Transpersonal Psychology annual conferences, and at the Nondual Wisdom and Psychotherapy conferences held at Mt. Madonna and in Berkeley, California.

Ms. Hunt is editor of *Love: A Fruit Always in Season, Daily Meditations by Mother Teresa of Calcutta*, with whom she worked for many years as Regional Link of the Co-Workers of Mother Teresa for Northern California. Her poems have been published in the journal, *Advaita-Satya-Amritam, Nectar of Non-Dual Truth*, and in *Your Head in the Tiger's Mouth, Talks in Bombay with Ramesh S. Balsekar*. In addition to Mother Teresa, significant teachers in her life include Ramana Maharshi, Ramesh Balsekar, and Adyashanti.

Lynn Marie Lumiere, M.A. is a licensed Marriage, Family Therapist with a transpersonal and somatic orientation. She has fifteen years experience working with trauma and trauma-related issues and is certified in a number of trauma recovery methods in addition to Somatic Experiencing. She brings 30 years of deep spiritual exploration to her work and is especially interested in embodied realization. Lynn Marie is co-author of *The Awakening West: Conversations with Today's New Western Spiritual Leaders*. Also, her chapter "Healing Trauma in the Eternal Now" will be part of an upcoming book on nondual wisdom and psychotherapy. Lynn Marie coordinated the 2002 Nondual Wisdom and Psychotherapy Conference and was also a presenter. In addition to adult individuals, she enjoys working with couples that are working through trauma-related issues in relationship as well as children and adolescents who have been traumatized.

Richard Miller, Ph.D. has been an internationally respected teacher and workshop leader, psychologist and writer for over 30 years. His writings and teachings are based upon a lifetime of inquiry into the nature of spiritual freedom and focus on the integration of the individual, interpersonal and impersonal dimensions of Self.

Co-founder of The International Association of Yoga Therapists and founding editor of its professional *Journal of Yoga Therapy,* Richard has published numerous articles related to the transformation and transcendence of body, mind and spirit. He lives with his wife and children in Sebastopol, California.

Jennifer Welwood, M.A., M.F.T., a graduate from Stanford University and the California Institute of Integral Studies, is a psychotherapist in private practice and teaches workshops in the U.S. and Europe. Her work integrates psychological and spiritual understandings and methods in the service of embodying our deeper nature. She has specialized in working with groups and couples since 1988.

John Welwood, Ph.D. is a clinical psychologist and psychotherapist in San Francisco, and an editor of *The Journal of Transpersonal Psychology.* His work, which focuses on psychological work in a spiritual context, integrates Eastern contemplative teachings with Western psychotherapeutic understanding. His books include *Awakening the Heart: East/West Approaches to Psychotherapy and the Healing Relationship* (Shambhala, 1983), *Journey of the Heart: The Path of Conscious Love* (HarperCollins, 1990), *Ordinary Magic: Everyday Life as Spiritual Path* (Shambhala, 1992), *Love and Awakening: Discovering the Sacred Path of Intmate Relationship* (HarperCollins, 1996) and *Towards a Psychology of Awakening: Buddhism, Psychotherapy, and the Path of Personal and Spiritual Transformation* (Shambhala, 2000).

Bryan Wittine, Ph.D. is a Jungian analyst in private practice and a member of the faculty at the C. G. Jung Institute of San Francisco, where he teaches on the relationship between mysticism and depth psychotherapy. The co-founder and former chair of the Department of Transpersonal Psychology at John F. Kennedy University, Orinda, California, he has taught at the California Institute of Integral Studies, the University of California, Berkeley, the Berkeley Psychotherapy Institute, and the Community Institute of Psychotherapy, San Rafael, California. The author of numerous papers on transpersonal psychotherapy and an international lecturer, he has trained in Eastern and Western contemplative practices, most notably Vajrayana Buddhism and Christian mysticism.

Index